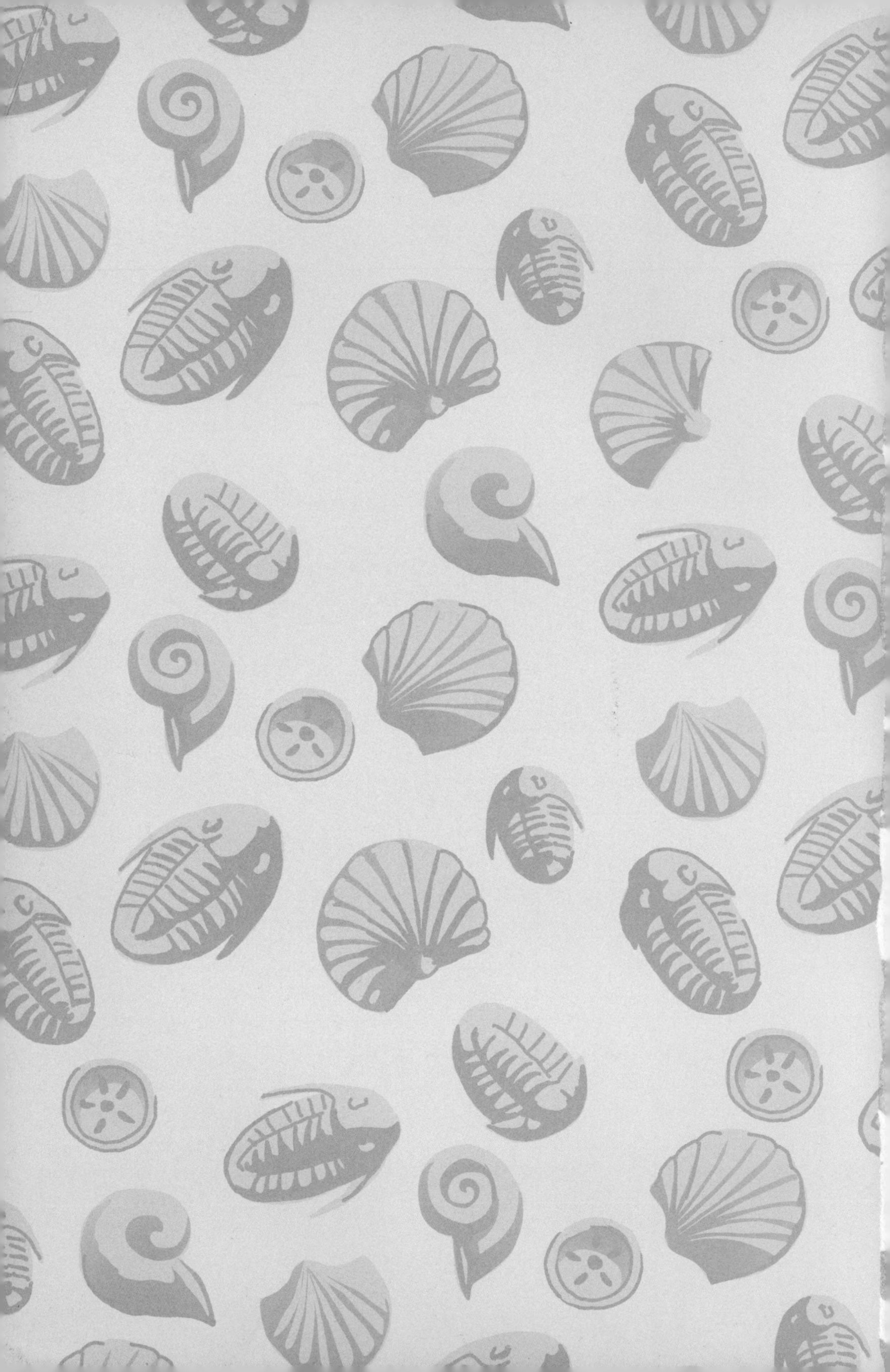

EARTH BEFORE US

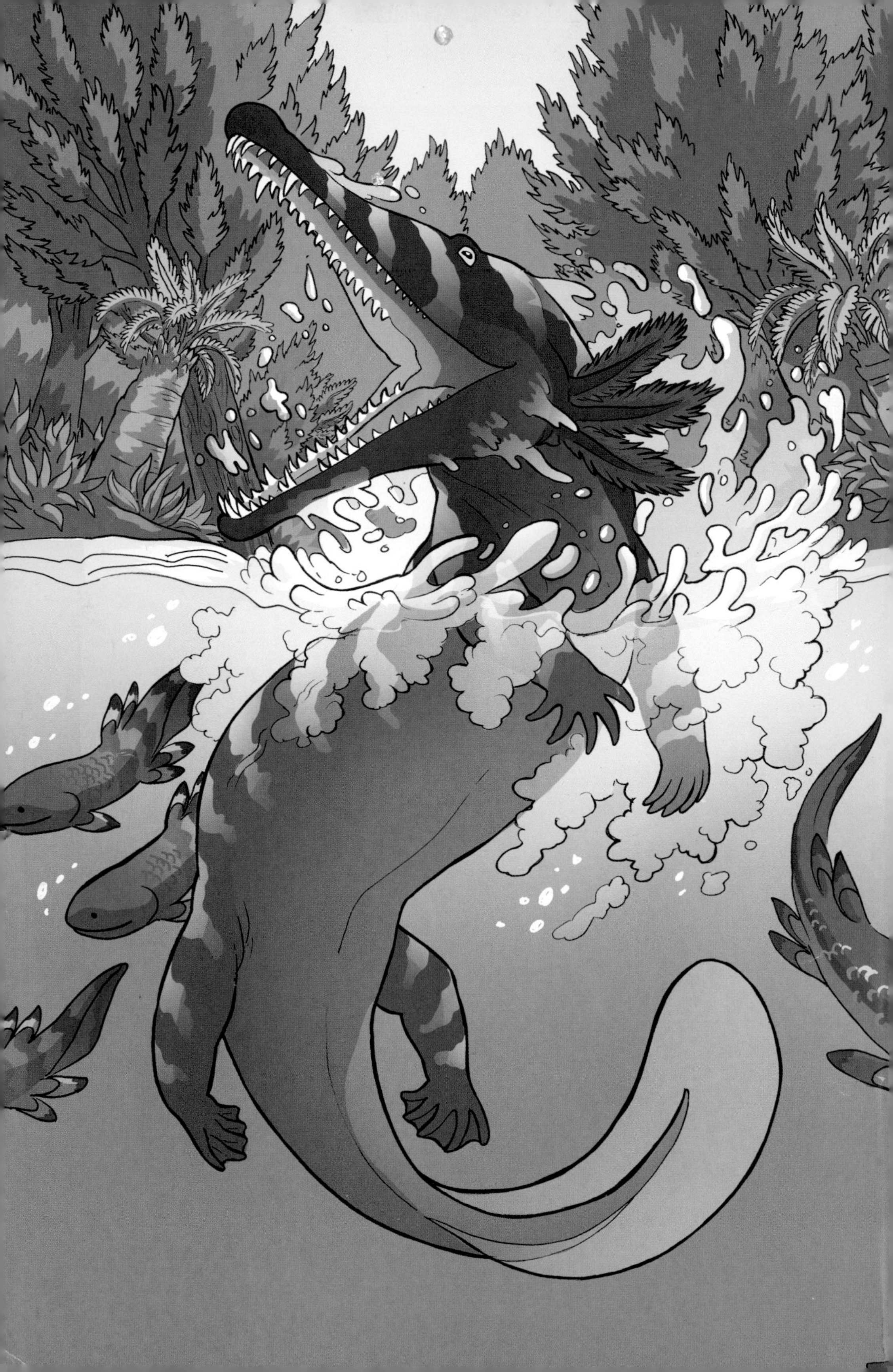

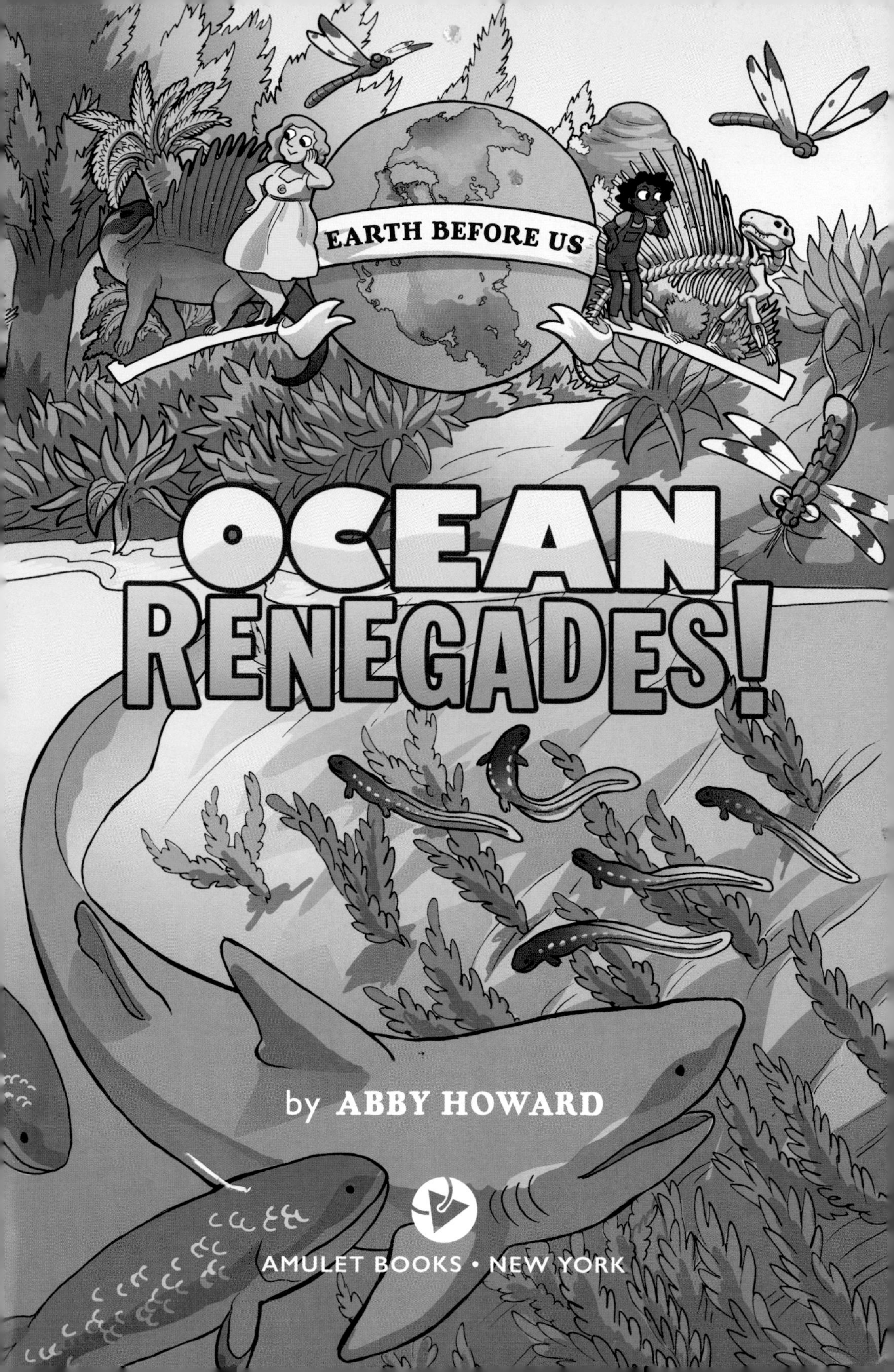

EARTH BEFORE US

OCEAN RENEGADES!

by **ABBY HOWARD**

AMULET BOOKS • NEW YORK

Library of Congress Cataloging-in-Publication Data
Names: Howard, Abby (Comic artist), author, illustrator.
Title: Ocean Renegrades! / by Abby Howard.
Description: New York: Amulet Books, 2018. | Series: Earth before us; #2 |
Summary: "Determined to show Ronnie just how interesting prehistoric life was BEFORE the age of the dinosaurs, Miss Lernin takes her back in time to the six parts of the Paleozoic era to study the earliest lifeforms on Earth, starting with the rise of the vertebrates"— Provided by publisher.
Identifiers: LCCN 2017052638 | ISBN 978-1-4197-3136-5 (hardcover POB)
Subjects: LCSH: Graphic novels. | CYAC: Graphic novels. | Prehistoric animals—Fiction. | Marine animals—Fiction. | Evolution—Fiction. | Time travel—Fiction.
Classification: LCC PZ7.7.H73 Oce 2018 | DDC 741.5/31—dc23

Printed and bound in China
10 9 8 7 6 5 4 3 2 1

Amulet Books are available at special discounts when purchased in quantity for premiums and promotions as well as fundraising or educational use. Special editions can also be created to specification. For details, contact specialsales@abramsbooks.com or the address below.

ABRAMS The Art of Books
195 Broadway, New York, NY 10007
abramsbooks.com

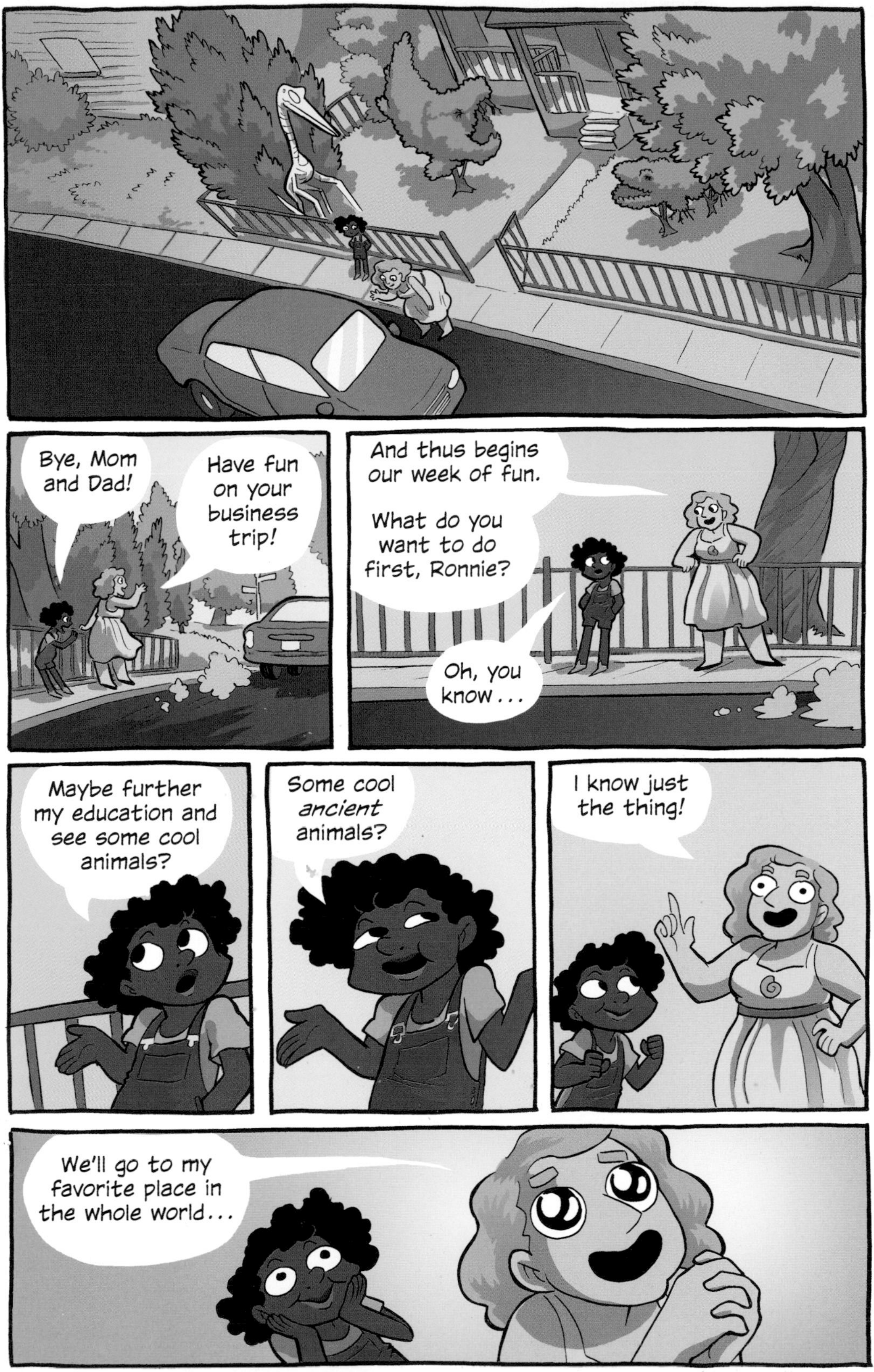
Bye, Mom and Dad!
Have fun on your business trip!
And thus begins our week of fun.
What do you want to do first, Ronnie?
Oh, you know...
Maybe further my education and see some cool animals?
Some cool *ancient* animals?
I know just the thing!
We'll go to my favorite place in the whole world...

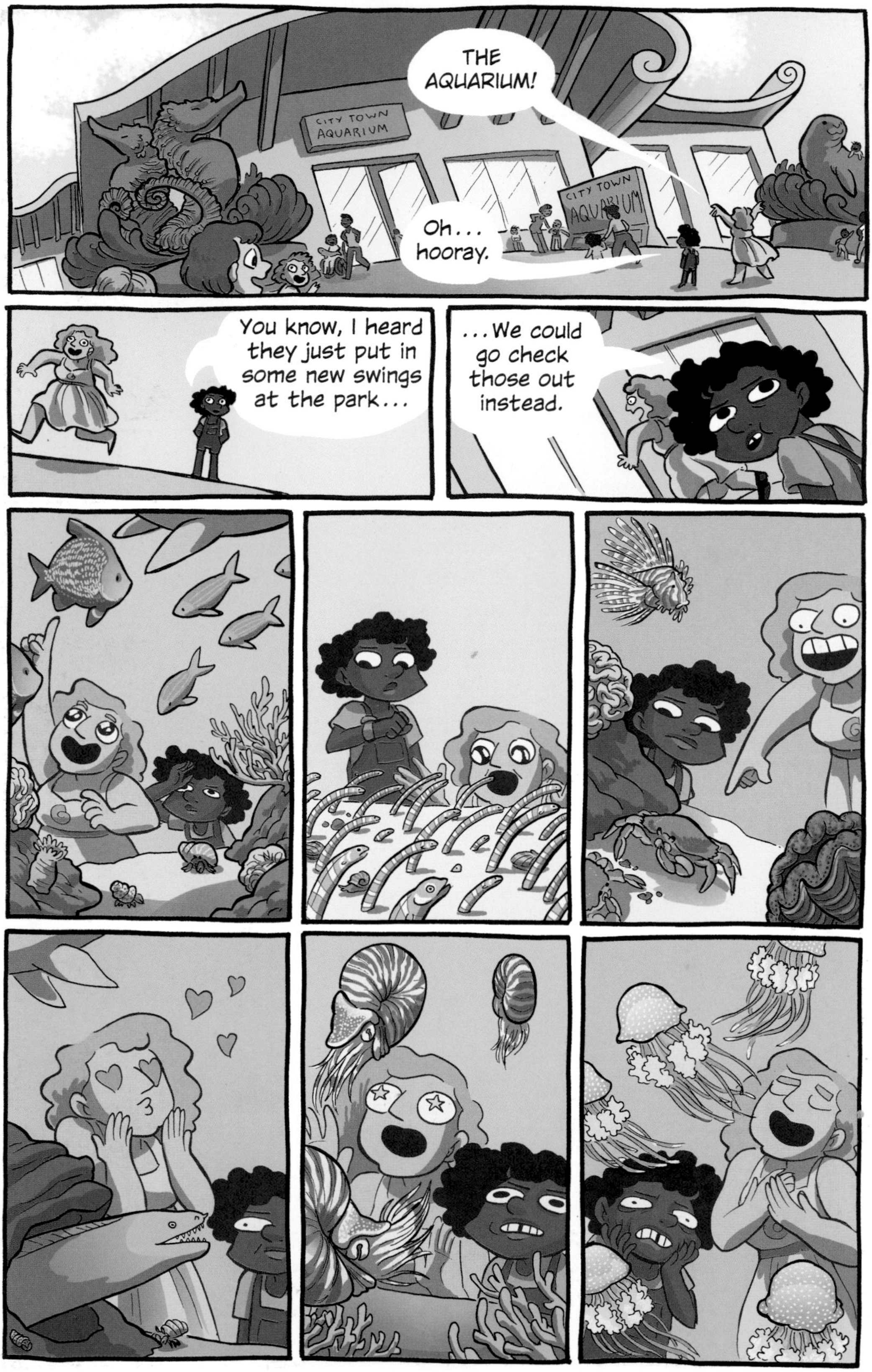
THE AQUARIUM!
CITY TOWN AQUARIUM
CITY TOWN AQUARIUM
Oh... hooray.
You know, I heard they just put in some new swings at the park...
...We could go check those out instead.

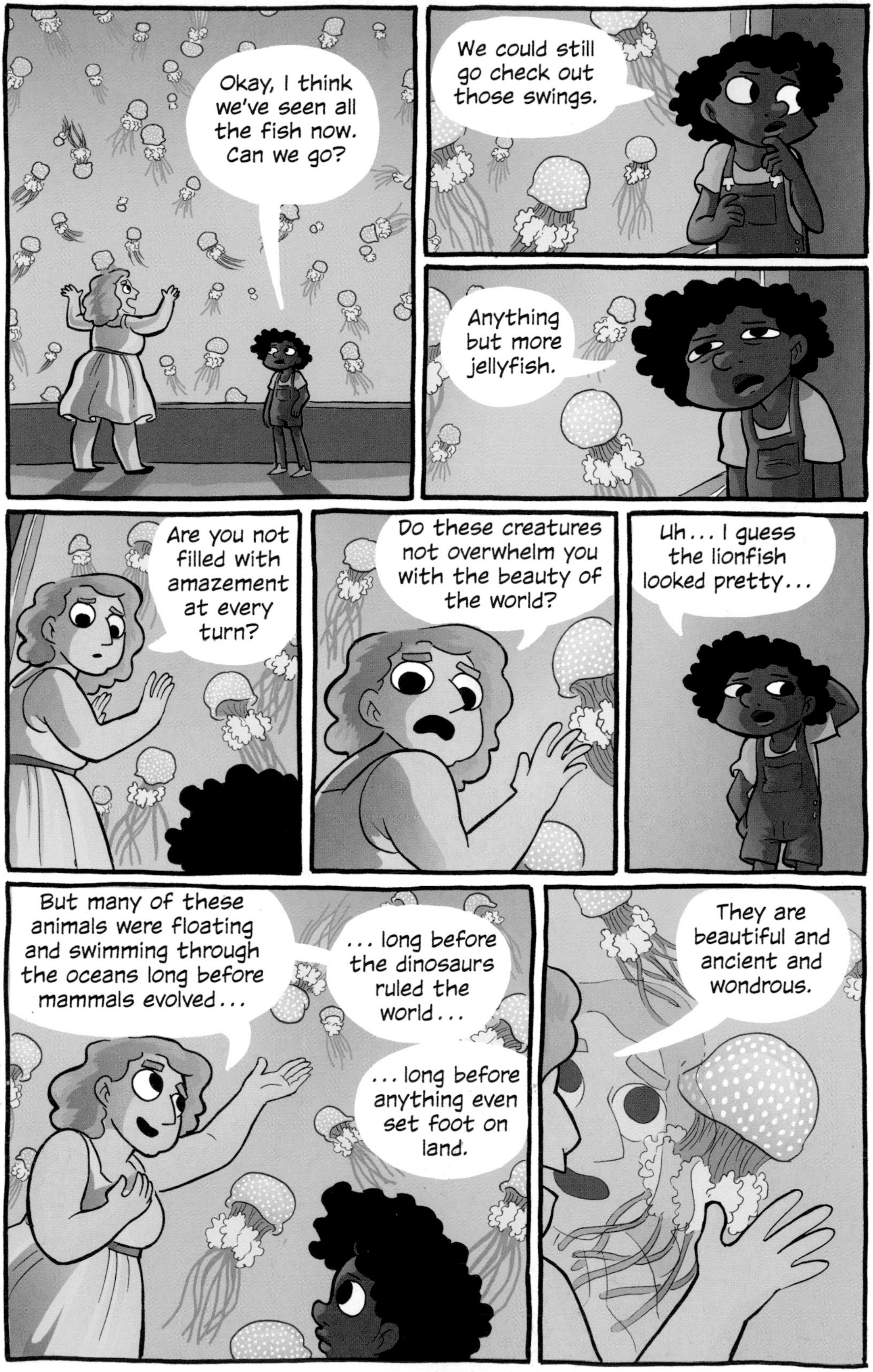
Okay, I think we've seen all the fish now. Can we go?
We could still go check out those swings.
Anything but more jellyfish.
Are you not filled with amazement at every turn?
Do these creatures not overwhelm you with the beauty of the world?
Uh... I guess the lionfish looked pretty...
But many of these animals were floating and swimming through the oceans long before mammals evolved...
... long before the dinosaurs ruled the world...
... long before anything even set foot on land.
They are beautiful and ancient and wondrous.

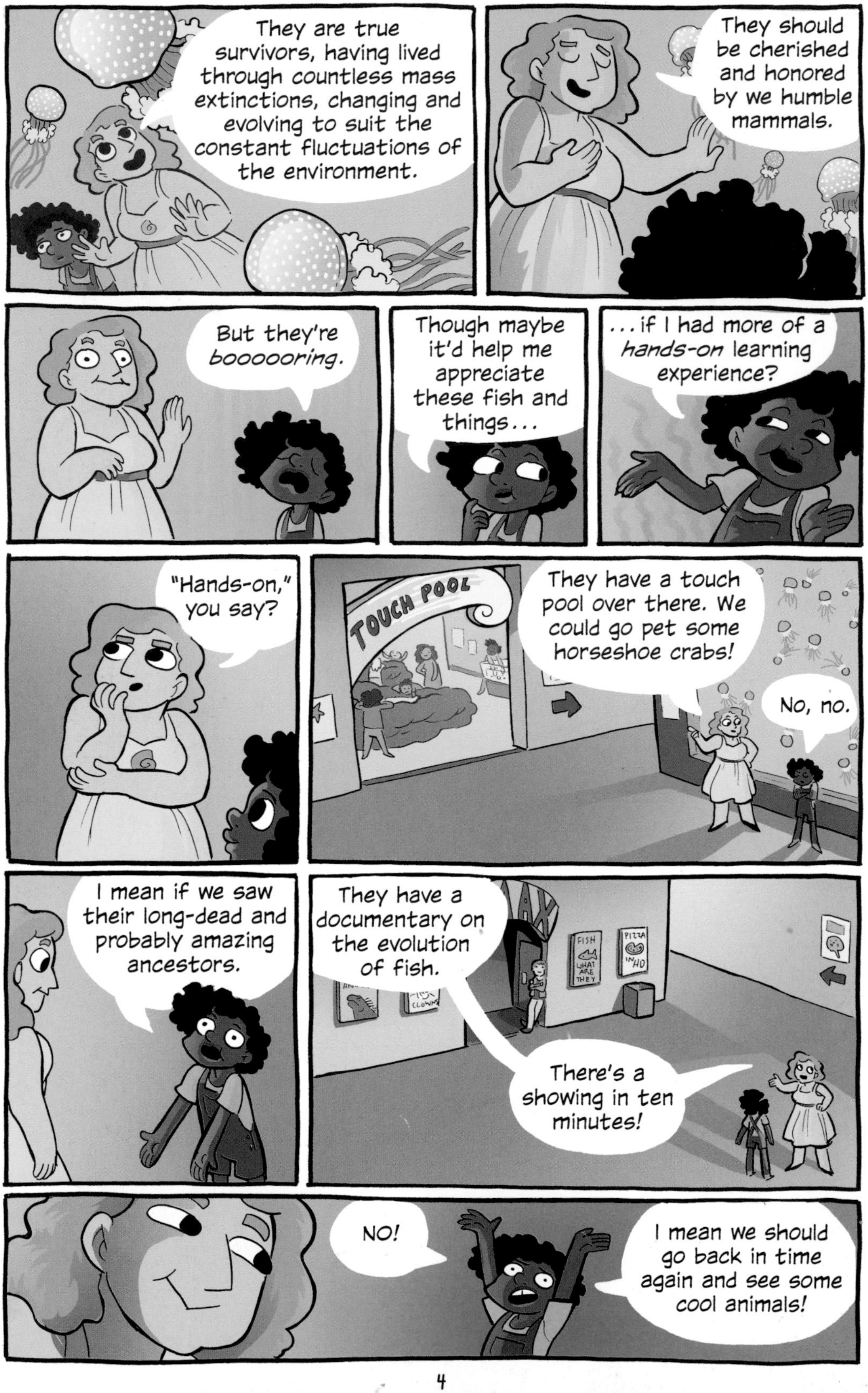

They are true survivors, having lived through countless mass extinctions, changing and evolving to suit the constant fluctuations of the environment.
They should be cherished and honored by we humble mammals.
But they're *boooooring*.
Though maybe it'd help me appreciate these fish and things...
...if I had more of a *hands-on* learning experience?
"Hands-on," you say?
TOUCH POOL
They have a touch pool over there. We could go pet some horseshoe crabs!
No, no.
I mean if we saw their long-dead and probably amazing ancestors.
They have a documentary on the evolution of fish.
FISH
WHAT ARE THEY
PIZZA
IN HD
There's a showing in ten minutes!
NO!
I mean we should go back in time again and see some cool animals!

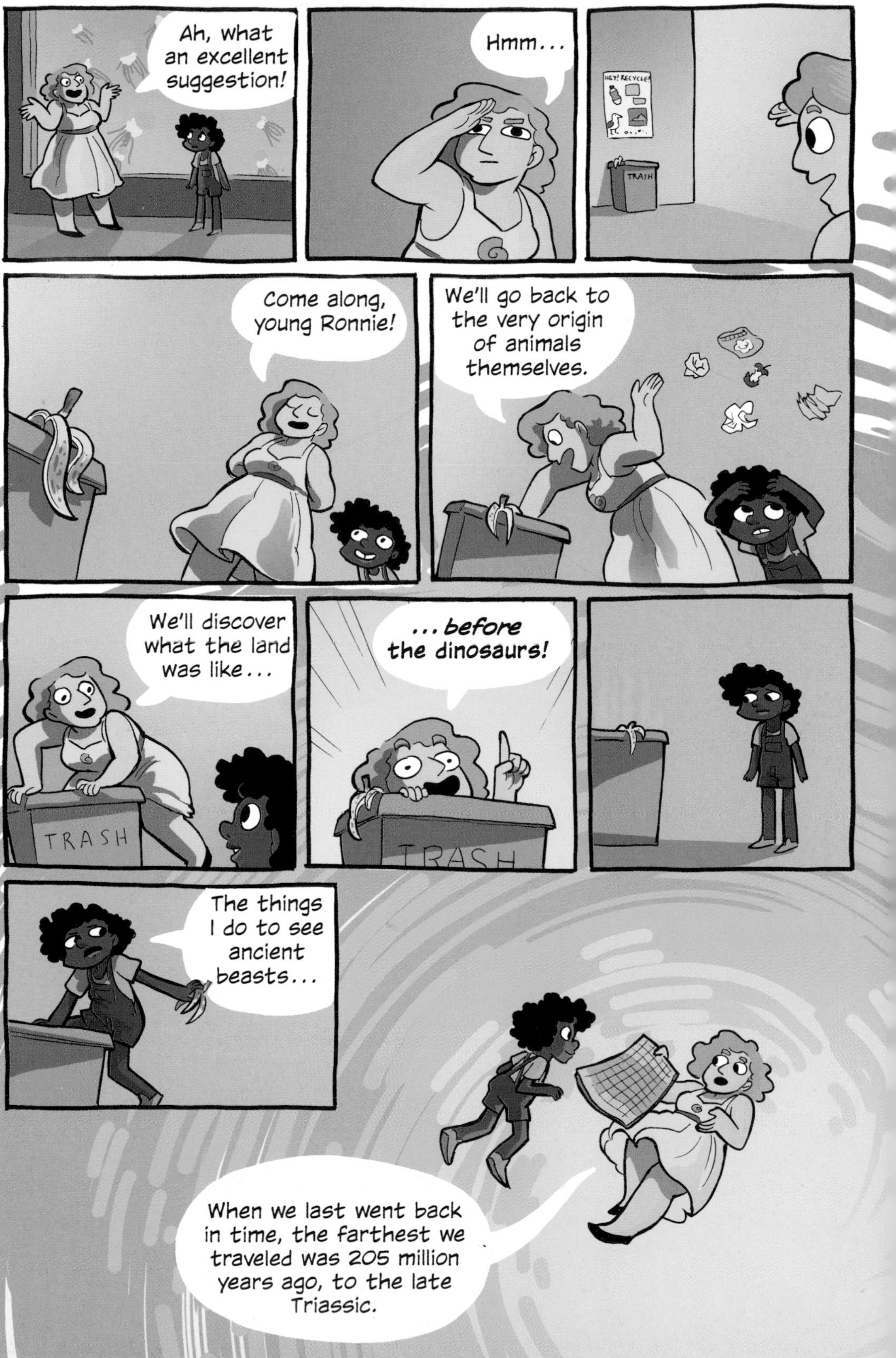
Ah, what an excellent suggestion!
Hmm...
HEY! RECYCLE!
TRASH
Come along, young Ronnie!
We'll go back to the very origin of animals themselves.
We'll discover what the land was like...
TRASH
...*before* the dinosaurs!
TRASH
The things I do to see ancient beasts...
When we last went back in time, the farthest we traveled was 205 million years ago, to the late Triassic.

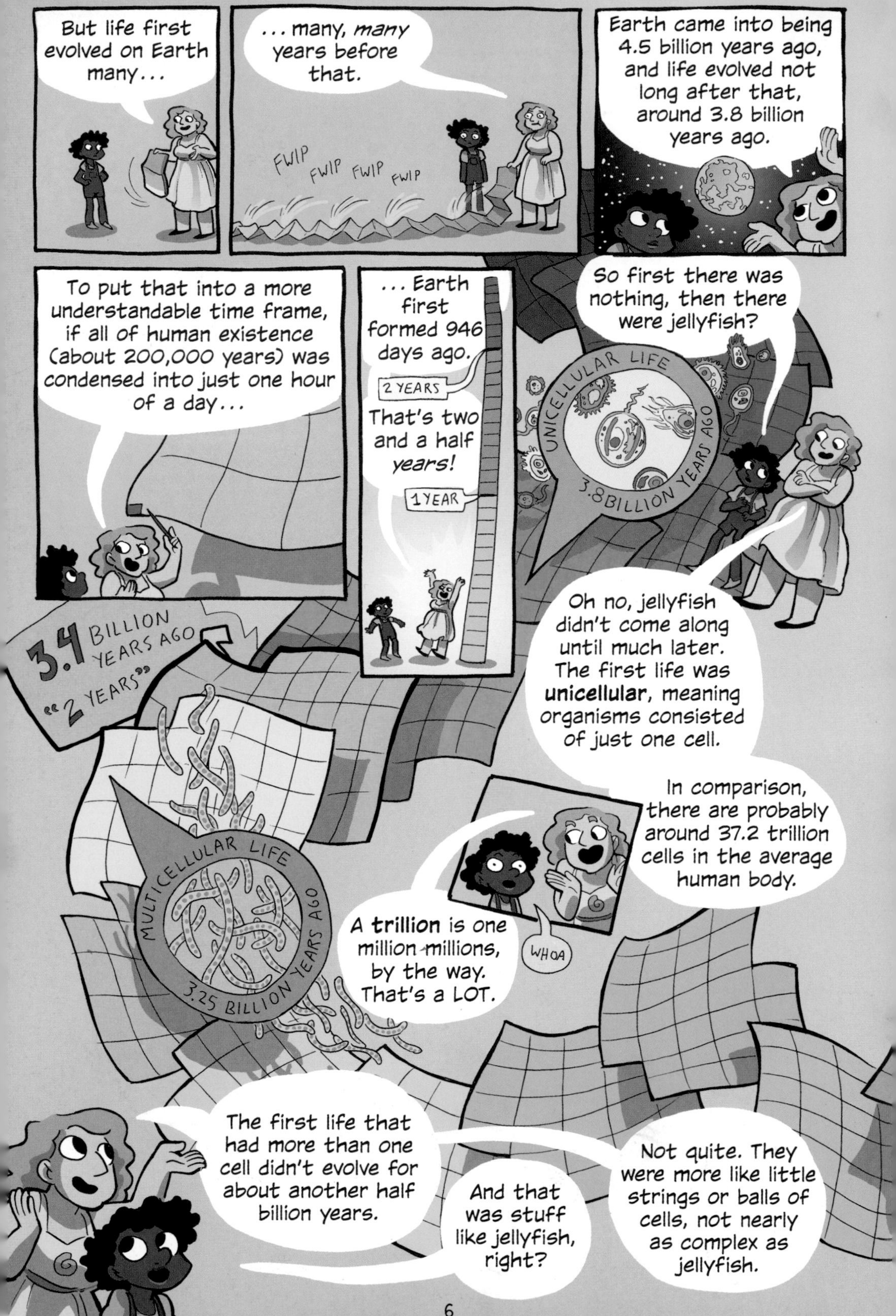
But life first evolved on Earth many...
...many, *many* years before that.
FWIP FWIP FWIP FWIP
Earth came into being 4.5 billion years ago, and life evolved not long after that, around 3.8 billion years ago.
To put that into a more understandable time frame, if all of human existence (about 200,000 years) was condensed into just one hour of a day...
...Earth first formed 946 days ago.
2 YEARS
That's two and a half *years*!
1 YEAR
So first there was nothing, then there were jellyfish?
UNICELLULAR LIFE
3.8 BILLION YEARS AGO
3.4 BILLION YEARS AGO
"2 YEARS"
Oh no, jellyfish didn't come along until much later. The first life was **unicellular**, meaning organisms consisted of just one cell.
In comparison, there are probably around 37.2 trillion cells in the average human body.
MULTICELLULAR LIFE
3.25 BILLION YEARS AGO
A **trillion** is one million millions, by the way. That's a LOT.
WHOA
The first life that had more than one cell didn't evolve for about another half billion years.
And that was stuff like jellyfish, right?
Not quite. They were more like little strings or balls of cells, not nearly as complex as jellyfish.

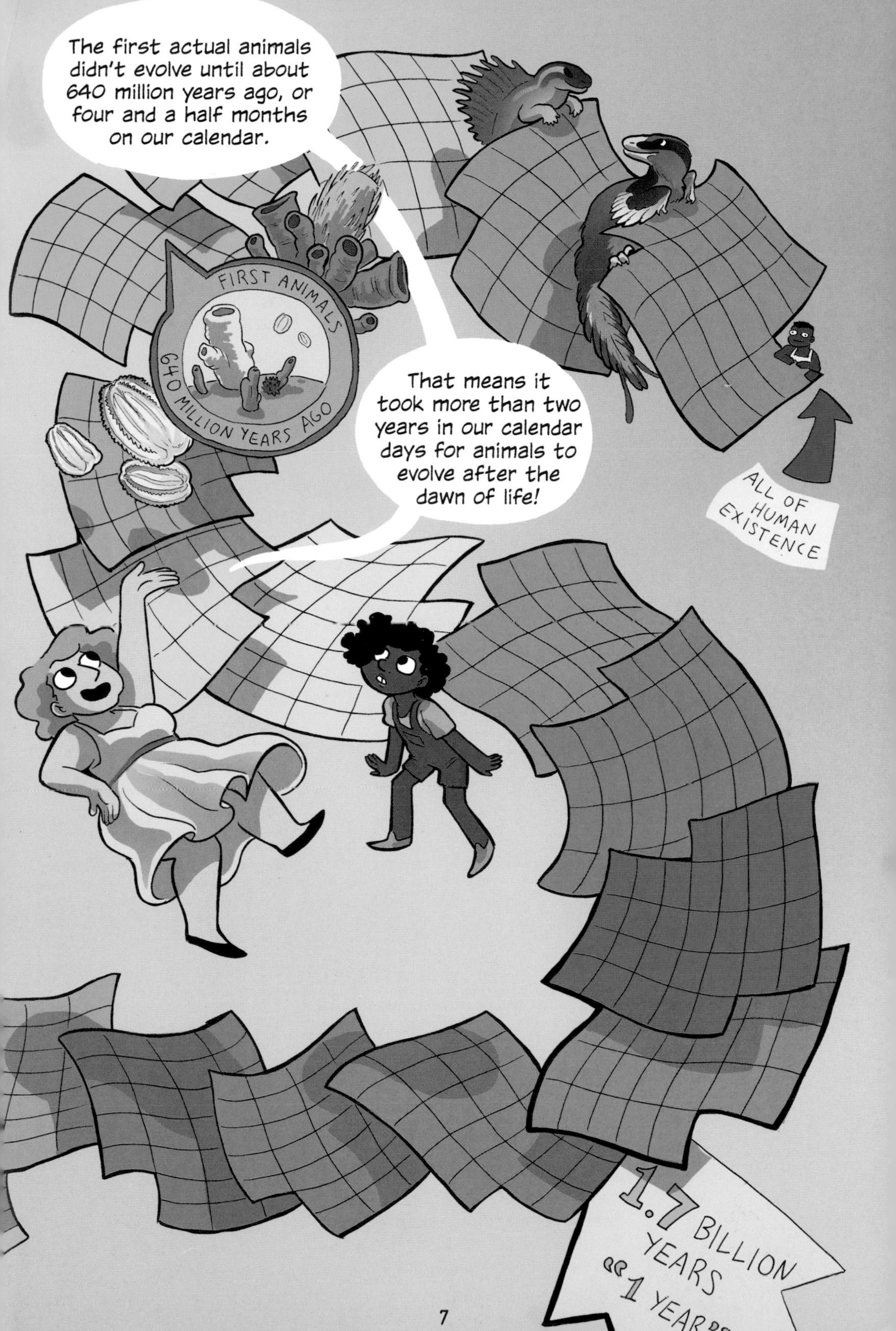
The first actual animals didn't evolve until about 640 million years ago, or four and a half months on our calendar.
FIRST ANIMALS
640 MILLION YEARS AGO
That means it took more than two years in our calendar days for animals to evolve after the dawn of life!
ALL OF HUMAN EXISTENCE
1.7 BILLION YEARS
"1 YEAR"

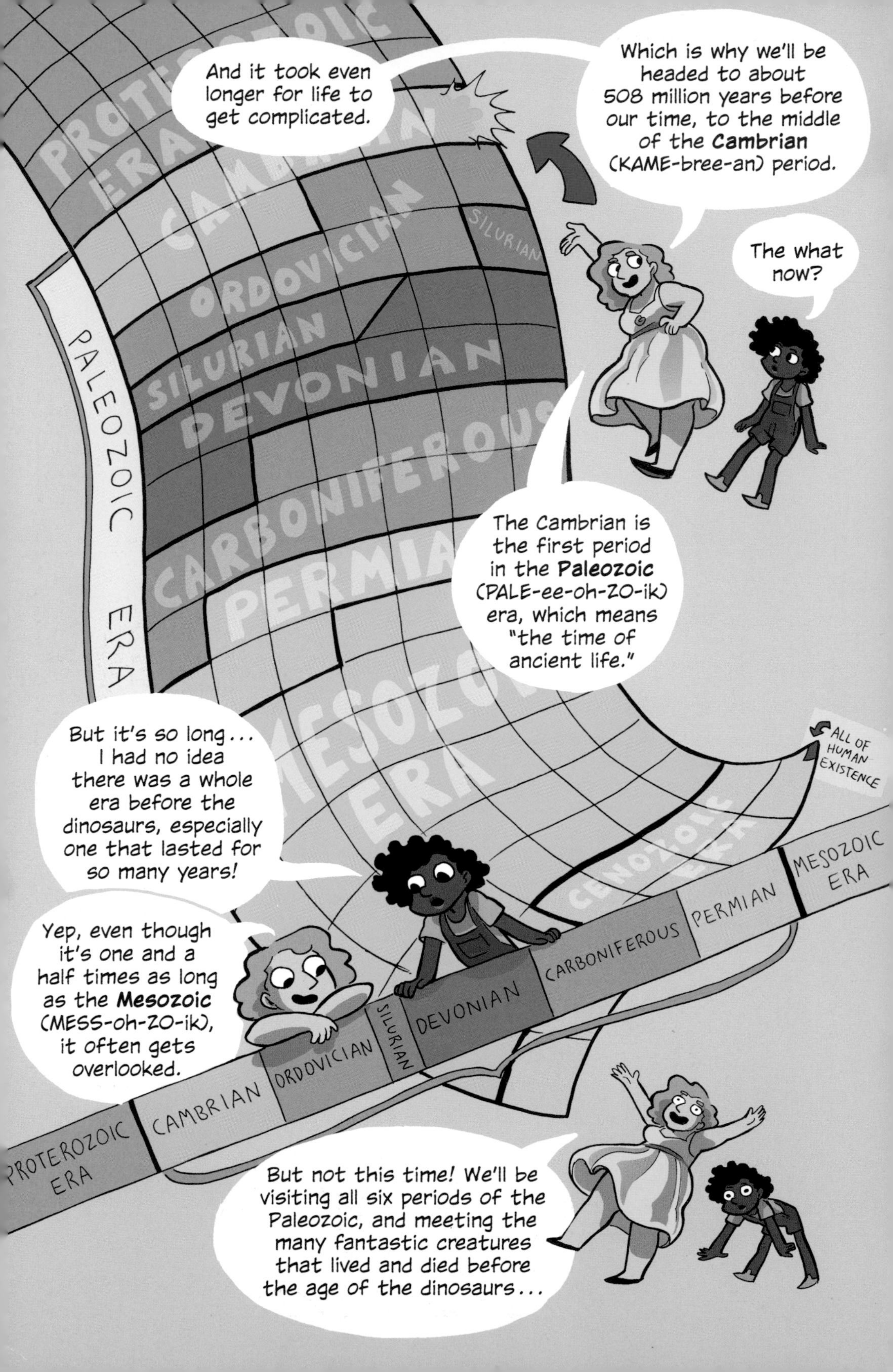
PROTEROZOIC ERA
CAMBRIAN
ORDOVICIAN
SILURIAN
SILURIAN
DEVONIAN
CARBONIFEROUS
PERMIAN
MESOZOIC ERA
CENOZOIC ERA
PALEOZOIC ERA
ALL OF HUMAN EXISTENCE
And it took even longer for life to get complicated.
Which is why we'll be headed to about 508 million years before our time, to the middle of the **Cambrian** (KAME-bree-an) period.
The what now?
The Cambrian is the first period in the **Paleozoic** (PALE-ee-oh-ZO-ik) era, which means "the time of ancient life."
But it's so long... I had no idea there was a whole era before the dinosaurs, especially one that lasted for so many years!
Yep, even though it's one and a half times as long as the **Mesozoic** (MESS-oh-ZO-ik), it often gets overlooked.
PROTEROZOIC ERA
CAMBRIAN
ORDOVICIAN
SILURIAN
DEVONIAN
CARBONIFEROUS
PERMIAN
MESOZOIC ERA
But not this time! We'll be visiting all six periods of the Paleozoic, and meeting the many fantastic creatures that lived and died before the age of the dinosaurs...

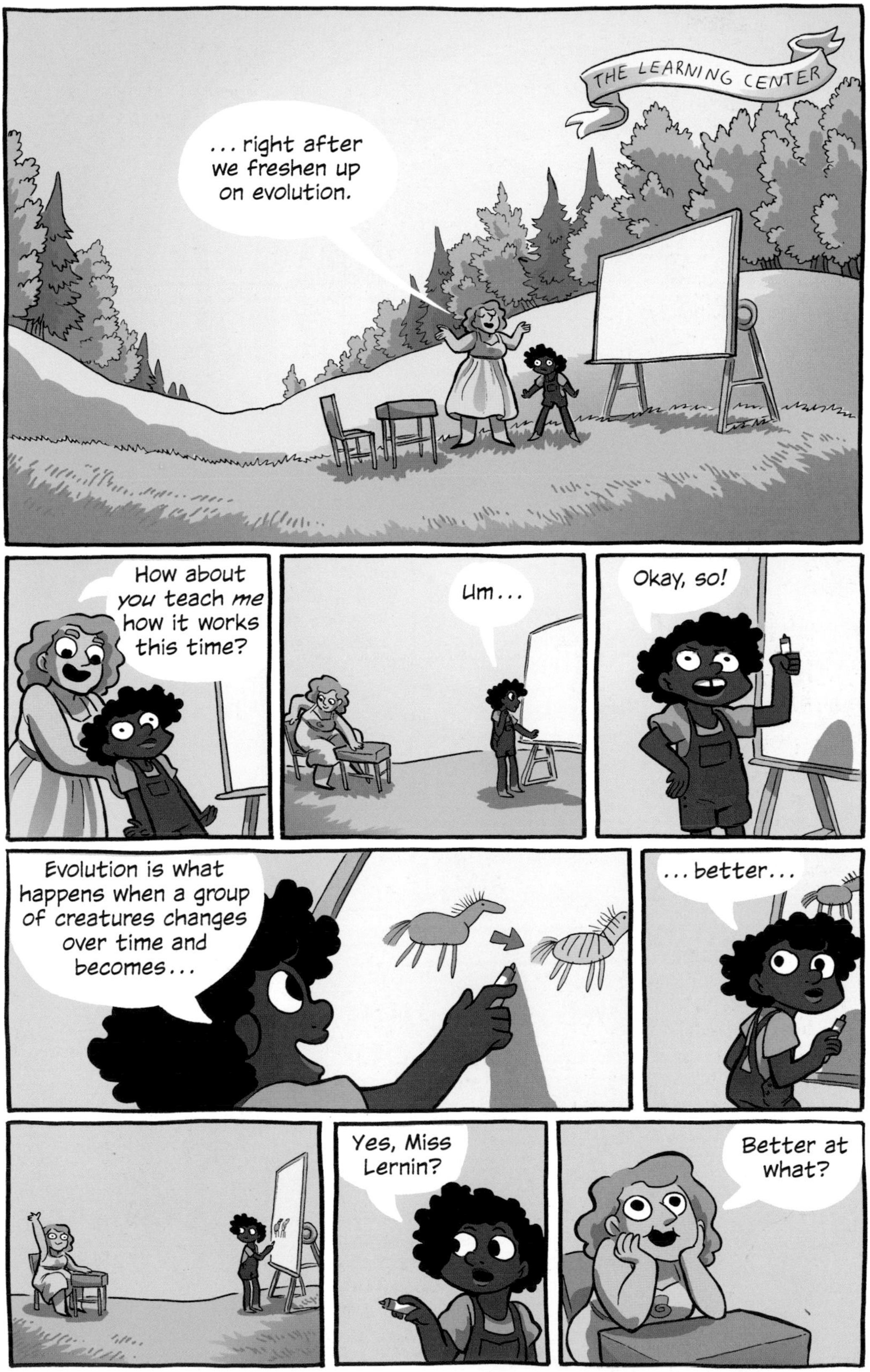
THE LEARNING CENTER
...right after we freshen up on evolution.
How about *you* teach *me* how it works this time?
Um...
Okay, so!
Evolution is what happens when a group of creatures changes over time and becomes...
...better...
Yes, Miss Lernin?
Better at what?

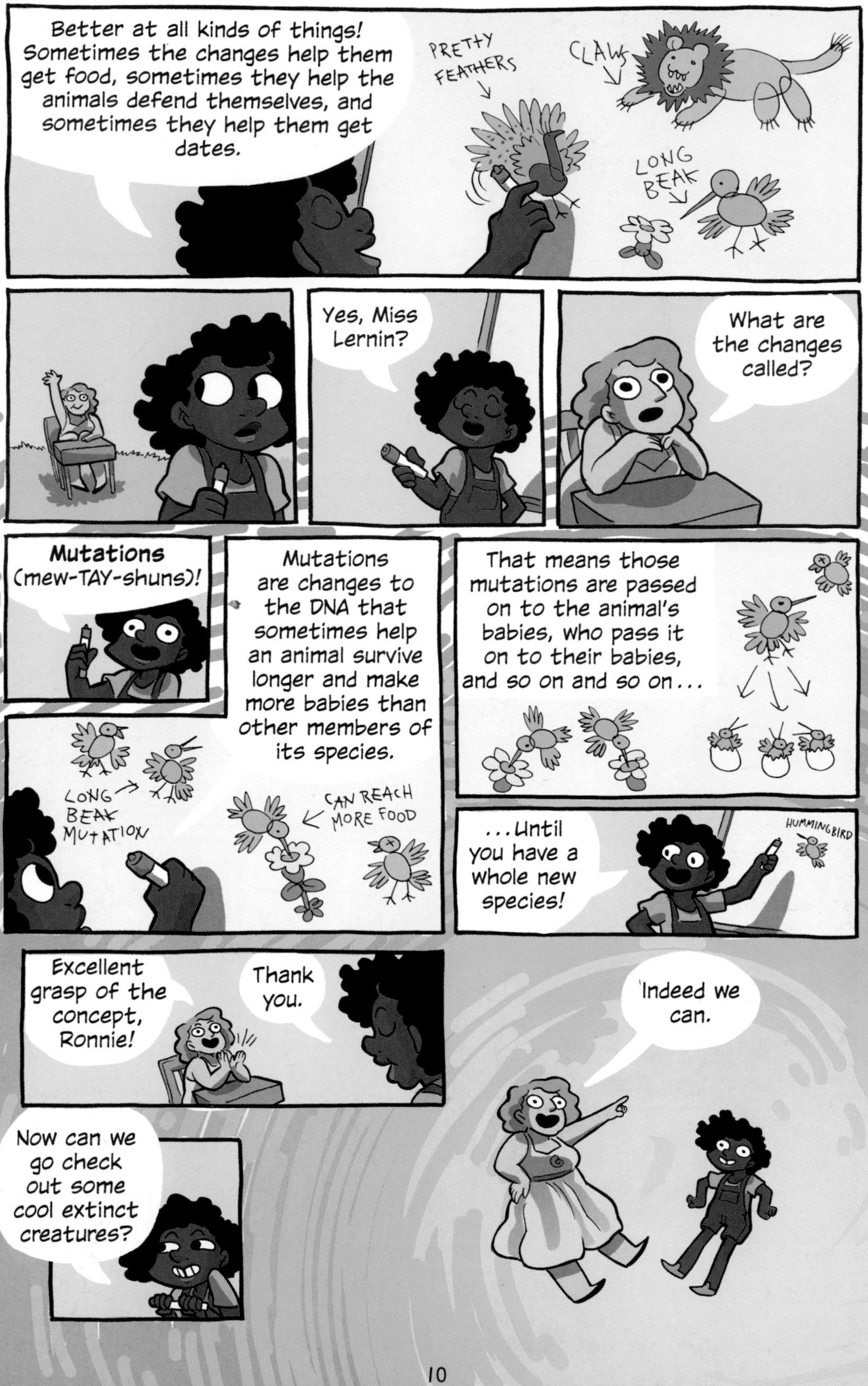
Better at all kinds of things! Sometimes the changes help them get food, sometimes they help the animals defend themselves, and sometimes they help them get dates.
PRETTY FEATHERS
CLAWS
LONG BEAK
Yes, Miss Lernin?
What are the changes called?
Mutations (mew-TAY-shuns)!
Mutations are changes to the DNA that sometimes help an animal survive longer and make more babies than other members of its species.
LONG BEAK MUTATION
CAN REACH MORE FOOD
That means those mutations are passed on to the animal's babies, who pass it on to their babies, and so on and so on...
...Until you have a whole new species!
HUMMINGBIRD
Excellent grasp of the concept, Ronnie!
Thank you.
Now can we go check out some cool extinct creatures?
Indeed we can.

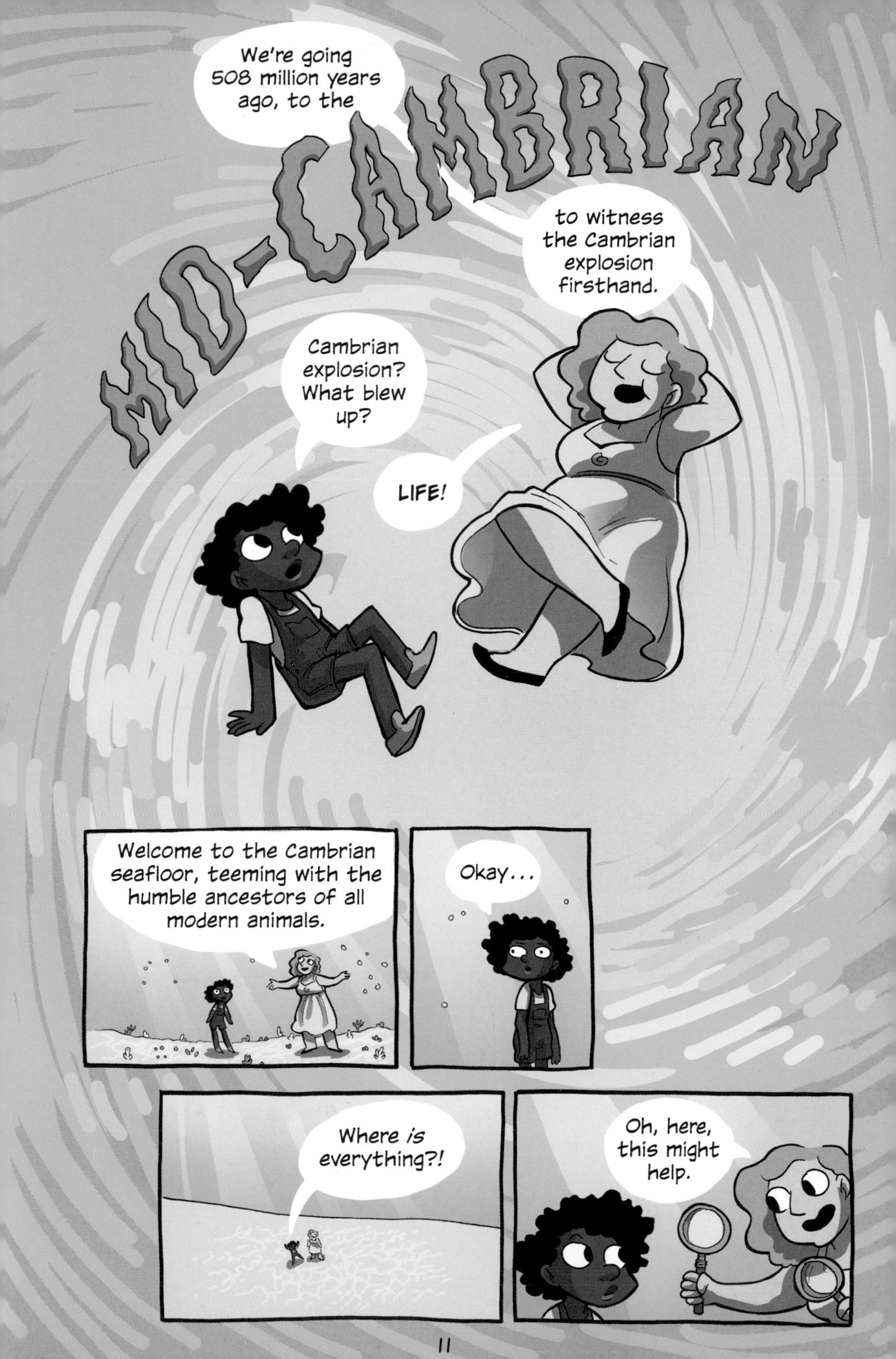
We're going 508 million years ago, to the
MID-CAMBRIAN
to witness the Cambrian explosion firsthand.
Cambrian explosion? What blew up?
LIFE!
Welcome to the Cambrian seafloor, teeming with the humble ancestors of all modern animals.
Okay...
Where *is* everything?!
Oh, here, this might help.

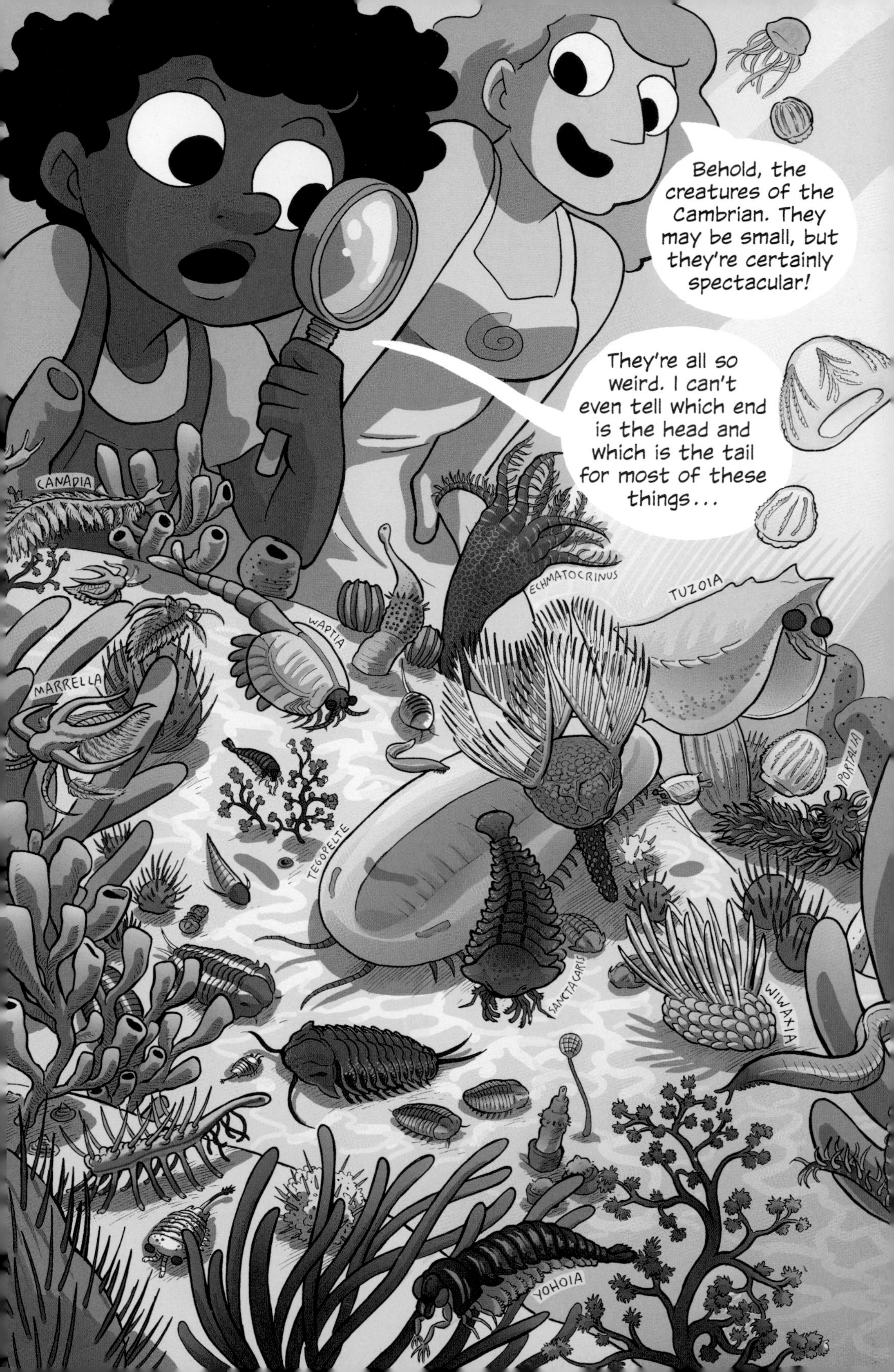
Behold, the creatures of the Cambrian. They may be small, but they're certainly spectacular!
They're all so weird. I can't even tell which end is the head and which is the tail for most of these things...
CANADIA
WAPTIA
ECHMATOCRINUS
TUZOIA
MARRELLA
PORTALIA
TEGOPELTE
SANCTACARIS
WIWAXIA
YOHOIA

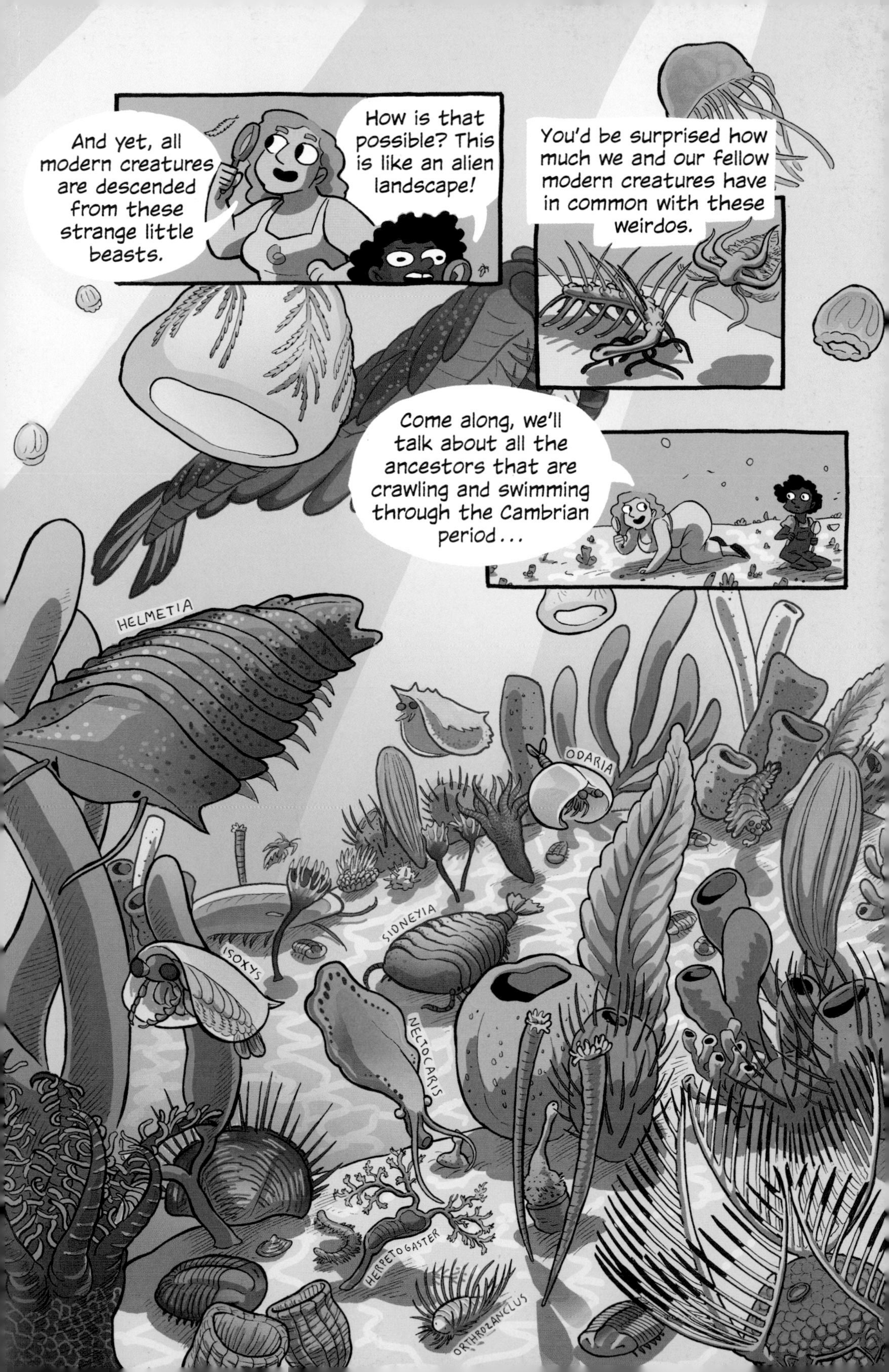
And yet, all modern creatures are descended from these strange little beasts.
How is that possible? This is like an alien landscape!
You'd be surprised how much we and our fellow modern creatures have in common with these weirdos.
Come along, we'll talk about all the ancestors that are crawling and swimming through the Cambrian period...
HELMETIA
ODARIA
SIDNEYIA
ISOXYS
NECTOCARIS
HERPETOGASTER
ORTHROZANCLUS

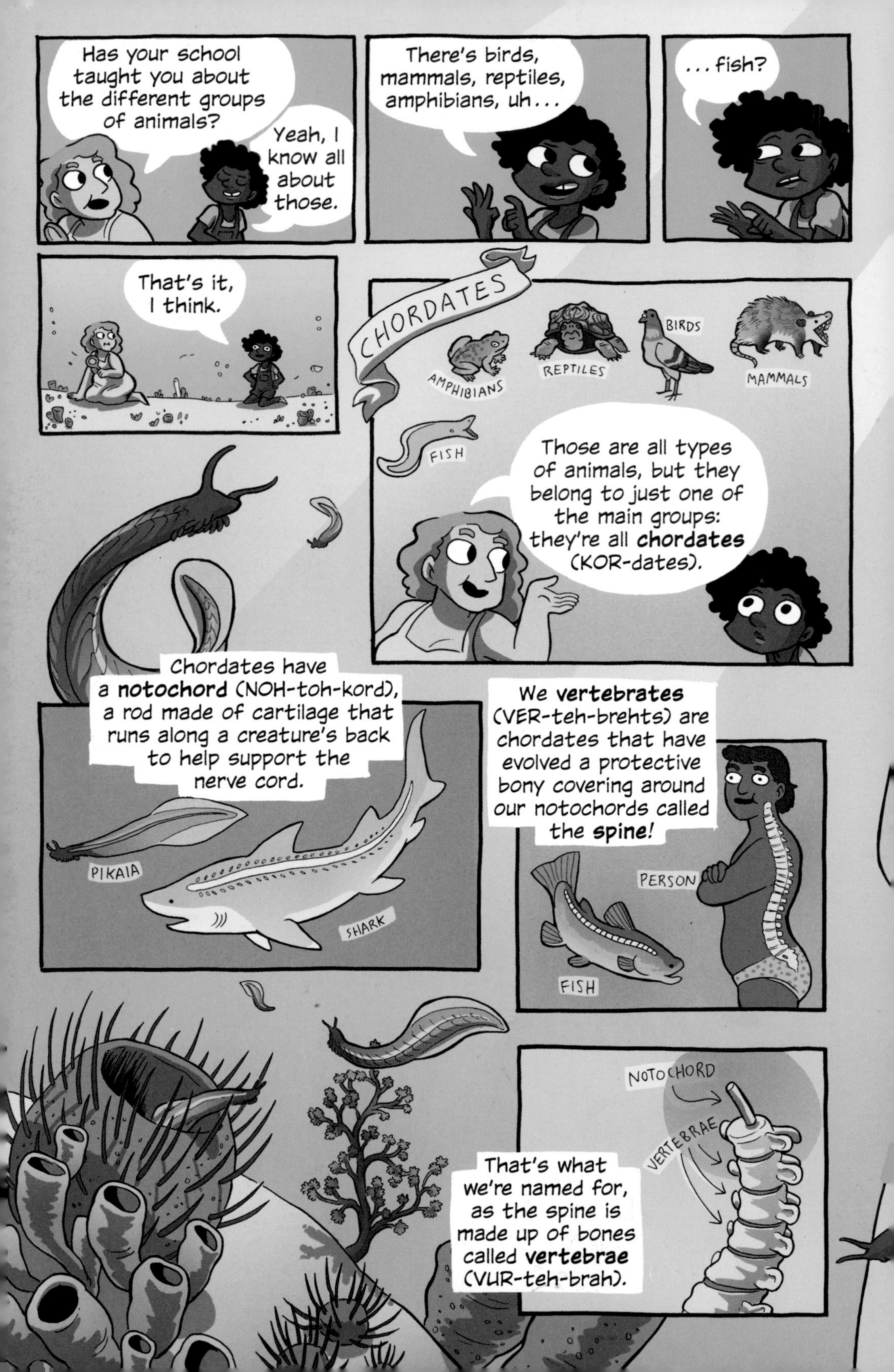

Has your school taught you about the different groups of animals?
Yeah, I know all about those.
There's birds, mammals, reptiles, amphibians, uh...
... fish?
That's it, I think.
CHORDATES
AMPHIBIANS
REPTILES
BIRDS
MAMMALS
FISH
Those are all types of animals, but they belong to just one of the main groups: they're all **chordates** (KOR-dates).
Chordates have a **notochord** (NOH-toh-kord), a rod made of cartilage that runs along a creature's back to help support the nerve cord.
PIKAIA
SHARK
We **vertebrates** (VER-teh-brehts) are chordates that have evolved a protective bony covering around our notochords called the **spine**!
PERSON
FISH
NOTOCHORD
VERTEBRAE
That's what we're named for, as the spine is made up of bones called **vertebrae** (VUR-teh-brah).

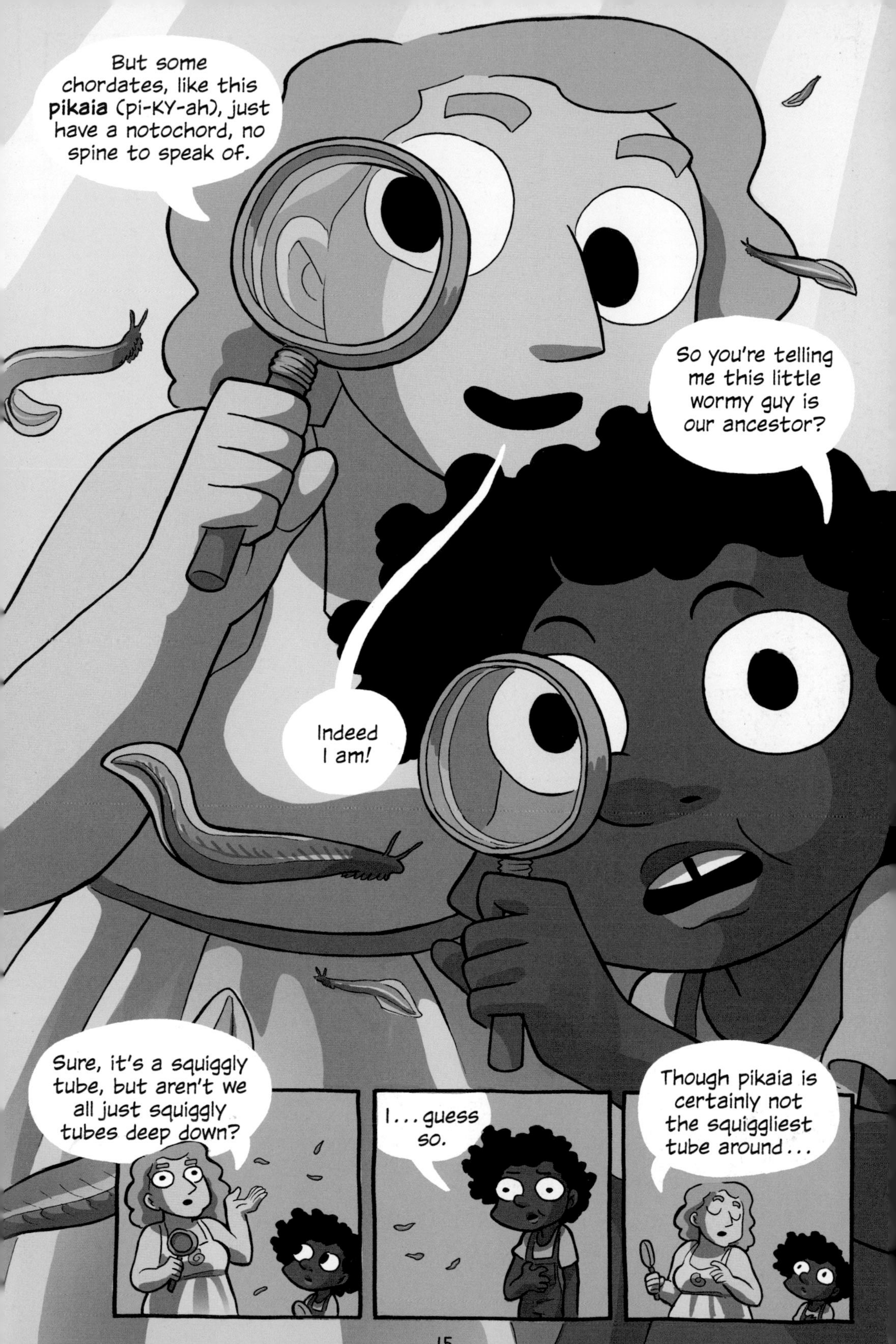
But some chordates, like this **pikaia** (pi-KY-ah), just have a notochord, no spine to speak of.
So you're telling me this little wormy guy is our ancestor?
Indeed I am!
Sure, it's a squiggly tube, but aren't we all just squiggly tubes deep down?
I... guess so.
Though pikaia is certainly not the squiggliest tube around...

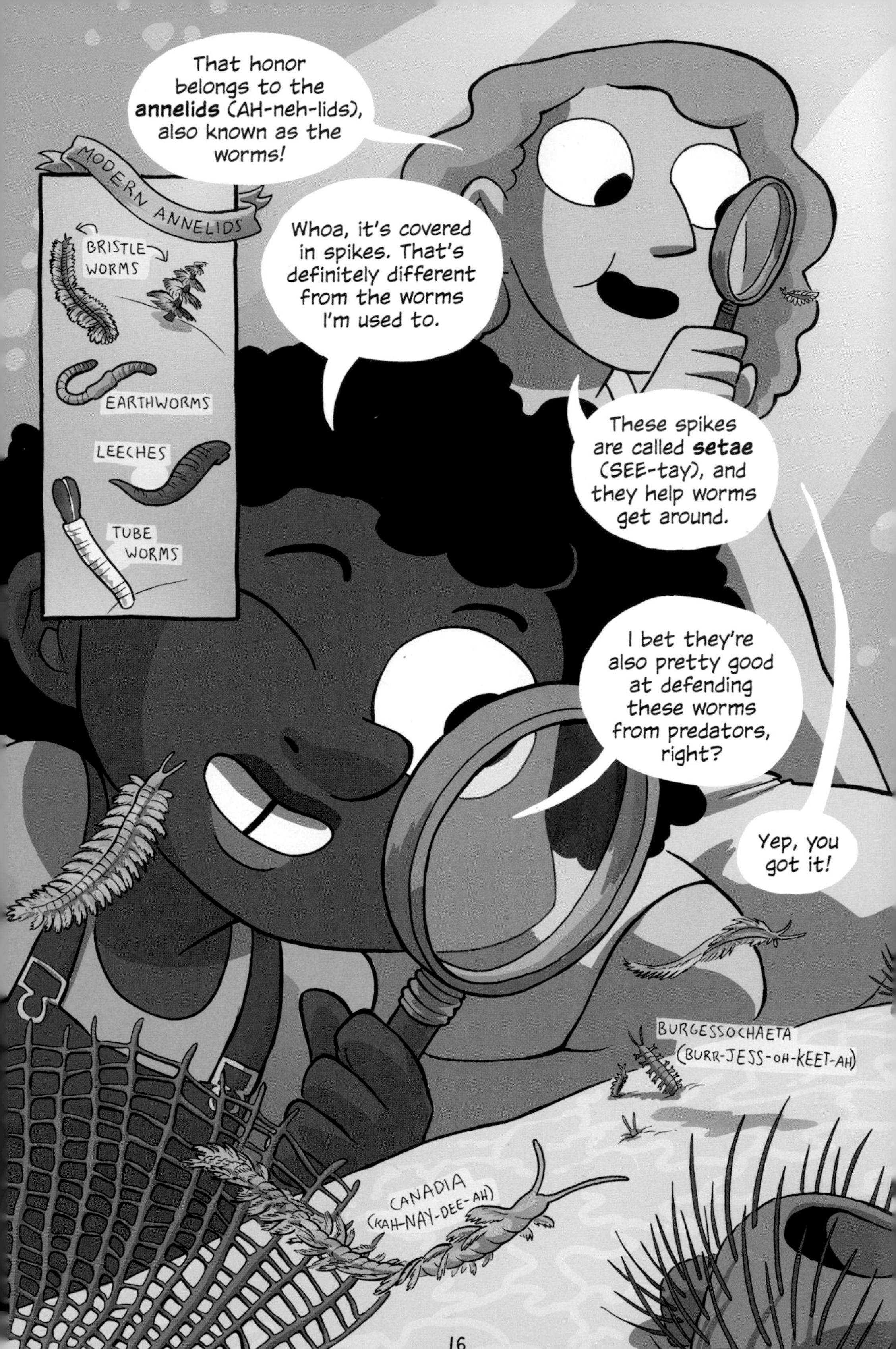
That honor belongs to the **annelids** (AH-neh-lids), also known as the worms!
MODERN ANNELIDS
BRISTLE WORMS
EARTHWORMS
LEECHES
TUBE WORMS
Whoa, it's covered in spikes. That's definitely different from the worms I'm used to.
These spikes are called **setae** (SEE-tay), and they help worms get around.
I bet they're also pretty good at defending these worms from predators, right?
Yep, you got it!
BURGESSOCHAETA (BURR-JESS-OH-KEET-AH)
CANADIA (KAH-NAY-DEE-AH)

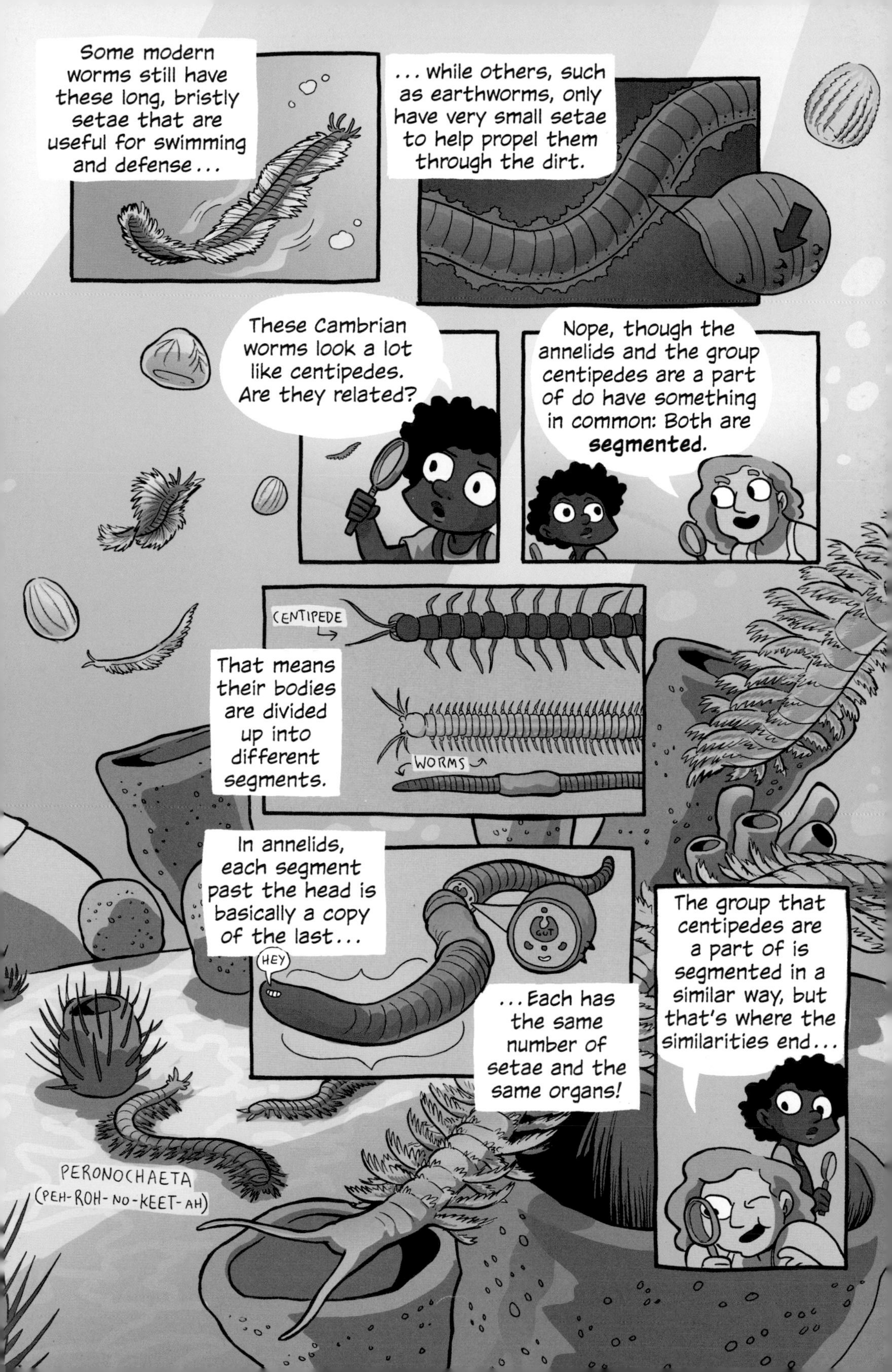
Some modern worms still have these long, bristly setae that are useful for swimming and defense...
...while others, such as earthworms, only have very small setae to help propel them through the dirt.
These Cambrian worms look a lot like centipedes. Are they related?
Nope, though the annelids and the group centipedes are a part of do have something in common: Both are **segmented**.
CENTIPEDE
That means their bodies are divided up into different segments.
WORMS
In annelids, each segment past the head is basically a copy of the last...
HEY
GUT
...Each has the same number of setae and the same organs!
The group that centipedes are a part of is segmented in a similar way, but that's where the similarities end...
PERONOCHAETA
(PEH-ROH-NO-KEET-AH)

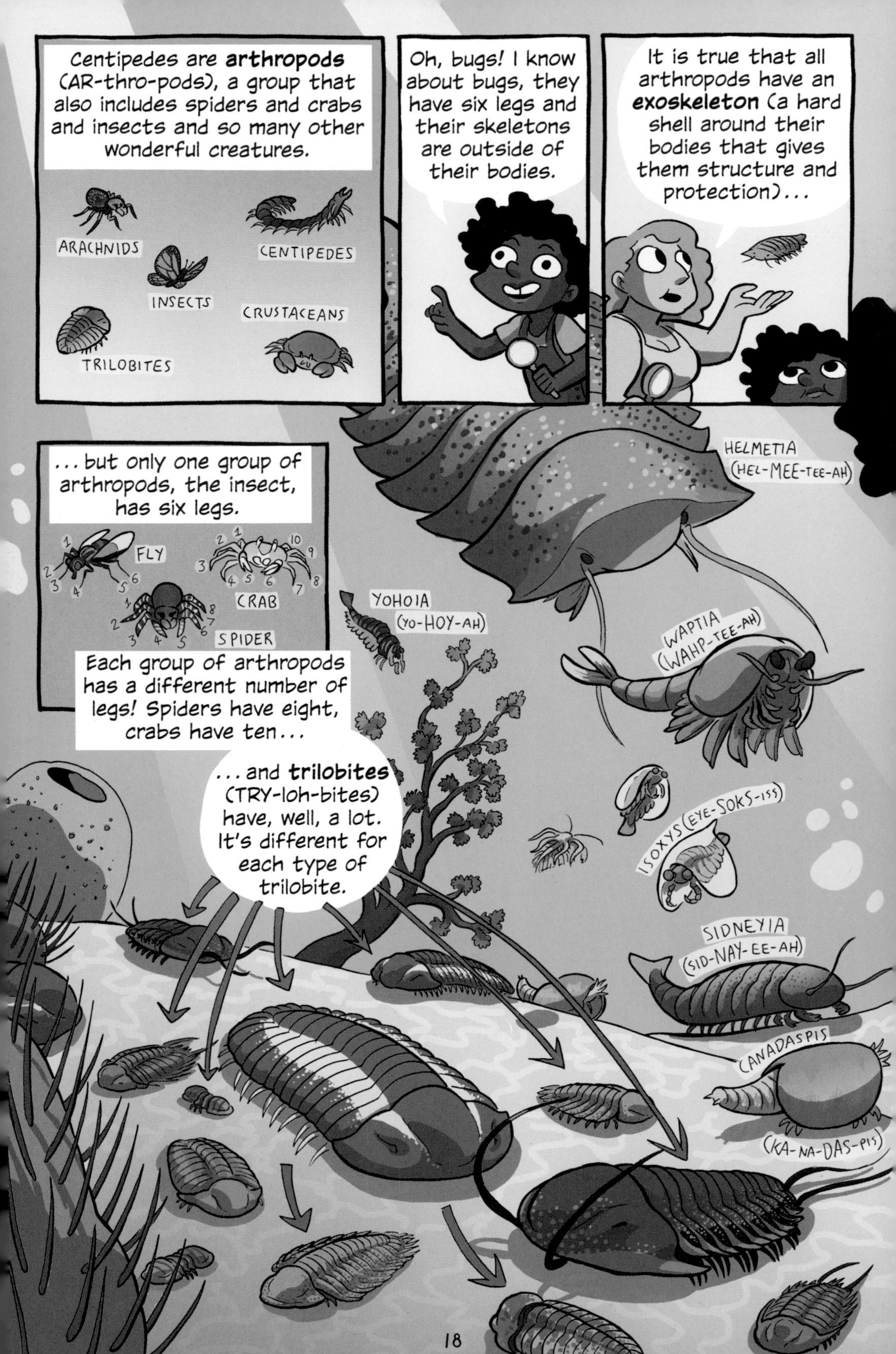

Centipedes are **arthropods** (AR-thro-pods), a group that also includes spiders and crabs and insects and so many other wonderful creatures.
ARACHNIDS
CENTIPEDES
INSECTS
CRUSTACEANS
TRILOBITES
Oh, bugs! I know about bugs, they have six legs and their skeletons are outside of their bodies.
It is true that all arthropods have an **exoskeleton** (a hard shell around their bodies that gives them structure and protection)...
HELMETIA
(HEL-MEE-TEE-AH)
...but only one group of arthropods, the insect, has six legs.
FLY
CRAB
SPIDER
YOHOIA
(YO-HOY-AH)
WAPTIA
(WAHP-TEE-AH)
Each group of arthropods has a different number of legs! Spiders have eight, crabs have ten...
...and **trilobites** (TRY-loh-bites) have, well, a lot. It's different for each type of trilobite.
ISOXYS (EYE-SOKS-ISS)
SIDNEYIA
(SID-NAY-EE-AH)
CANADASPIS
(KA-NA-DAS-PIS)

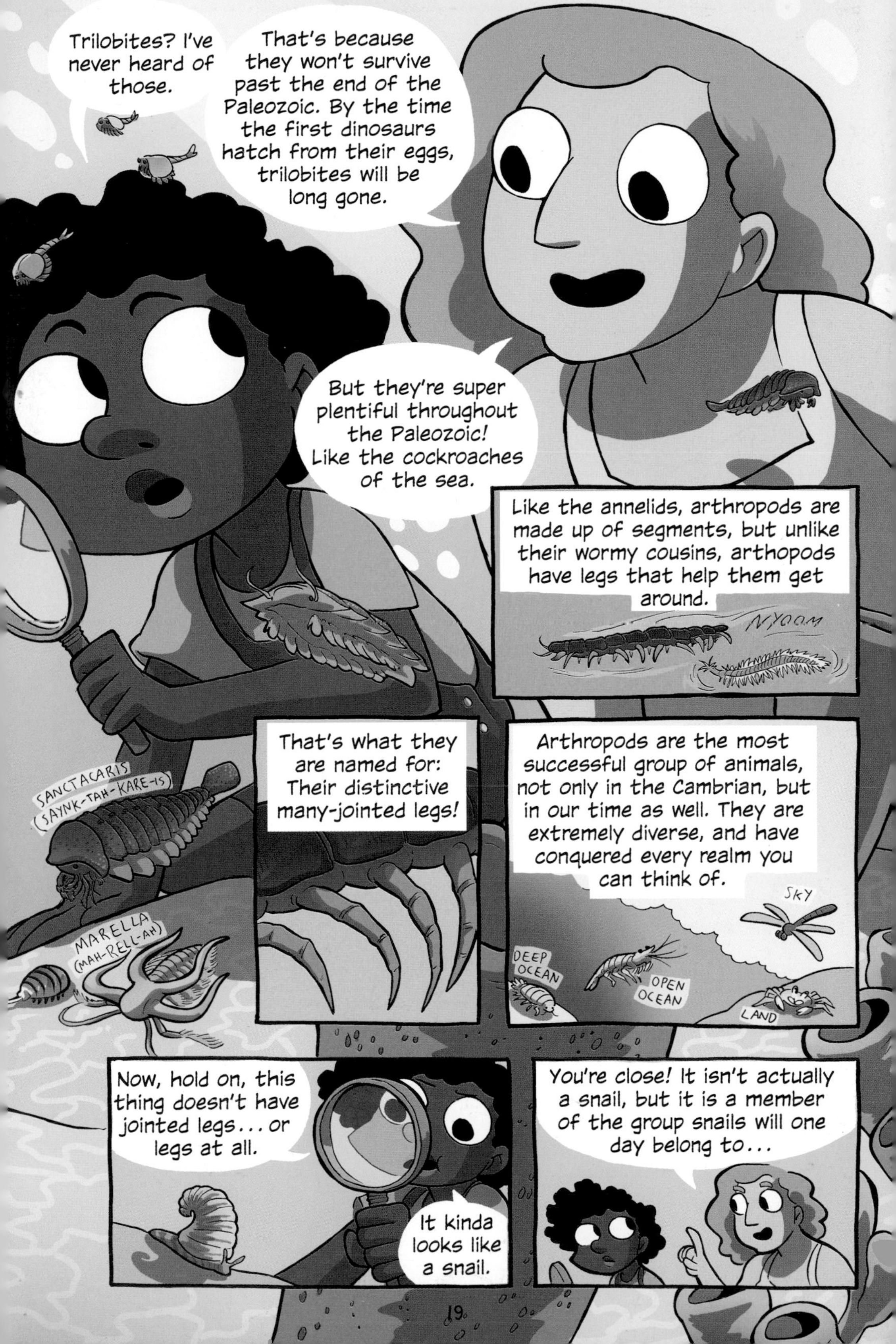

Trilobites? I've never heard of those.
That's because they won't survive past the end of the Paleozoic. By the time the first dinosaurs hatch from their eggs, trilobites will be long gone.
But they're super plentiful throughout the Paleozoic! Like the cockroaches of the sea.
Like the annelids, arthropods are made up of segments, but unlike their wormy cousins, arthopods have legs that help them get around.
NYOOM
SANCTACARIS (SAYNK-TAH-KARE-IS)
MARELLA (MAH-RELL-AH)
That's what they are named for: Their distinctive many-jointed legs!
Arthropods are the most successful group of animals, not only in the Cambrian, but in our time as well. They are extremely diverse, and have conquered every realm you can think of.
SKY
DEEP OCEAN
OPEN OCEAN
LAND
Now, hold on, this thing doesn't have jointed legs... or legs at all.
It kinda looks like a snail.
You're close! It isn't actually a snail, but it is a member of the group snails will one day belong to...

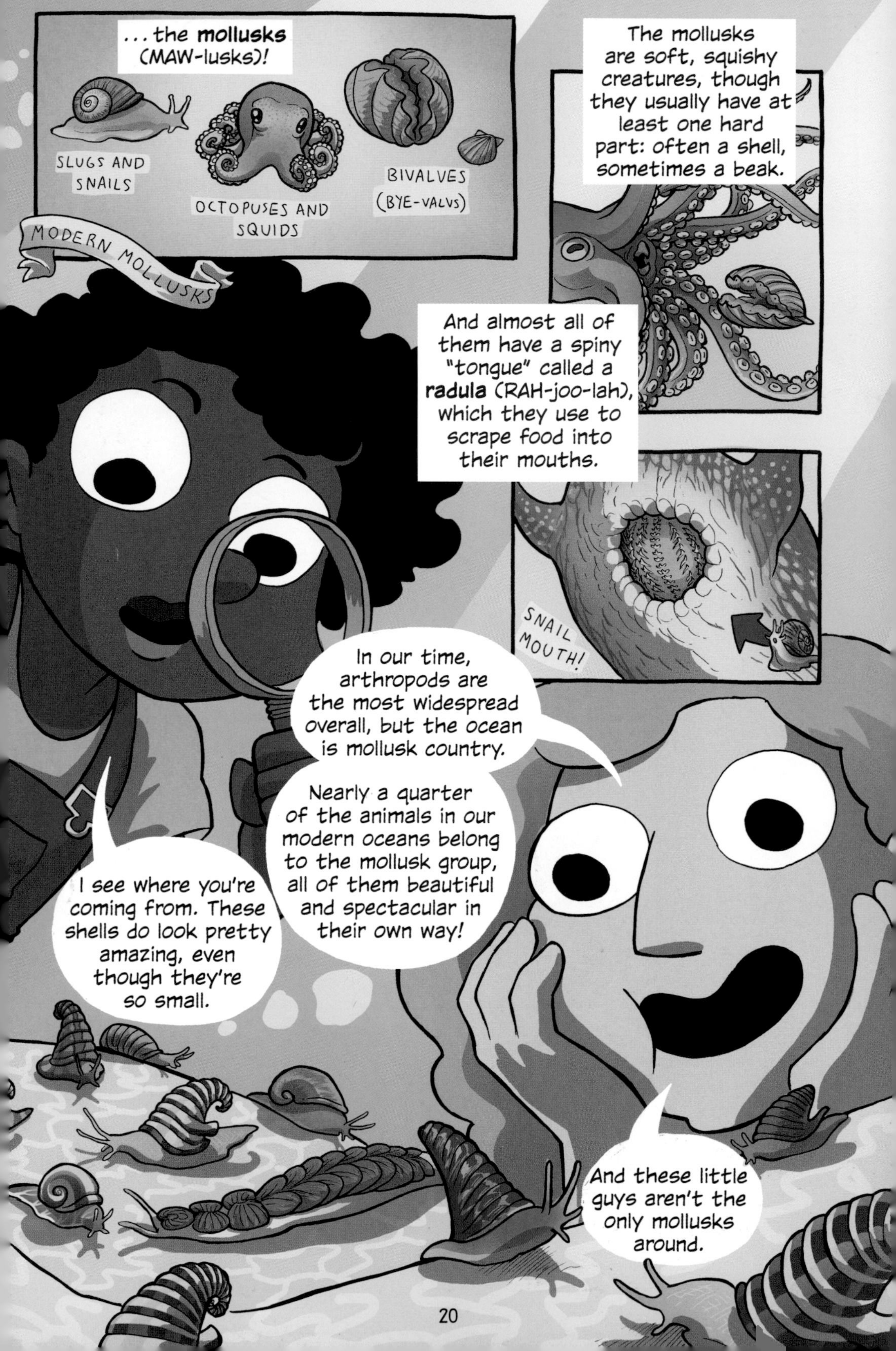
...the **mollusks** (MAW-lusks)!
SLUGS AND SNAILS
OCTOPUSES AND SQUIDS
BIVALVES (BYE-VALVS)
MODERN MOLLUSKS
The mollusks are soft, squishy creatures, though they usually have at least one hard part: often a shell, sometimes a beak.
And almost all of them have a spiny "tongue" called a **radula** (RAH-joo-lah), which they use to scrape food into their mouths.
SNAIL MOUTH!
In our time, arthropods are the most widespread overall, but the ocean is mollusk country.
Nearly a quarter of the animals in our modern oceans belong to the mollusk group, all of them beautiful and spectacular in their own way!
I see where you're coming from. These shells do look pretty amazing, even though they're so small.
And these little guys aren't the only mollusks around.

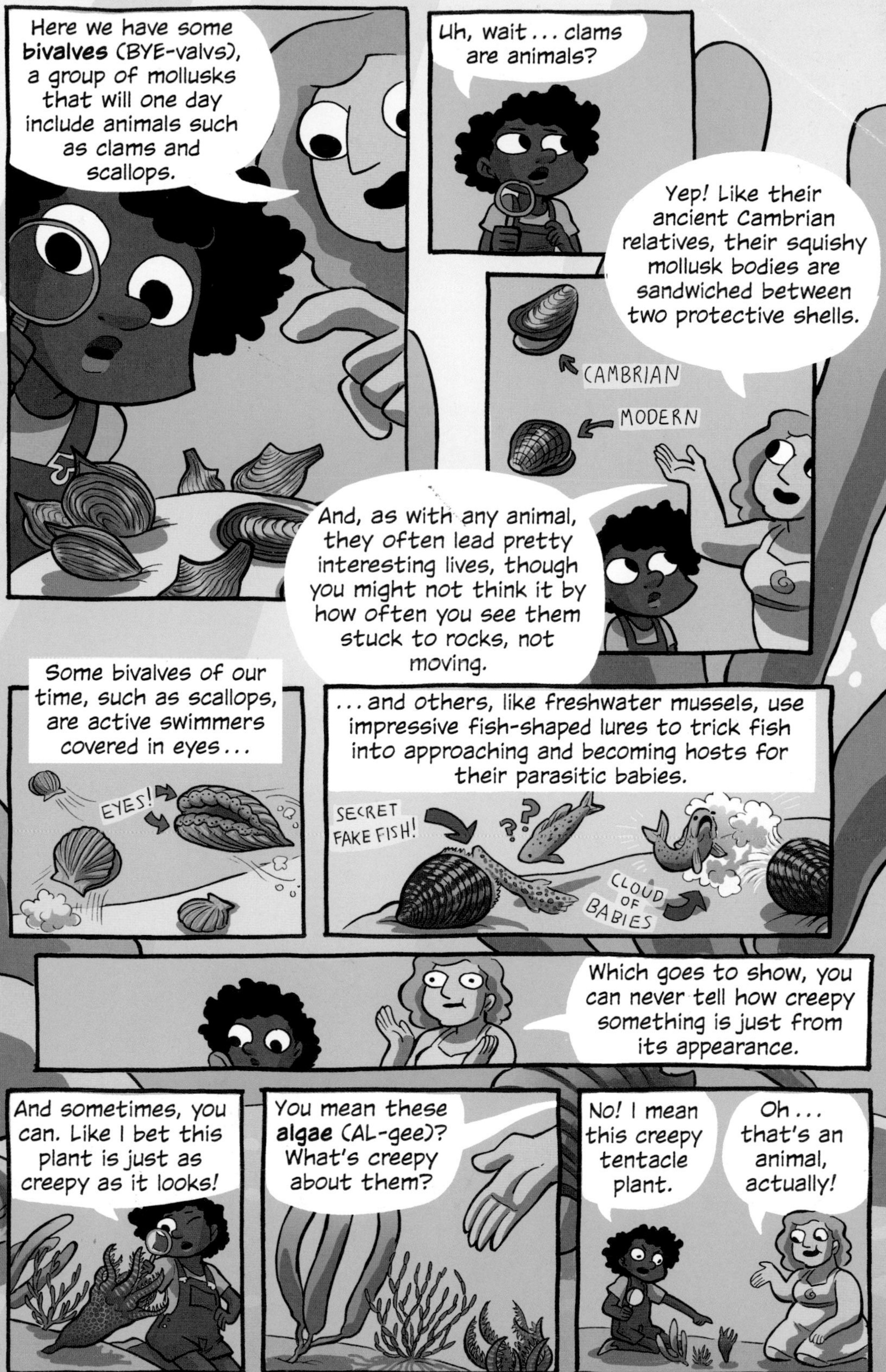
Here we have some bivalves (BYE-valvs), a group of mollusks that will one day include animals such as clams and scallops.
Uh, wait... clams are animals?
Yep! Like their ancient Cambrian relatives, their squishy mollusk bodies are sandwiched between two protective shells.
CAMBRIAN
MODERN
And, as with any animal, they often lead pretty interesting lives, though you might not think it by how often you see them stuck to rocks, not moving.
Some bivalves of our time, such as scallops, are active swimmers covered in eyes...
EYES!
...and others, like freshwater mussels, use impressive fish-shaped lures to trick fish into approaching and becoming hosts for their parasitic babies.
SECRET FAKE FISH!
? ?
CLOUD OF BABIES
Which goes to show, you can never tell how creepy something is just from its appearance.
And sometimes, you can. Like I bet this plant is just as creepy as it looks!
You mean these algae (AL-gee)? What's creepy about them?
No! I mean this creepy tentacle plant.
Oh... that's an animal, actually!

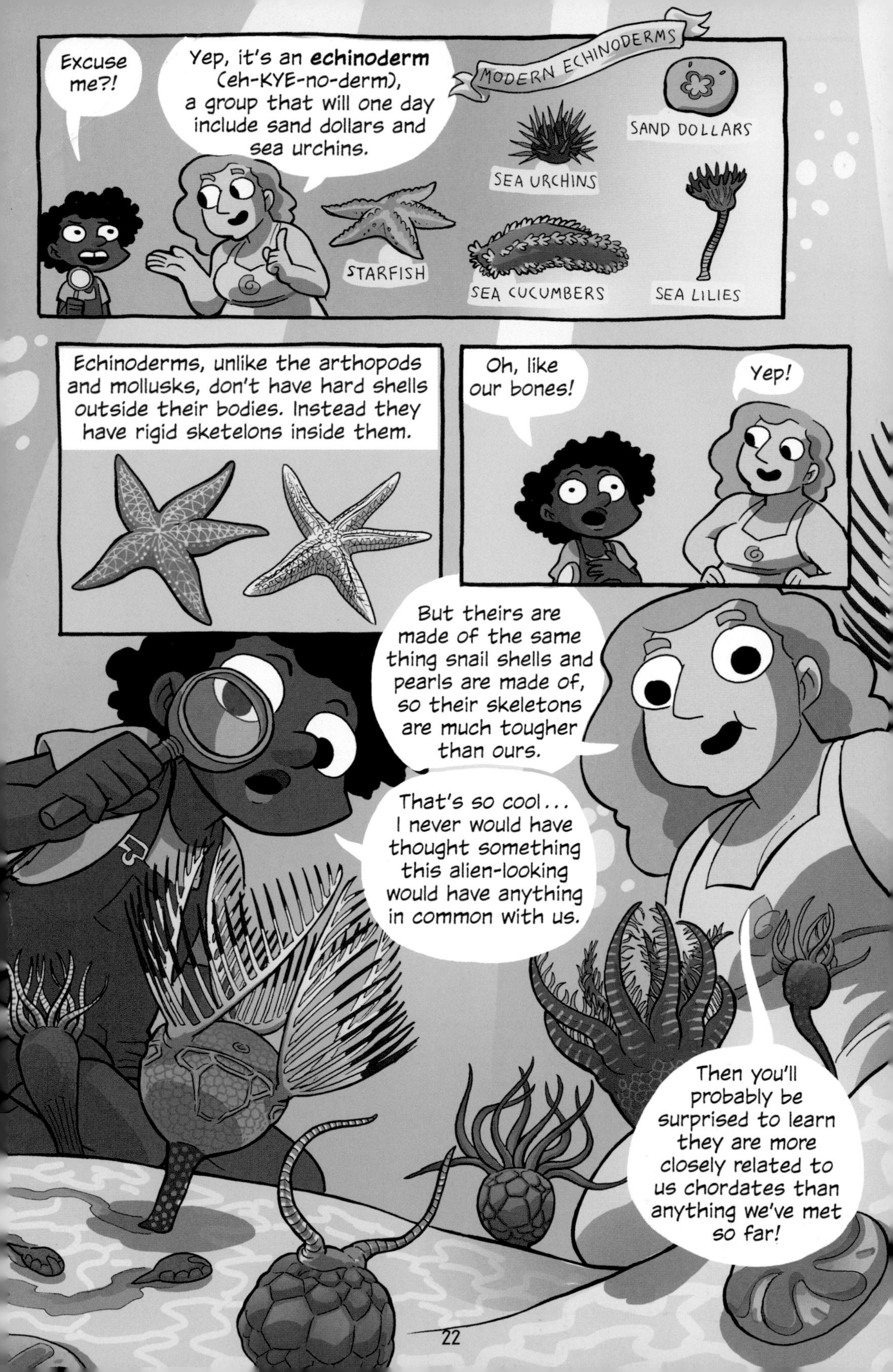
Excuse me?!
Yep, it's an **echinoderm** (eh-KYE-no-derm), a group that will one day include sand dollars and sea urchins.
MODERN ECHINODERMS
SAND DOLLARS
SEA URCHINS
STARFISH
SEA CUCUMBERS
SEA LILIES
Echinoderms, unlike the arthopods and mollusks, don't have hard shells outside their bodies. Instead they have rigid sketelons inside them.
Oh, like our bones!
Yep!
But theirs are made of the same thing snail shells and pearls are made of, so their skeletons are much tougher than ours.
That's so cool... I never would have thought something this alien-looking would have anything in common with us.
Then you'll probably be surprised to learn they are more closely related to us chordates than anything we've met so far!

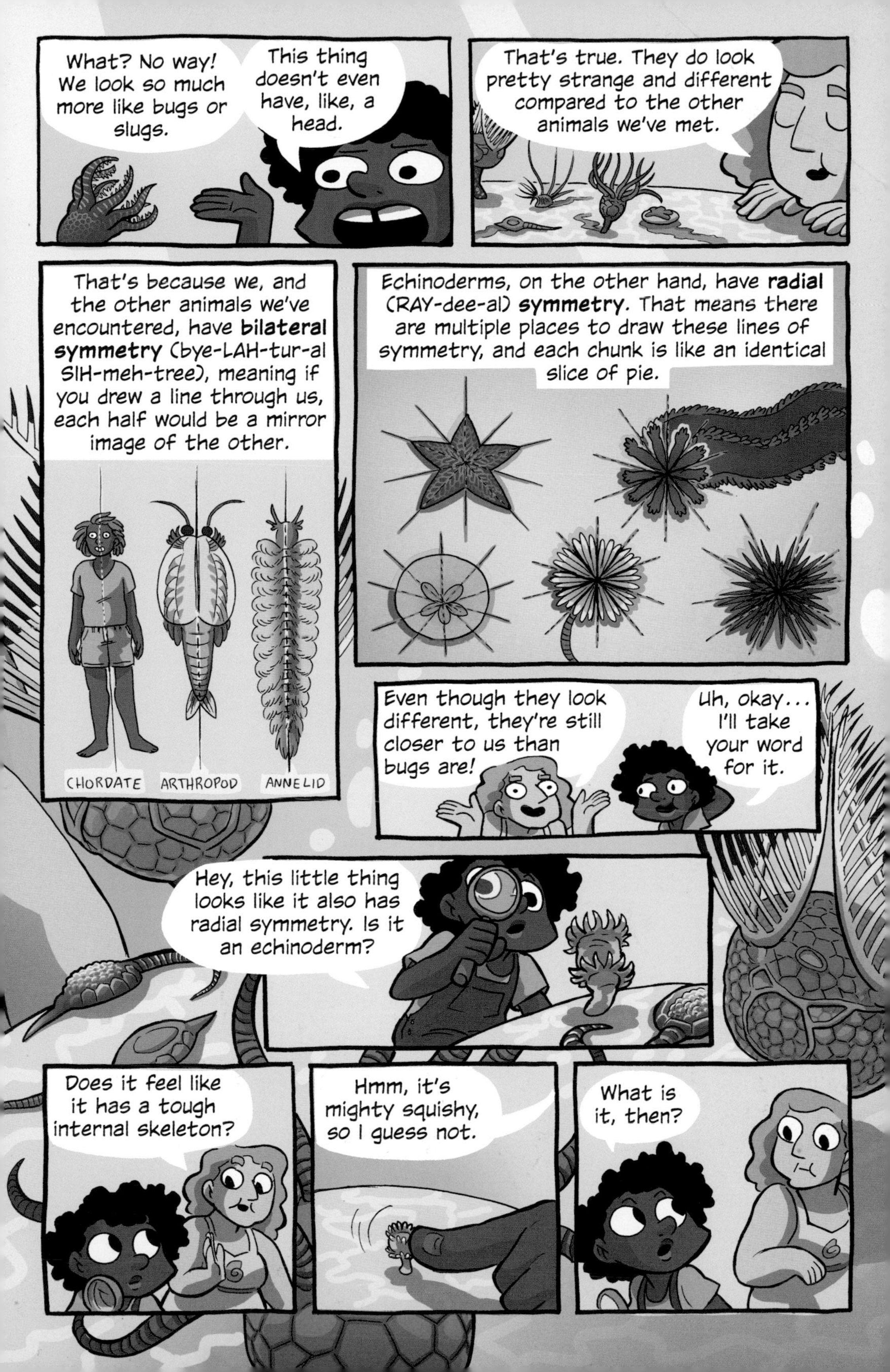
What? No way! We look so much more like bugs or slugs.
This thing doesn't even have, like, a head.
That's true. They do look pretty strange and different compared to the other animals we've met.
That's because we, and the other animals we've encountered, have **bilateral symmetry** (bye-LAH-tur-al SIH-meh-tree), meaning if you drew a line through us, each half would be a mirror image of the other.
CHORDATE
ARTHROPOD
ANNELID
Echinoderms, on the other hand, have **radial** (RAY-dee-al) **symmetry**. That means there are multiple places to draw these lines of symmetry, and each chunk is like an identical slice of pie.
Even though they look different, they're still closer to us than bugs are!
Uh, okay... I'll take your word for it.
Hey, this little thing looks like it also has radial symmetry. Is it an echinoderm?
Does it feel like it has a tough internal skeleton?
Hmm, it's mighty squishy, so I guess not.
What is it, then?

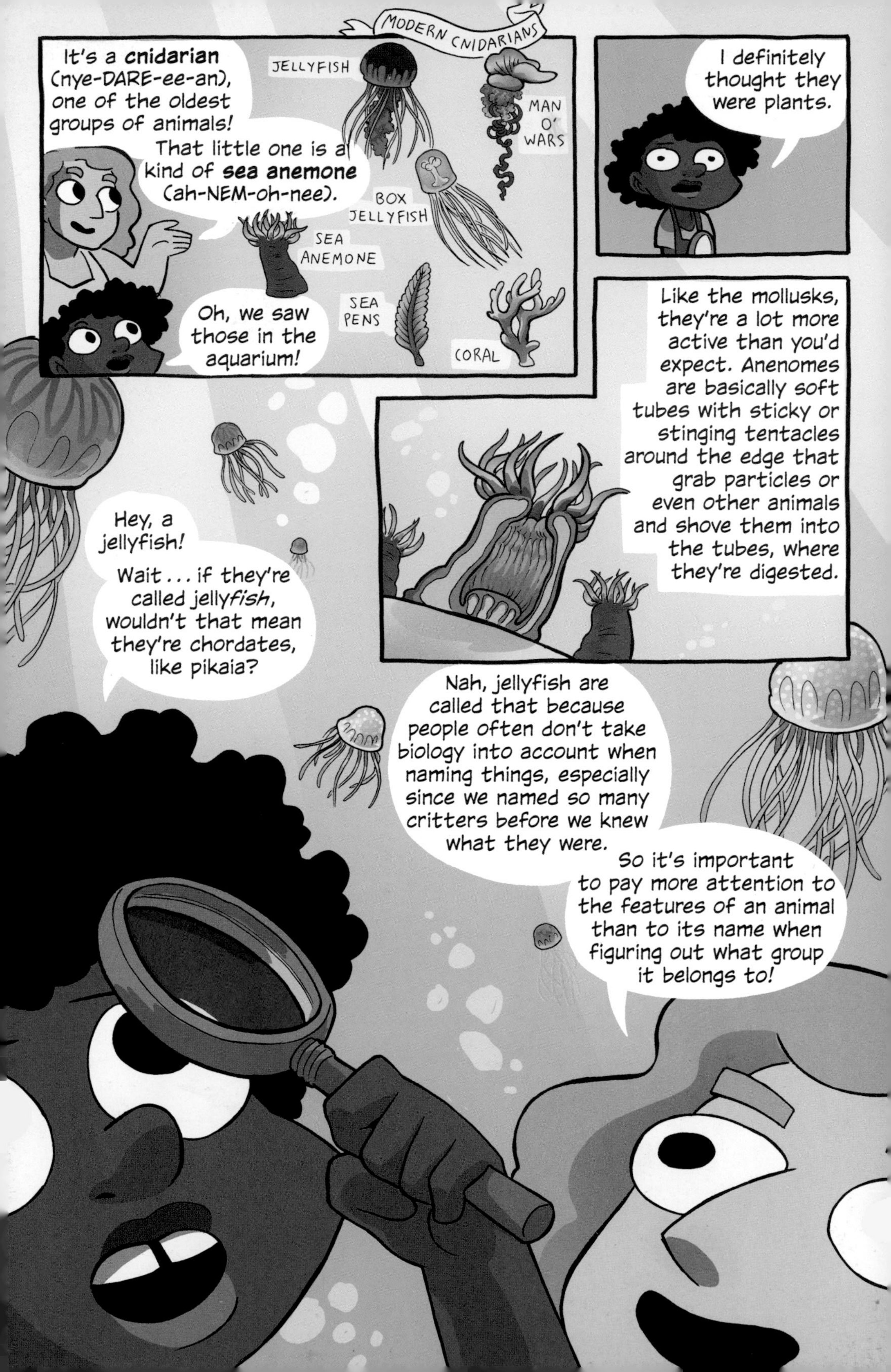
MODERN CNIDARIANS
It's a **cnidarian** (nye-DARE-ee-an), one of the oldest groups of animals!
That little one is a kind of **sea anemone** (ah-NEM-oh-nee).
JELLYFISH
MAN O' WARS
BOX JELLYFISH
SEA ANEMONE
SEA PENS
CORAL
Oh, we saw those in the aquarium!
I definitely thought they were plants.
Like the mollusks, they're a lot more active than you'd expect. Anemones are basically soft tubes with sticky or stinging tentacles around the edge that grab particles or even other animals and shove them into the tubes, where they're digested.
Hey, a jellyfish!
Wait . . . if they're called jelly*fish*, wouldn't that mean they're chordates, like pikaia?
Nah, jellyfish are called that because people often don't take biology into account when naming things, especially since we named so many critters before we knew what they were.
So it's important to pay more attention to the features of an animal than to its name when figuring out what group it belongs to!

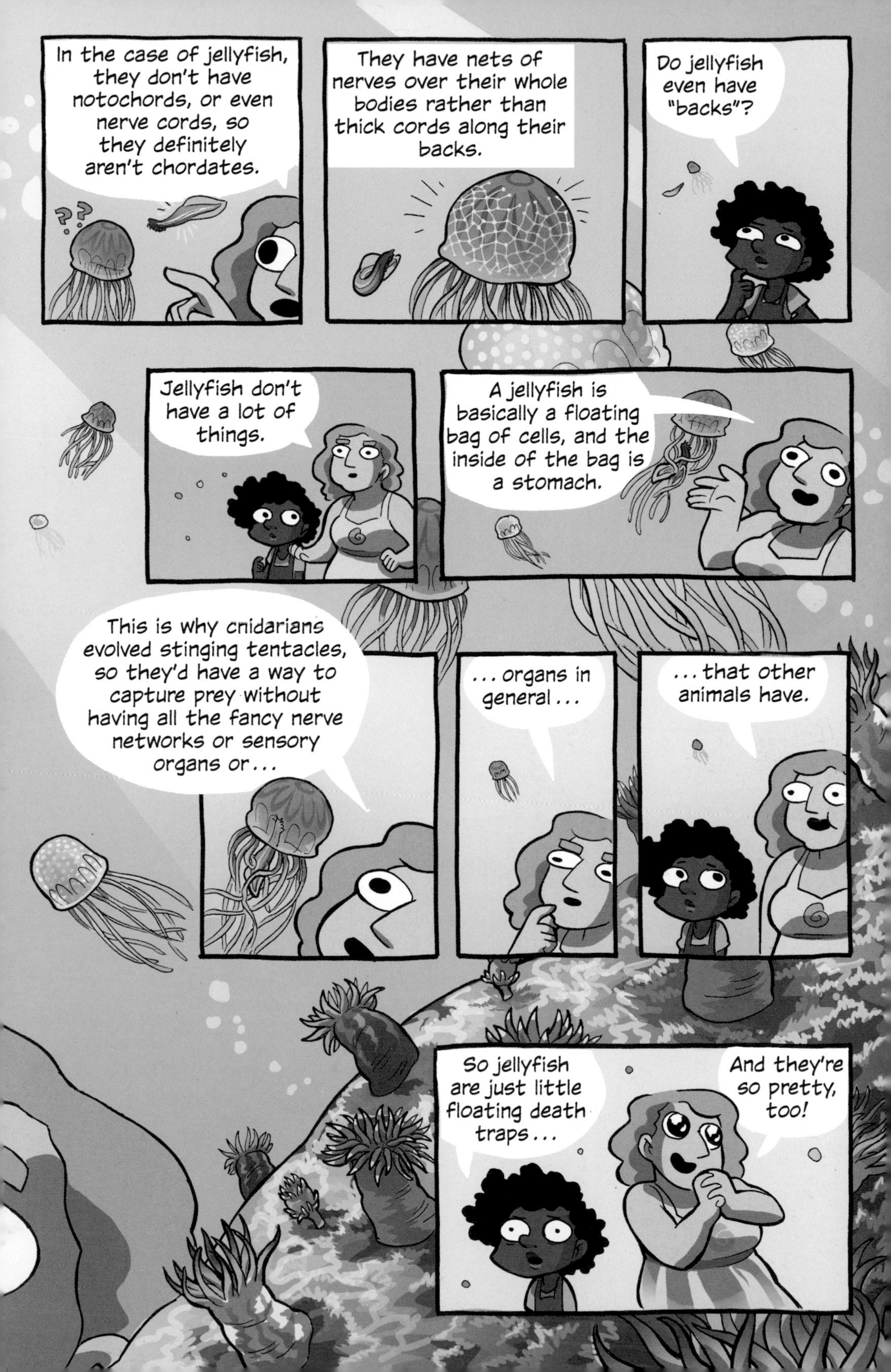
In the case of jellyfish, they don't have notochords, or even nerve cords, so they definitely aren't chordates.
??
They have nets of nerves over their whole bodies rather than thick cords along their backs.
Do jellyfish even have "backs"?
Jellyfish don't have a lot of things.
A jellyfish is basically a floating bag of cells, and the inside of the bag is a stomach.
This is why cnidarians evolved stinging tentacles, so they'd have a way to capture prey without having all the fancy nerve networks or sensory organs or...
...organs in general...
...that other animals have.
So jellyfish are just little floating death traps...
And they're so pretty, too!

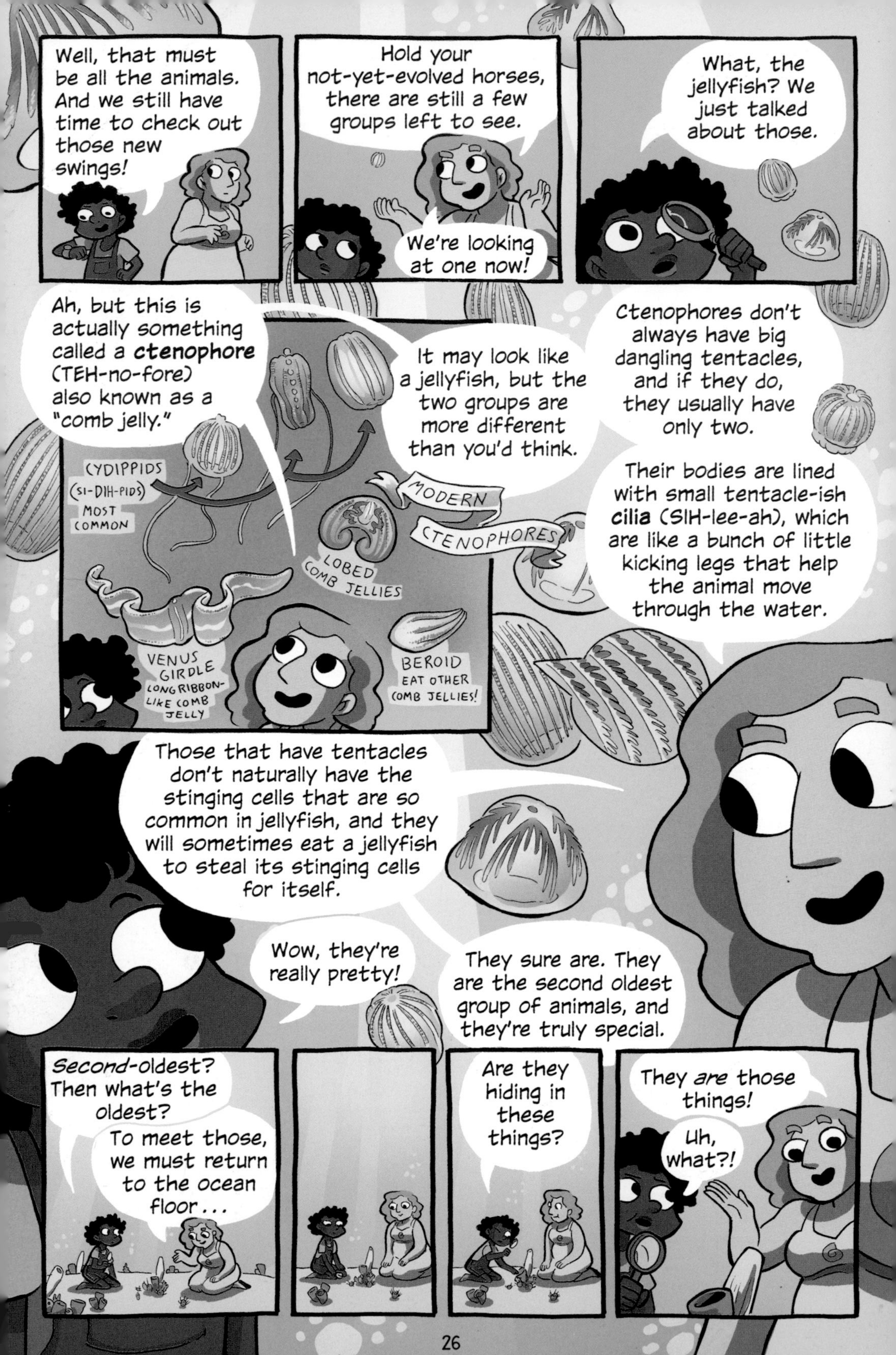

Well, that must be all the animals. And we still have time to check out those new swings!
Hold your not-yet-evolved horses, there are still a few groups left to see.
We're looking at one now!
What, the jellyfish? We just talked about those.
Ah, but this is actually something called a **ctenophore** (TEH-no-fore) also known as a "comb jelly."
It may look like a jellyfish, but the two groups are more different than you'd think.
CYDIPPIDS (SI-DIH-PIDS) MOST COMMON
MODERN CTENOPHORES
LOBED COMB JELLIES
VENUS GIRDLE LONG RIBBON-LIKE COMB JELLY
BEROID EAT OTHER COMB JELLIES!
Ctenophores don't always have big dangling tentacles, and if they do, they usually have only two.
Their bodies are lined with small tentacle-ish **cilia** (SIH-lee-ah), which are like a bunch of little kicking legs that help the animal move through the water.
Those that have tentacles don't naturally have the stinging cells that are so common in jellyfish, and they will sometimes eat a jellyfish to steal its stinging cells for itself.
Wow, they're really pretty!
They sure are. They are the second oldest group of animals, and they're truly special.
Second-oldest? Then what's the oldest?
To meet those, we must return to the ocean floor . . .
Are they hiding in these things?
They *are* those things!
Uh, what?!

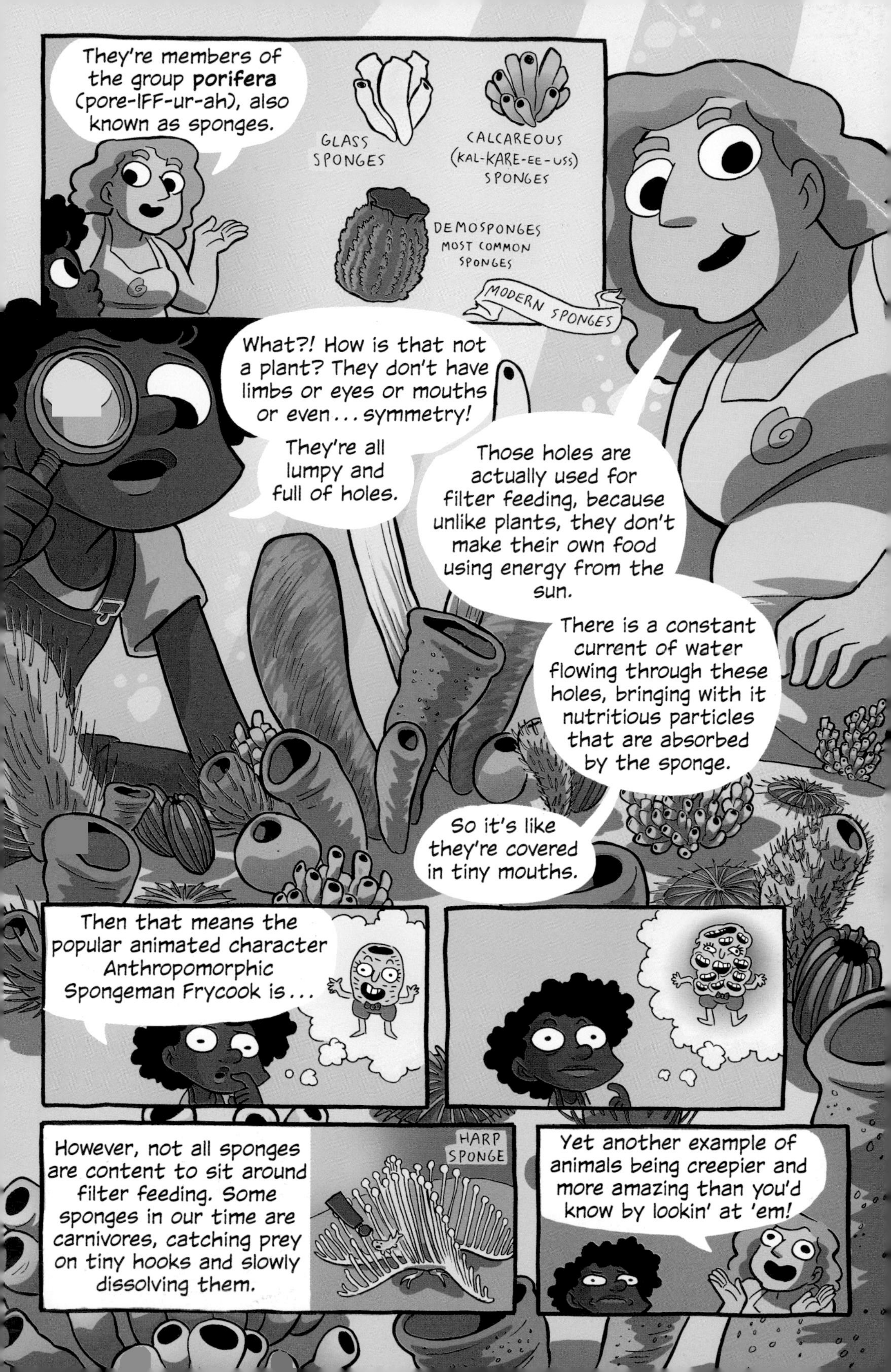
They're members of the group **porifera** (pore-IFF-ur-ah), also known as sponges.
GLASS SPONGES
CALCAREOUS (KAL-KARE-EE-USS) SPONGES
DEMOSPONGES MOST COMMON SPONGES
MODERN SPONGES
What?! How is that not a plant? They don't have limbs or eyes or mouths or even . . . symmetry!
They're all lumpy and full of holes.
Those holes are actually used for filter feeding, because unlike plants, they don't make their own food using energy from the sun.
There is a constant current of water flowing through these holes, bringing with it nutritious particles that are absorbed by the sponge.
So it's like they're covered in tiny mouths.
Then that means the popular animated character Anthropomorphic Spongeman Frycook is . . .
However, not all sponges are content to sit around filter feeding. Some sponges in our time are carnivores, catching prey on tiny hooks and slowly dissolving them.
HARP SPONGE
Yet another example of animals being creepier and more amazing than you'd know by lookin' at 'em!

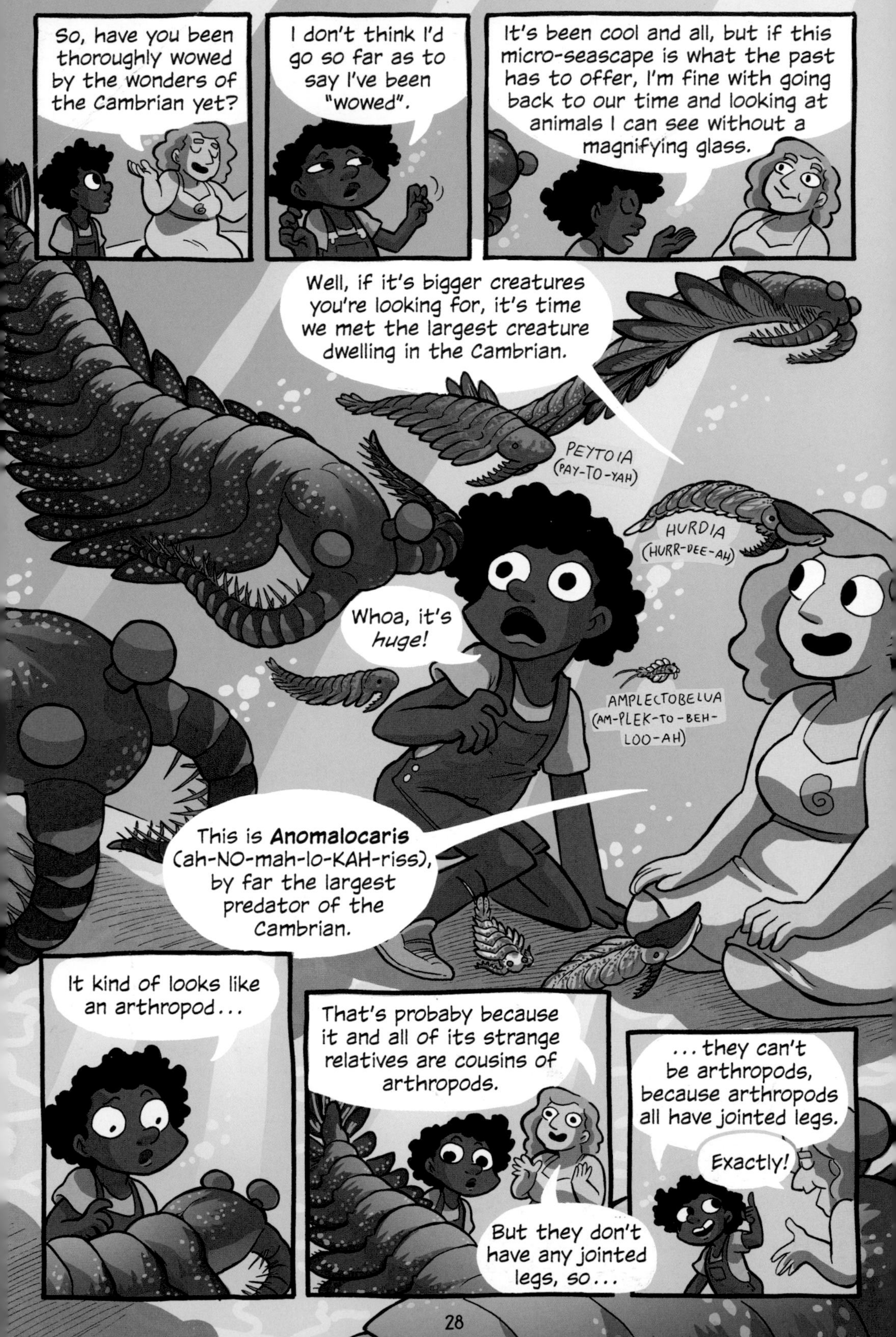
So, have you been thoroughly wowed by the wonders of the Cambrian yet?
I don't think I'd go so far as to say I've been "wowed".
It's been cool and all, but if this micro-seascape is what the past has to offer, I'm fine with going back to our time and looking at animals I can see without a magnifying glass.
Well, if it's bigger creatures you're looking for, it's time we met the largest creature dwelling in the Cambrian.
PEYTOIA (PAY-TO-YAH)
HURDIA (HURR-DEE-AH)
Whoa, it's *huge!*
AMPLECTOBELUA (AM-PLEK-TO-BEH-LOO-AH)
This is **Anomalocaris** (ah-NO-mah-lo-KAH-riss), by far the largest predator of the Cambrian.
It kind of looks like an arthropod...
That's probaby because it and all of its strange relatives are cousins of arthropods.
But they don't have any jointed legs, so...
...they can't be arthropods, because arthropods all have jointed legs.
Exactly!

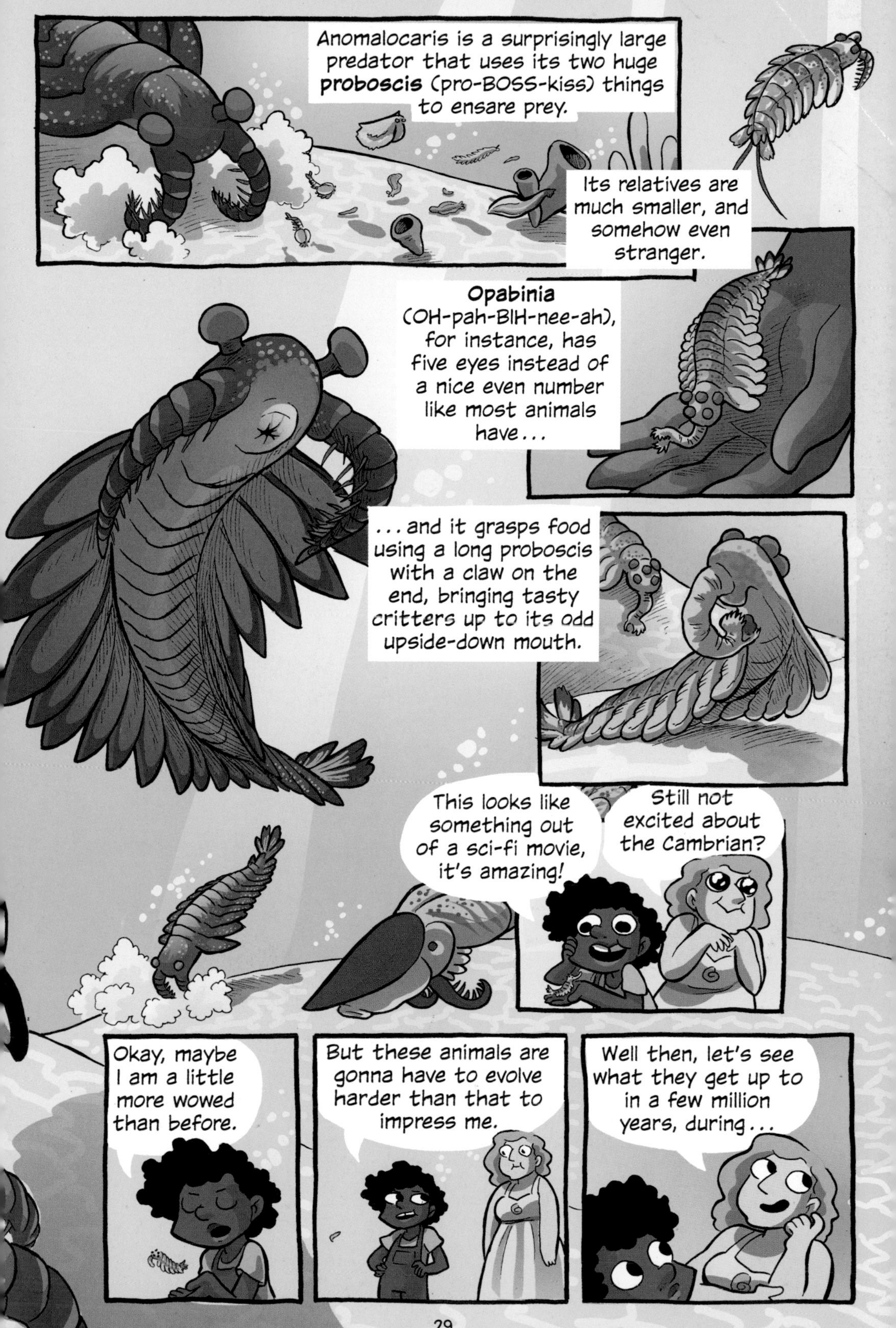
Anomalocaris is a surprisingly large predator that uses its two huge **proboscis** (pro-BOSS-kiss) things to ensare prey.
Its relatives are much smaller, and somehow even stranger.
Opabinia (OH-pah-BIH-nee-ah), for instance, has five eyes instead of a nice even number like most animals have...
...and it grasps food using a long proboscis with a claw on the end, bringing tasty critters up to its odd upside-down mouth.
This looks like something out of a sci-fi movie, it's amazing!
Still not excited about the Cambrian?
Okay, maybe I am a little more wowed than before.
But these animals are gonna have to evolve harder than that to impress me.
Well then, let's see what they get up to in a few million years, during...

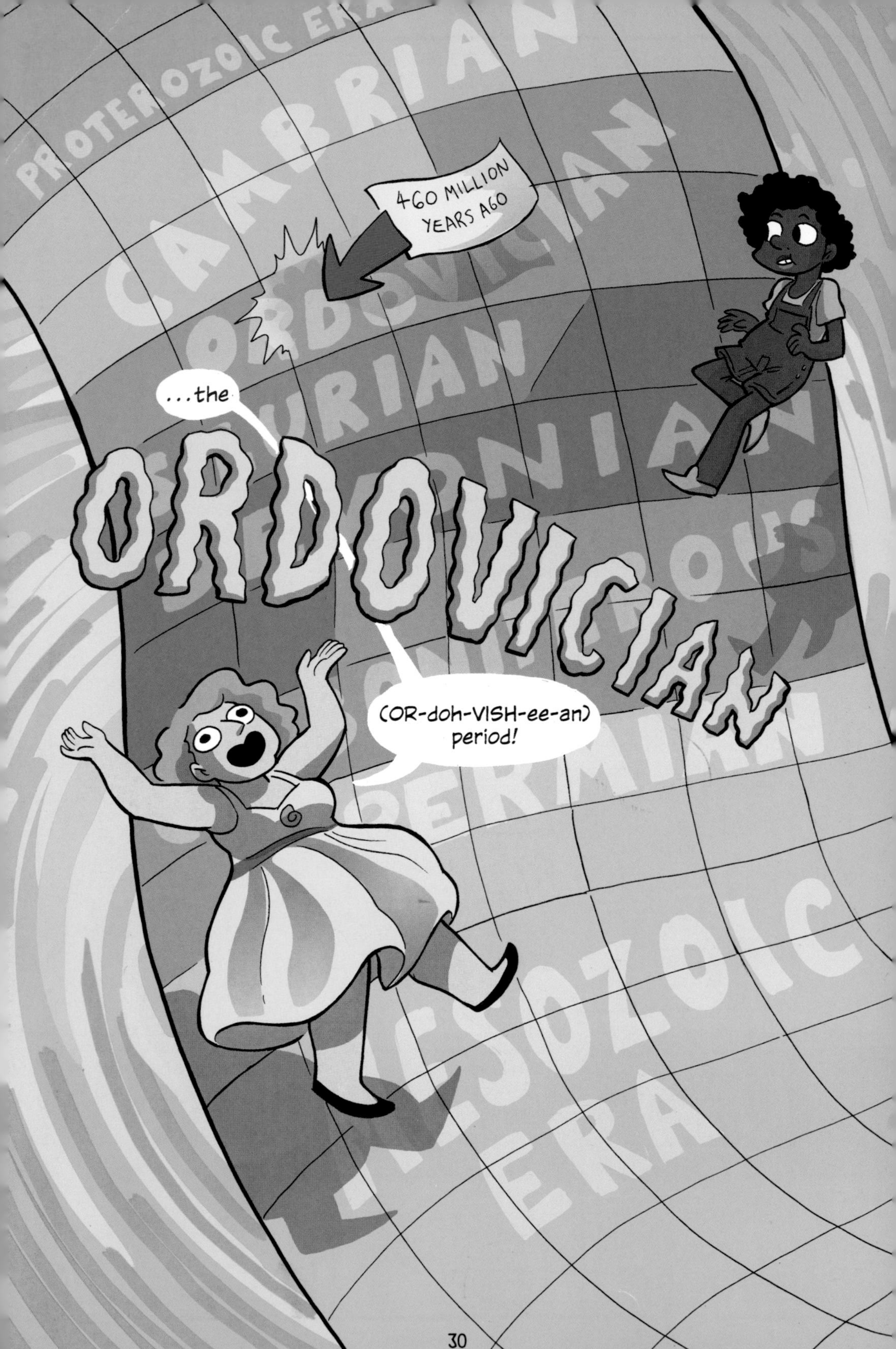
CAMBRIAN
460 MILLION YEARS AGO
...the
ORDOVICIAN
(OR-doh-VISH-ee-an) period!
PERMIAN

The last chordates we met were pretty small and squiggly.

Now, in the Ordovician, they're considerably bigger and covered in thick plates of armor for protection.

Fun fact: The plates are made of enamel, the same stuff our teeth are made of! So it's like their skin is covered in huge teeth that protect them from harm.

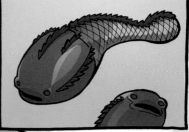

Now that's more like it! And do they have backbones, too?

Yep, they're full-on vertebrates now! Though they're still lacking a few things that we have.

Most importantly, they don't have a jaw, the bone that opens and closes our mouths and helps us hold and chew our food.

ASTRASPIS (AHS-TRAS-PIS)

ARANDASPIS (AH-RAN-DAS-PIS)

SACABAMBASPIS (SAY-KA-BAM-BASS-PIS)

They eat by sucking things up into their mouths. It's not a bad way to eat, but it's not quite as effective as a nice crunching jaw.

SLUUURP...

Though, I guess I'm biased, with my jaw and all.

Hey, these plants look new, too.

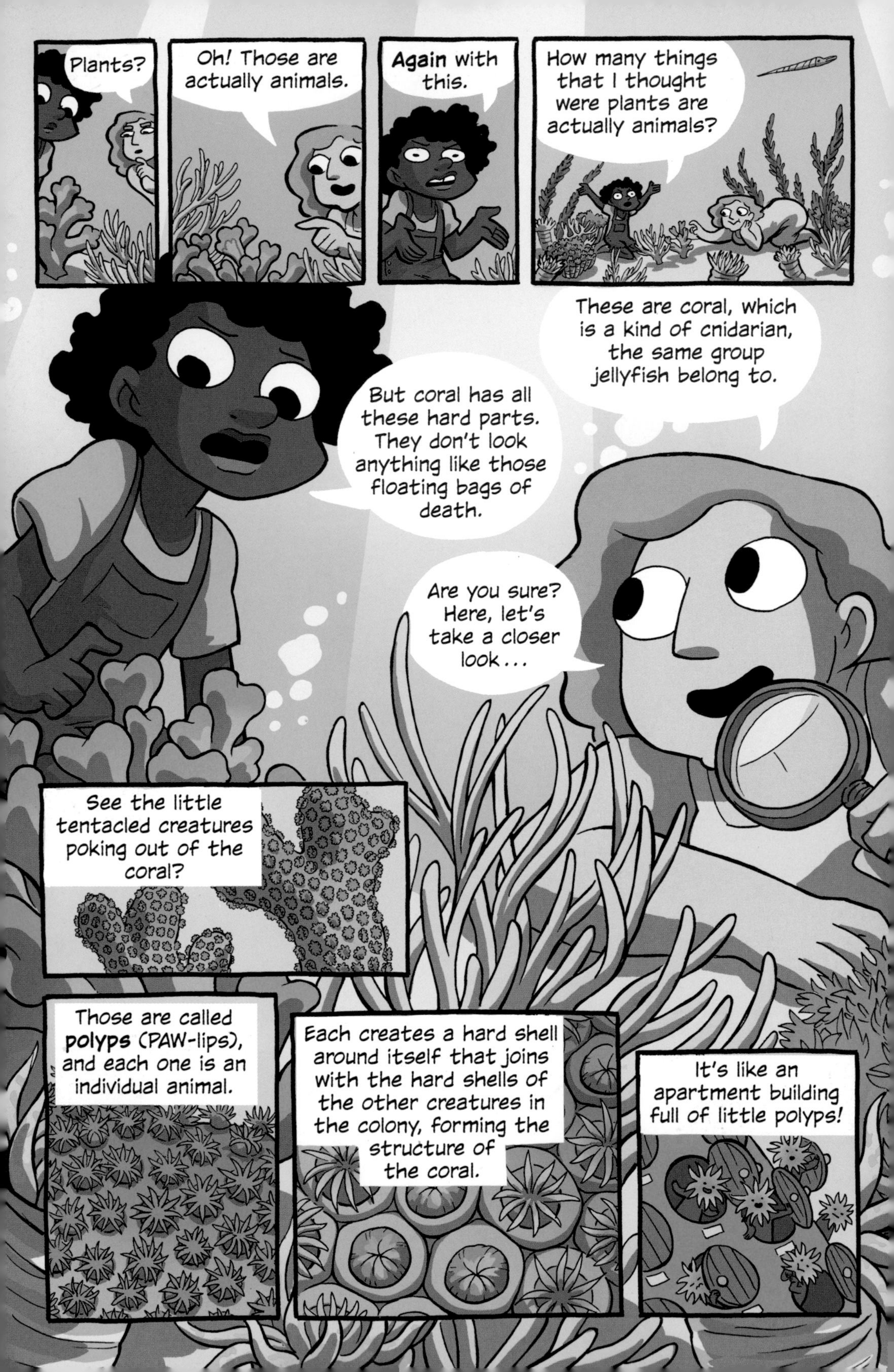

Plants?
Oh! Those are actually animals.
Again with this.
How many things that I thought were plants are actually animals?
These are coral, which is a kind of cnidarian, the same group jellyfish belong to.
But coral has all these hard parts. They don't look anything like those floating bags of death.
Are you sure? Here, let's take a closer look . . .
See the little tentacled creatures poking out of the coral?
Those are called **polyps** (PAW-lips), and each one is an individual animal.
Each creates a hard shell around itself that joins with the hard shells of the other creatures in the colony, forming the structure of the coral.
It's like an apartment building full of little polyps!

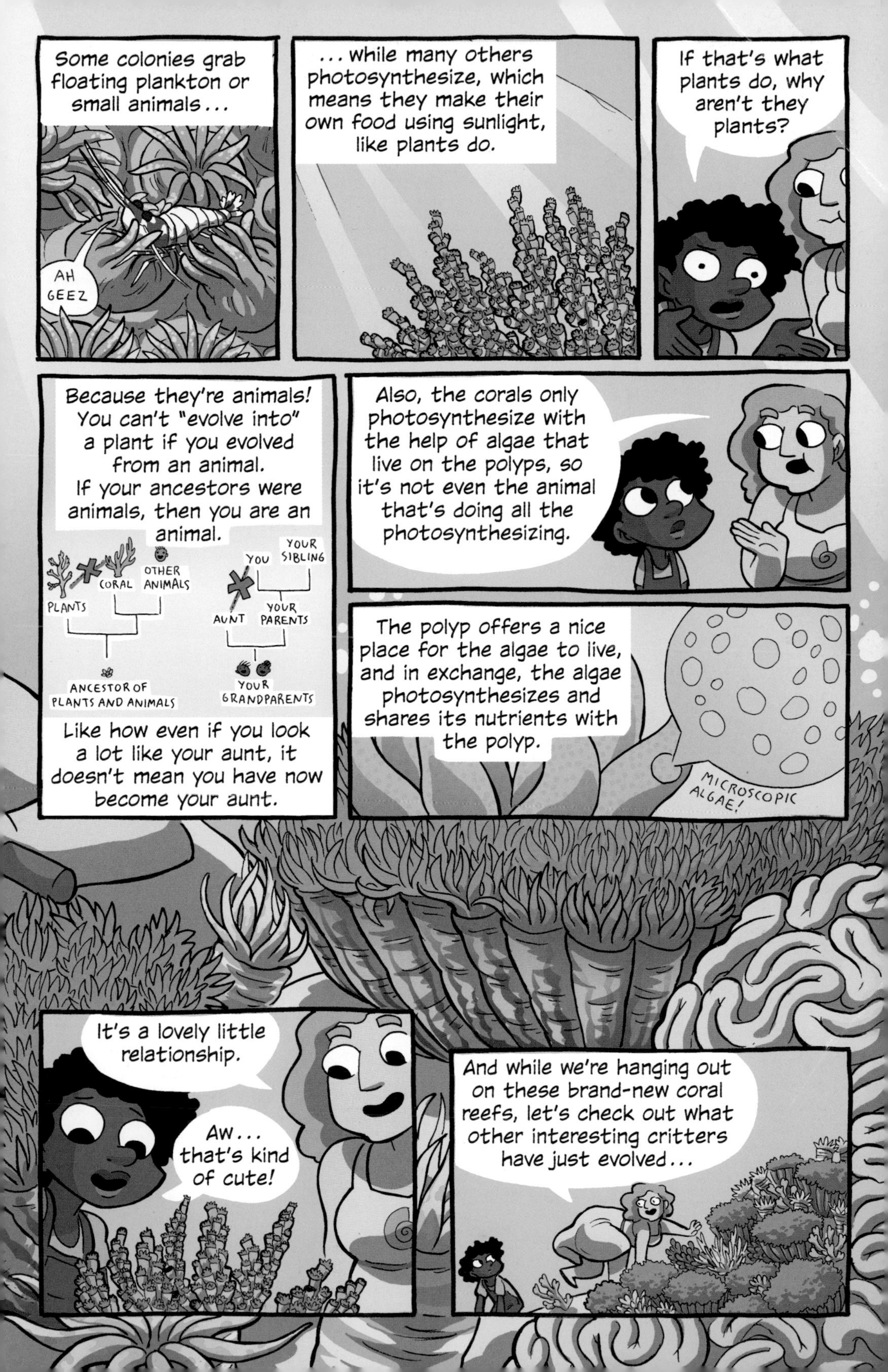

Some colonies grab floating plankton or small animals...
AH GEEZ
... while many others photosynthesize, which means they make their own food using sunlight, like plants do.
If that's what plants do, why aren't they plants?
Because they're animals! You can't "evolve into" a plant if you evolved from an animal. If your ancestors were animals, then you are an animal.
PLANTS
CORAL
OTHER ANIMALS
ANCESTOR OF PLANTS AND ANIMALS
YOU
YOUR SIBLING
AUNT
YOUR PARENTS
YOUR GRANDPARENTS
Like how even if you look a lot like your aunt, it doesn't mean you have now become your aunt.
Also, the corals only photosynthesize with the help of algae that live on the polyps, so it's not even the animal that's doing all the photosynthesizing.
The polyp offers a nice place for the algae to live, and in exchange, the algae photosynthesizes and shares its nutrients with the polyp.
MICROSCOPIC ALGAE!
It's a lovely little relationship.
Aw... that's kind of cute!
And while we're hanging out on these brand-new coral reefs, let's check out what other interesting critters have just evolved...

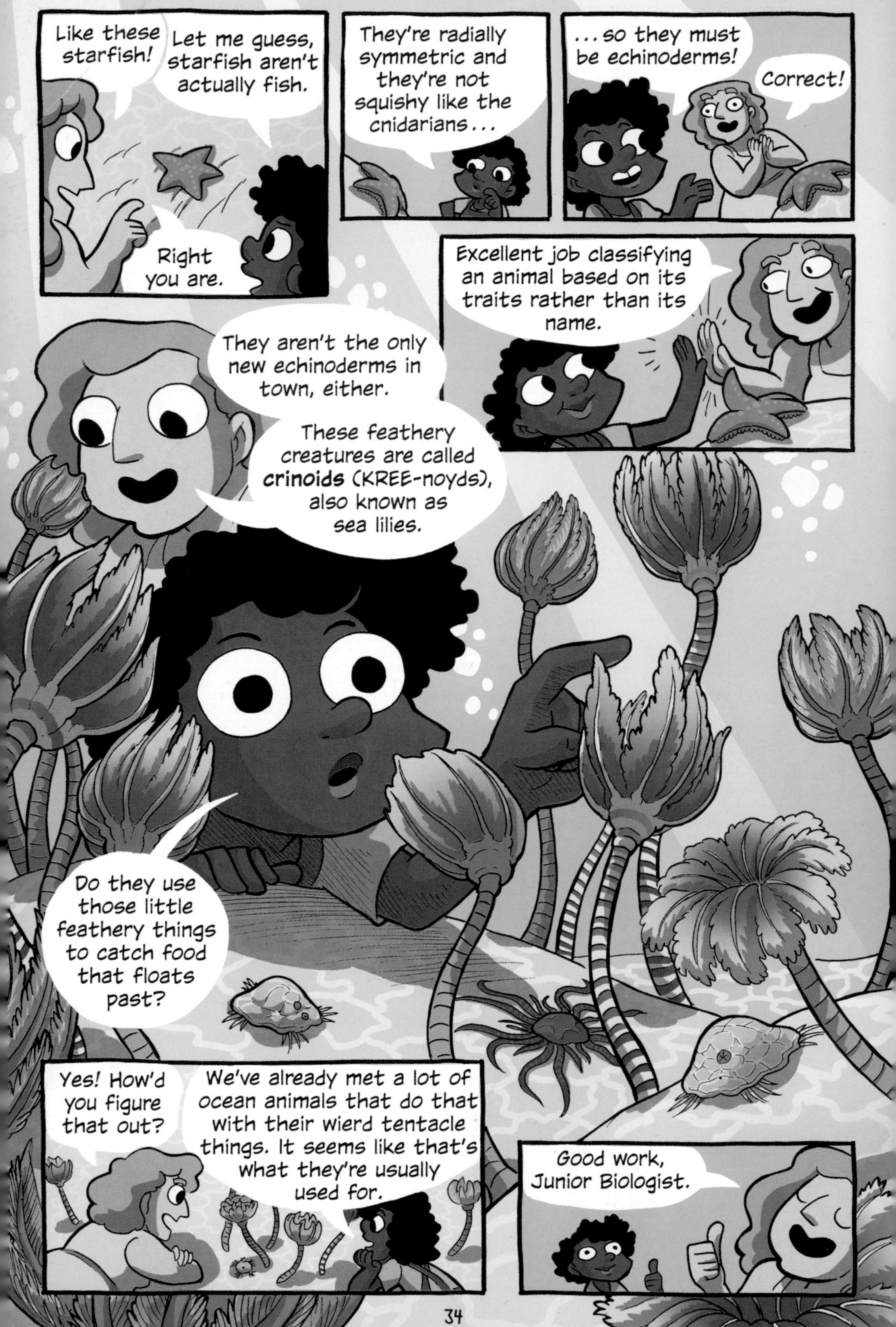
Like these starfish!
Let me guess, starfish aren't actually fish.
Right you are.
They're radially symmetric and they're not squishy like the cnidarians...
...so they must be echinoderms!
Correct!
Excellent job classifying an animal based on its traits rather than its name.
They aren't the only new echinoderms in town, either.
These feathery creatures are called **crinoids** (KREE-noyds), also known as sea lilies.
Do they use those little feathery things to catch food that floats past?
Yes! How'd you figure that out?
We've already met a lot of ocean animals that do that with their wierd tentacle things. It seems like that's what they're usually used for.
Good work, Junior Biologist.

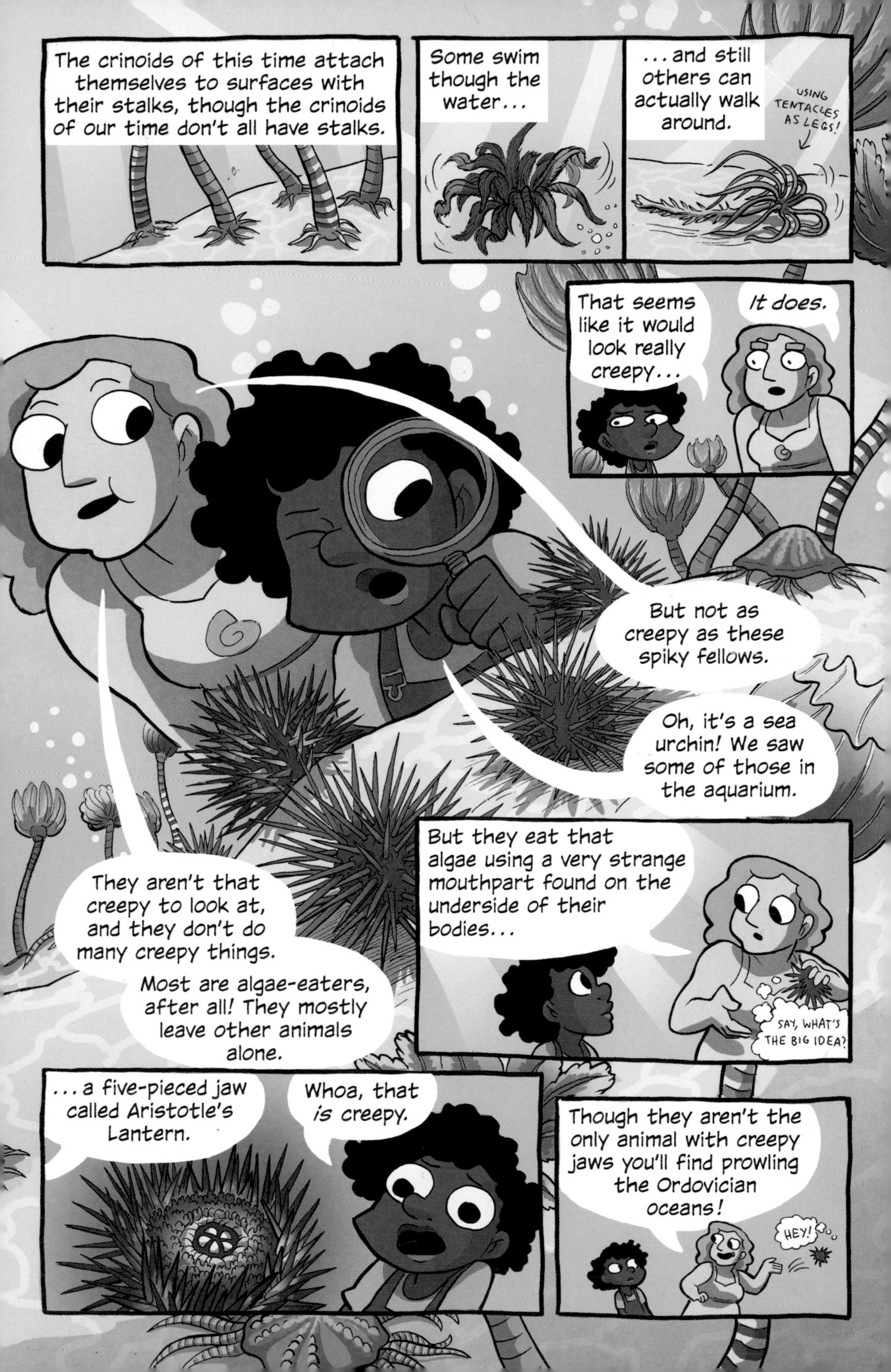

The crinoids of this time attach themselves to surfaces with their stalks, though the crinoids of our time don't all have stalks.
Some swim though the water...
...and still others can actually walk around.
USING TENTACLES AS LEGS!
That seems like it would look really creepy...
It does.
But not as creepy as these spiky fellows.
Oh, it's a sea urchin! We saw some of those in the aquarium.
They aren't that creepy to look at, and they don't do many creepy things.
Most are algae-eaters, after all! They mostly leave other animals alone.
But they eat that algae using a very strange mouthpart found on the underside of their bodies...
SAY, WHAT'S THE BIG IDEA?
...a five-pieced jaw called Aristotle's Lantern.
Whoa, that is creepy.
Though they aren't the only animal with creepy jaws you'll find prowling the Ordovician oceans!
HEY!

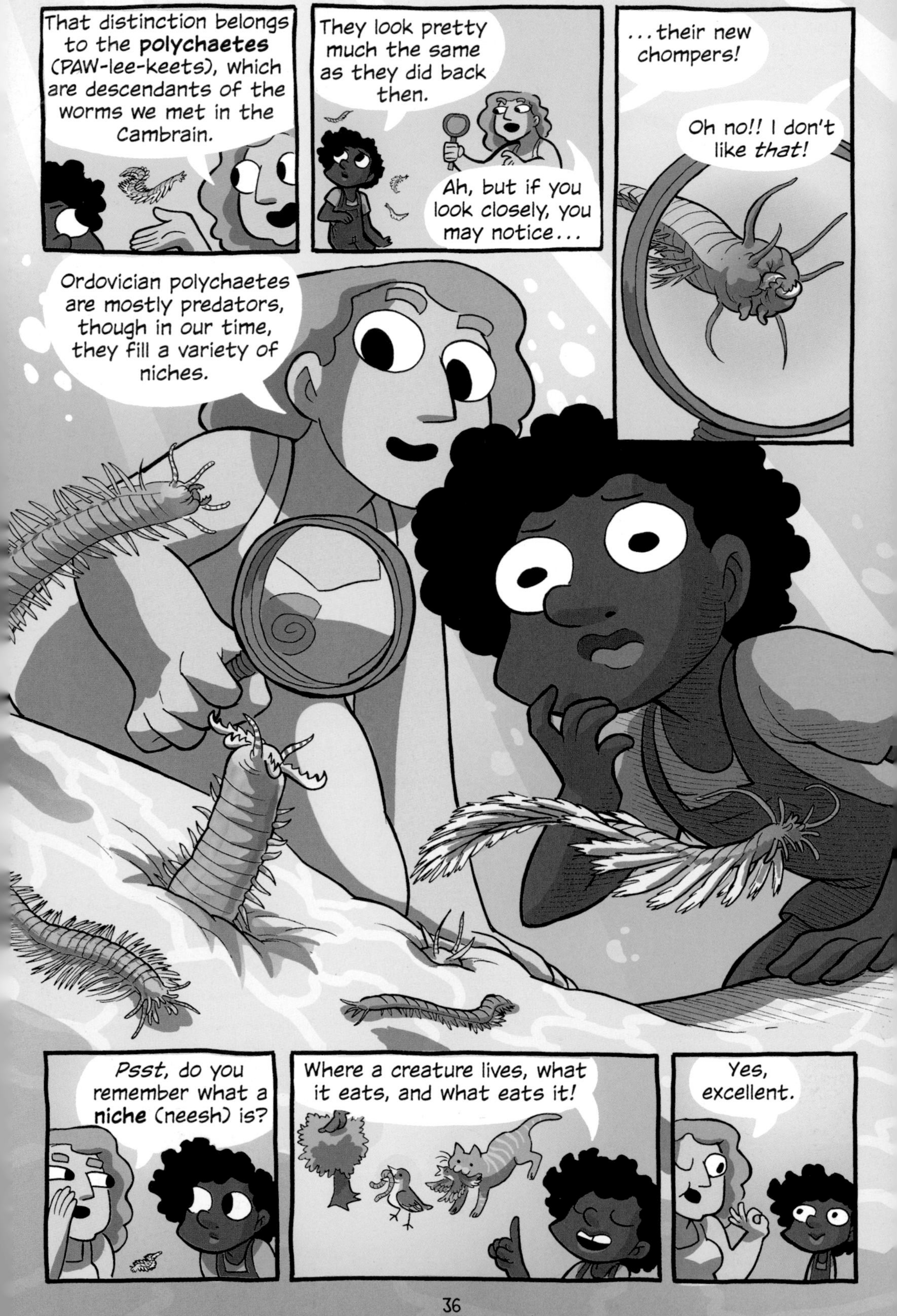
That distinction belongs to the **polychaetes** (PAW-lee-keets), which are descendants of the worms we met in the Cambrain.
They look pretty much the same as they did back then.
Ah, but if you look closely, you may notice...
...their new chompers!
Oh no!! I don't like *that*!
Ordovician polychaetes are mostly predators, though in our time, they fill a variety of niches.
Psst, do you remember what a **niche** (neesh) is?
Where a creature lives, what it eats, and what eats it!
Yes, excellent.

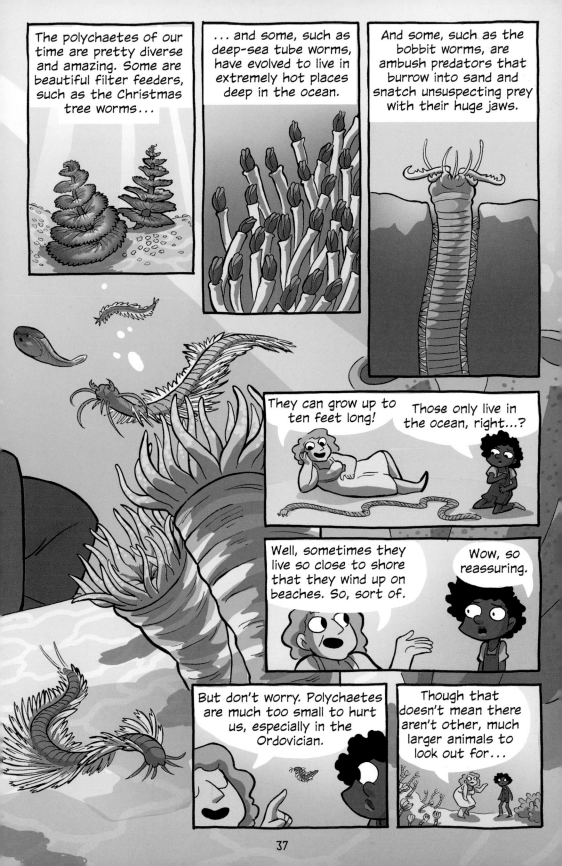

The polychaetes of our time are pretty diverse and amazing. Some are beautiful filter feeders, such as the Christmas tree worms...

... and some, such as deep-sea tube worms, have evolved to live in extremely hot places deep in the ocean.

And some, such as the bobbit worms, are ambush predators that burrow into sand and snatch unsuspecting prey with their huge jaws.

They can grow up to ten feet long!

Those only live in the ocean, right...?

Well, sometimes they live so close to shore that they wind up on beaches. So, sort of.

Wow, so reassuring.

But don't worry. Polychaetes are much too small to hurt us, especially in the Ordovician.

Though that doesn't mean there aren't other, much larger animals to look out for...

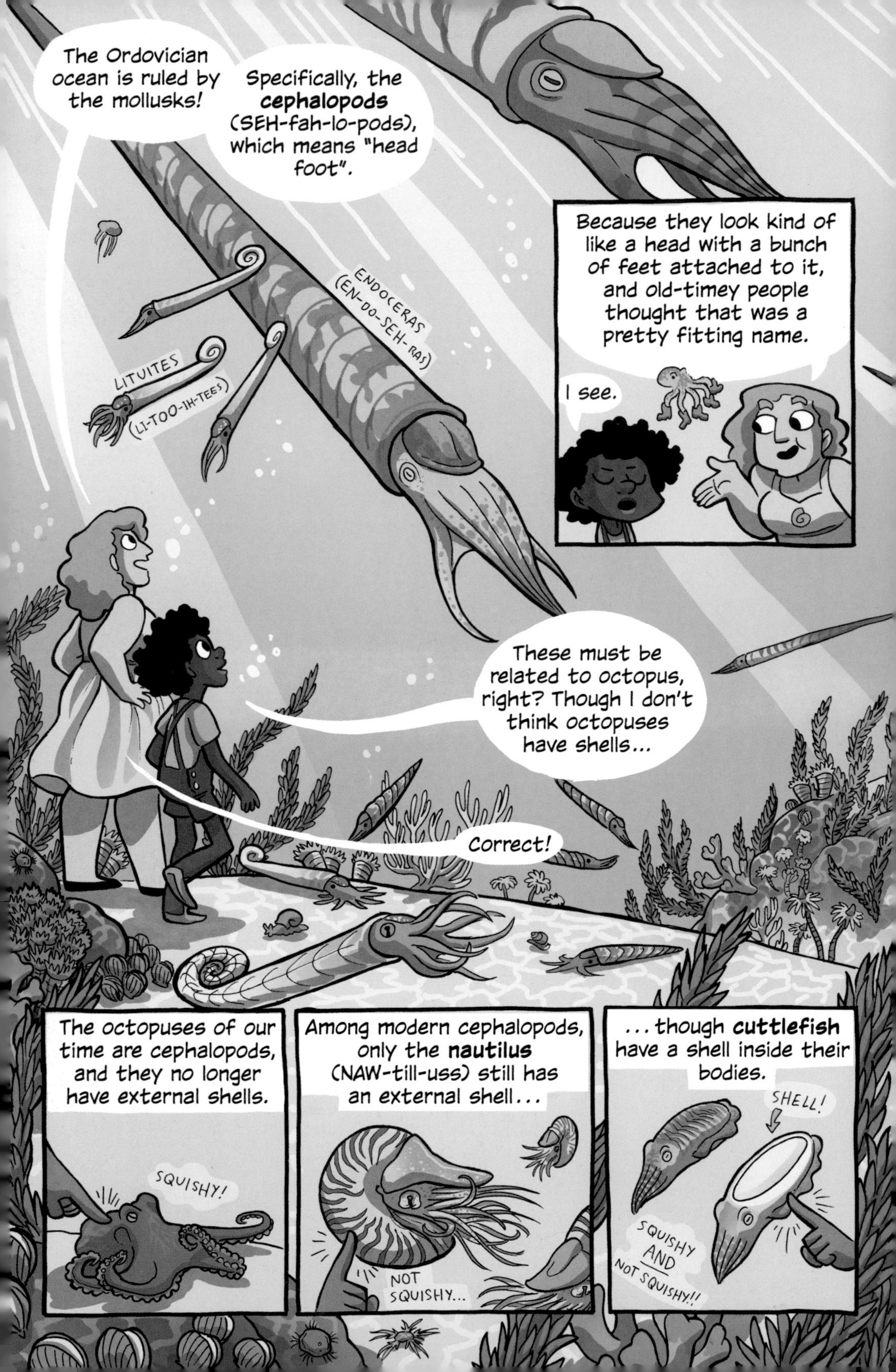
The Ordovician ocean is ruled by the mollusks!
Specifically, the **cephalopods** (SEH-fah-lo-pods), which means "head foot".
Because they look kind of like a head with a bunch of feet attached to it, and old-timey people thought that was a pretty fitting name.
I see.
ENDOCERAS (EN-DO-SEH-RAS)
LITUITES (LI-TOO-IH-TEES)
These must be related to octopus, right? Though I don't think octopuses have shells...
Correct!
The octopuses of our time are cephalopods, and they no longer have external shells.
SQUISHY!
Among modern cephalopods, only the **nautilus** (NAW-till-uss) still has an external shell...
NOT SQUISHY...
...though **cuttlefish** have a shell inside their bodies.
SHELL!
SQUISHY AND NOT SQUISHY!!

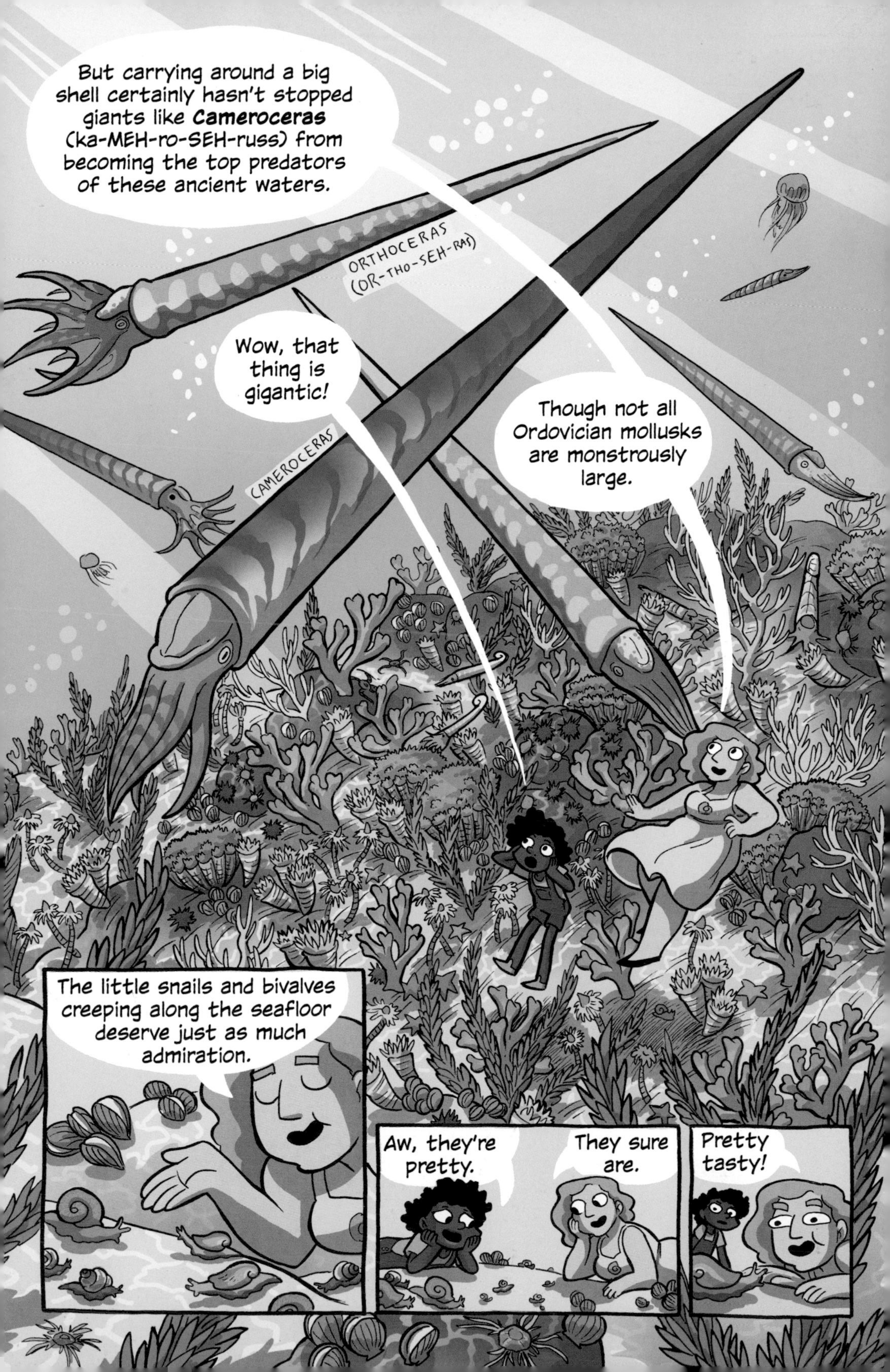

But carrying around a big shell certainly hasn't stopped giants like **Cameroceras** (ka-MEH-ro-SEH-russ) from becoming the top predators of these ancient waters.
ORTHOCERAS (OR-THO-SEH-RAS)
CAMEROCERAS
Wow, that thing is gigantic!
Though not all Ordovician mollusks are monstrously large.
The little snails and bivalves creeping along the seafloor deserve just as much admiration.
Aw, they're pretty.
They sure are.
Pretty tasty!

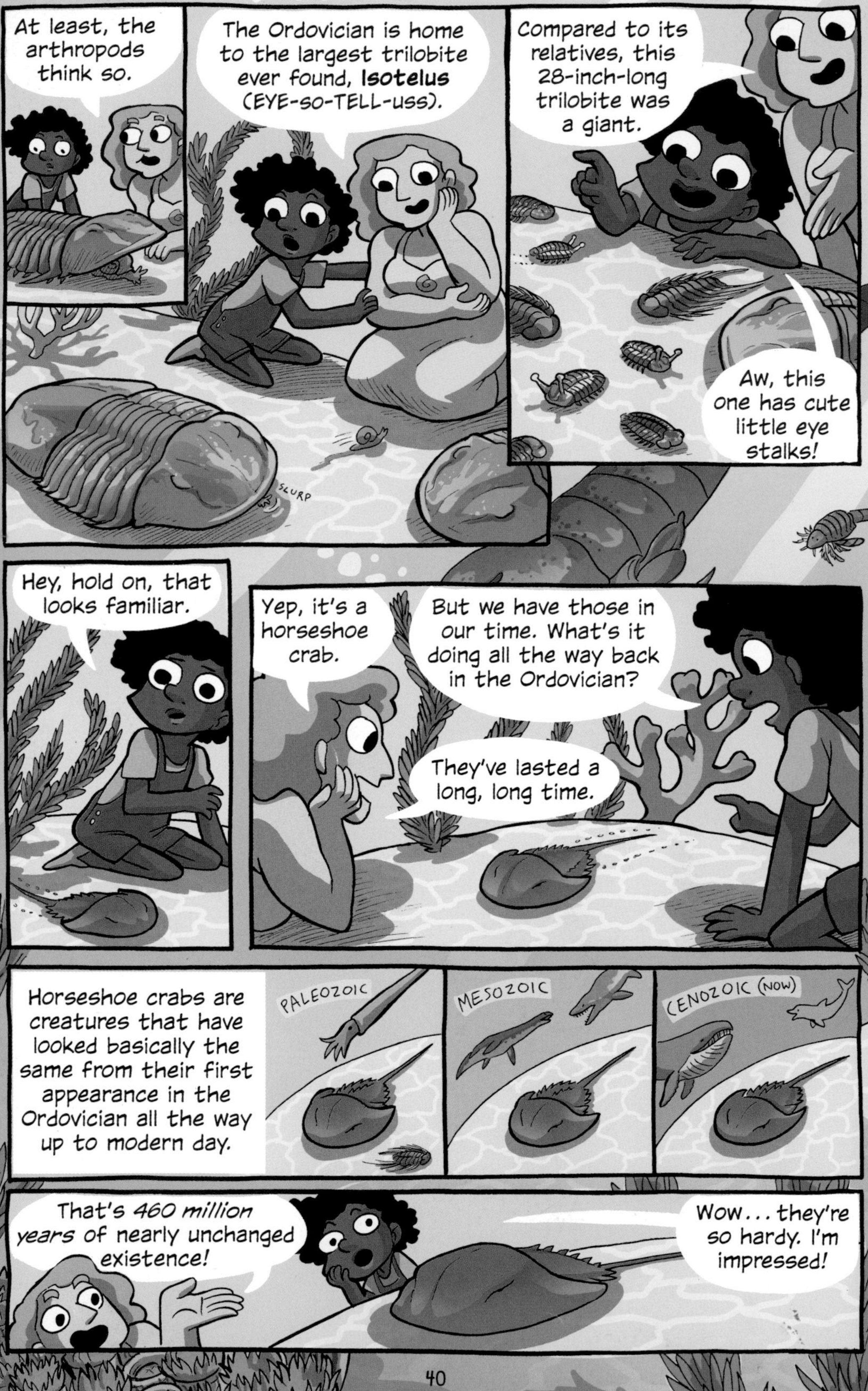
At least, the arthropods think so.
The Ordovician is home to the largest trilobite ever found, **Isotelus** (EYE-so-TELL-uss).
Compared to its relatives, this 28-inch-long trilobite was a giant.
Aw, this one has cute little eye stalks!
SLURP
Hey, hold on, that looks familiar.
Yep, it's a horseshoe crab.
But we have those in our time. What's it doing all the way back in the Ordovician?
They've lasted a long, long time.
Horseshoe crabs are creatures that have looked basically the same from their first appearance in the Ordovician all the way up to modern day.
PALEOZOIC
MESOZOIC
CENOZOIC (NOW)
That's *460 million years* of nearly unchanged existence!
Wow... they're so hardy. I'm impressed!

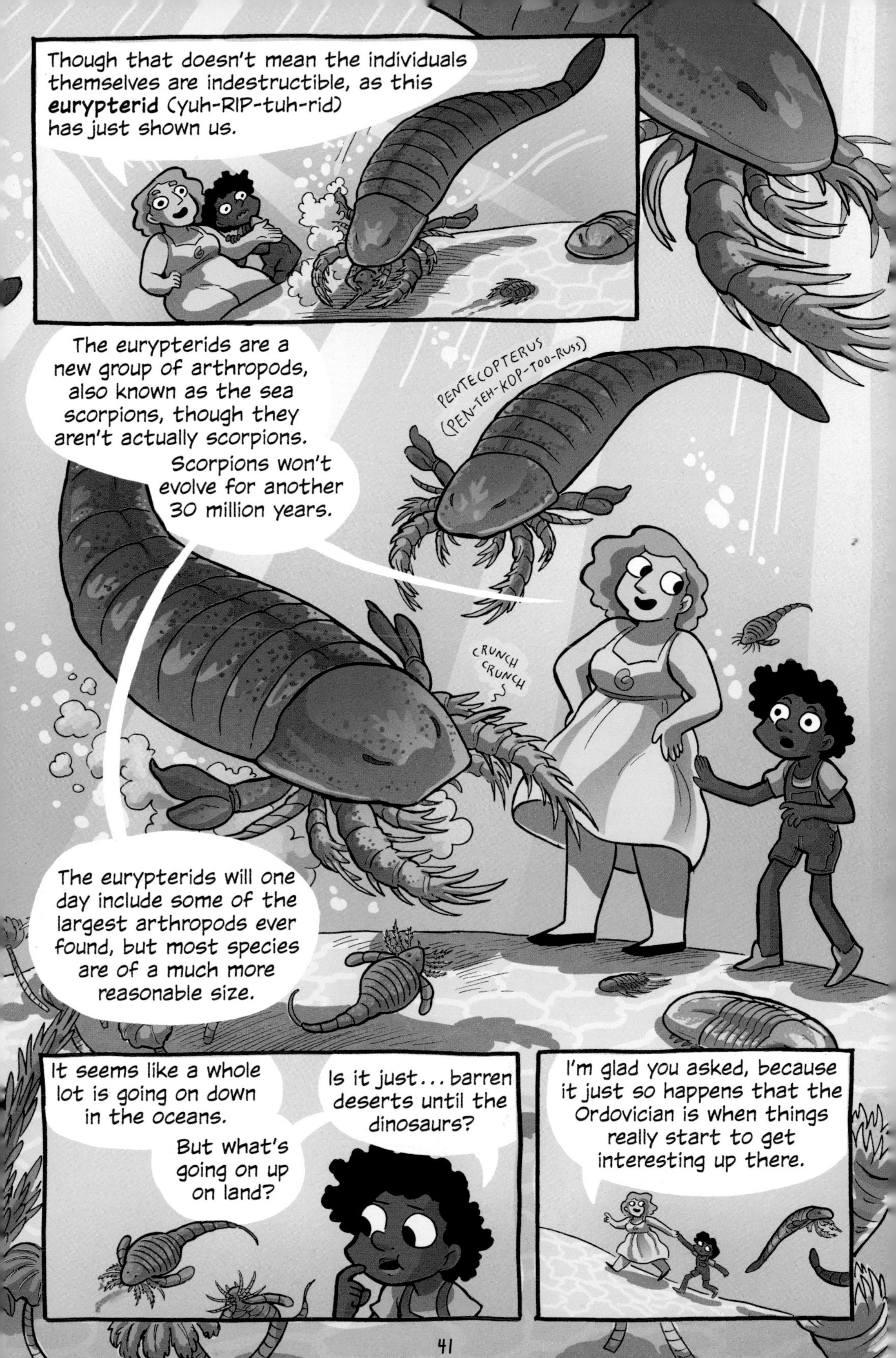

Though that doesn't mean the individuals themselves are indestructible, as this **eurypterid** (yuh-RIP-tuh-rid) has just shown us.
The eurypterids are a new group of arthropods, also known as the sea scorpions, though they aren't actually scorpions.
Scorpions won't evolve for another 30 million years.
PENTECOPTERUS (PEN-TEH-KOP-TOO-RUSS)
CRUNCH CRUNCH
The eurypterids will one day include some of the largest arthropods ever found, but most species are of a much more reasonable size.
It seems like a whole lot is going on down in the oceans.
But what's going on up on land?
Is it just... barren deserts until the dinosaurs?
I'm glad you asked, because it just so happens that the Ordovician is when things really start to get interesting up there.

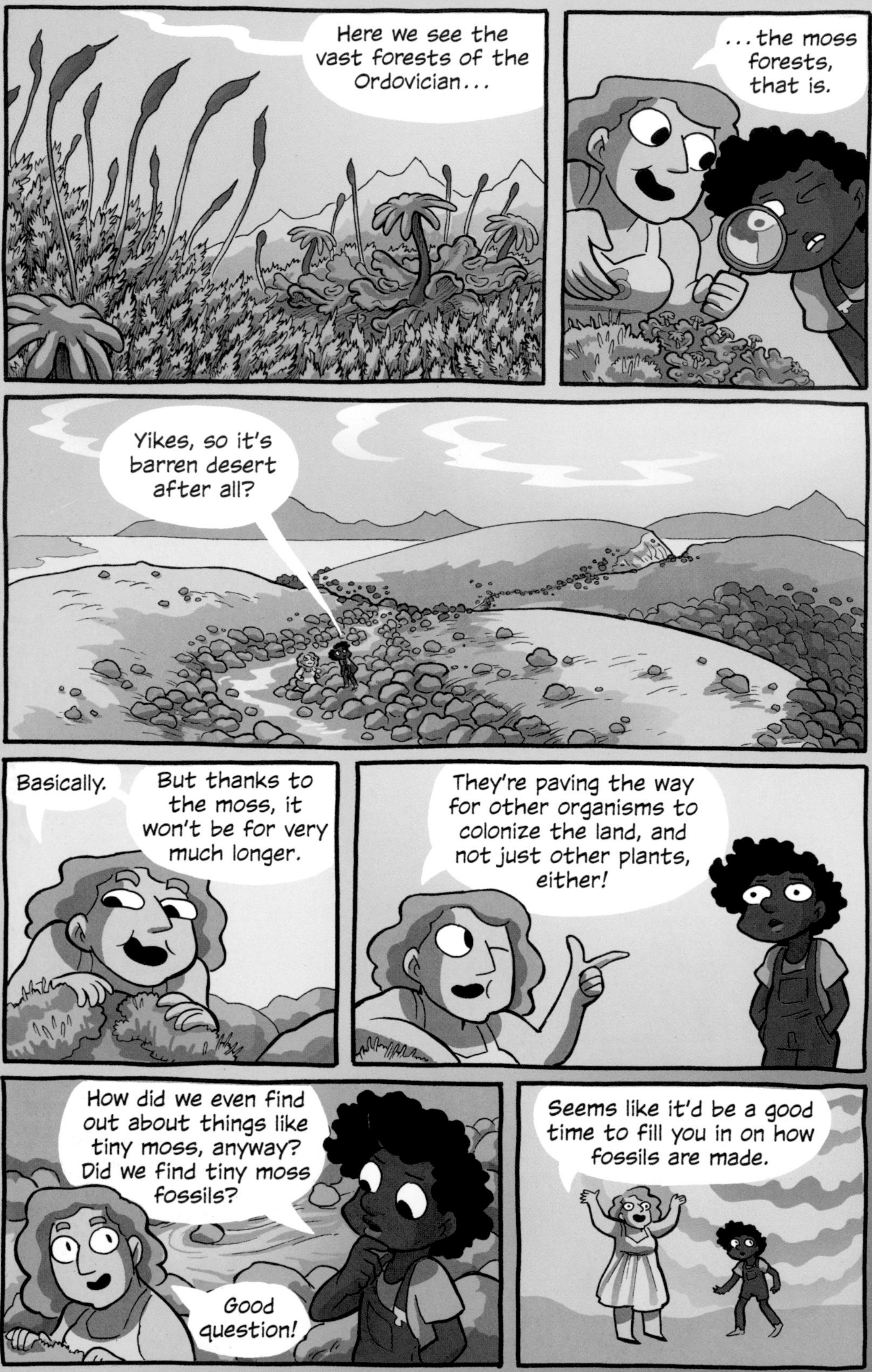
Here we see the vast forests of the Ordovician...
...the moss forests, that is.
Yikes, so it's barren desert after all?
Basically.
But thanks to the moss, it won't be for very much longer.
They're paving the way for other organisms to colonize the land, and not just other plants, either!
How did we even find out about things like tiny moss, anyway? Did we find tiny moss fossils?
Good question!
Seems like it'd be a good time to fill you in on how fossils are made.

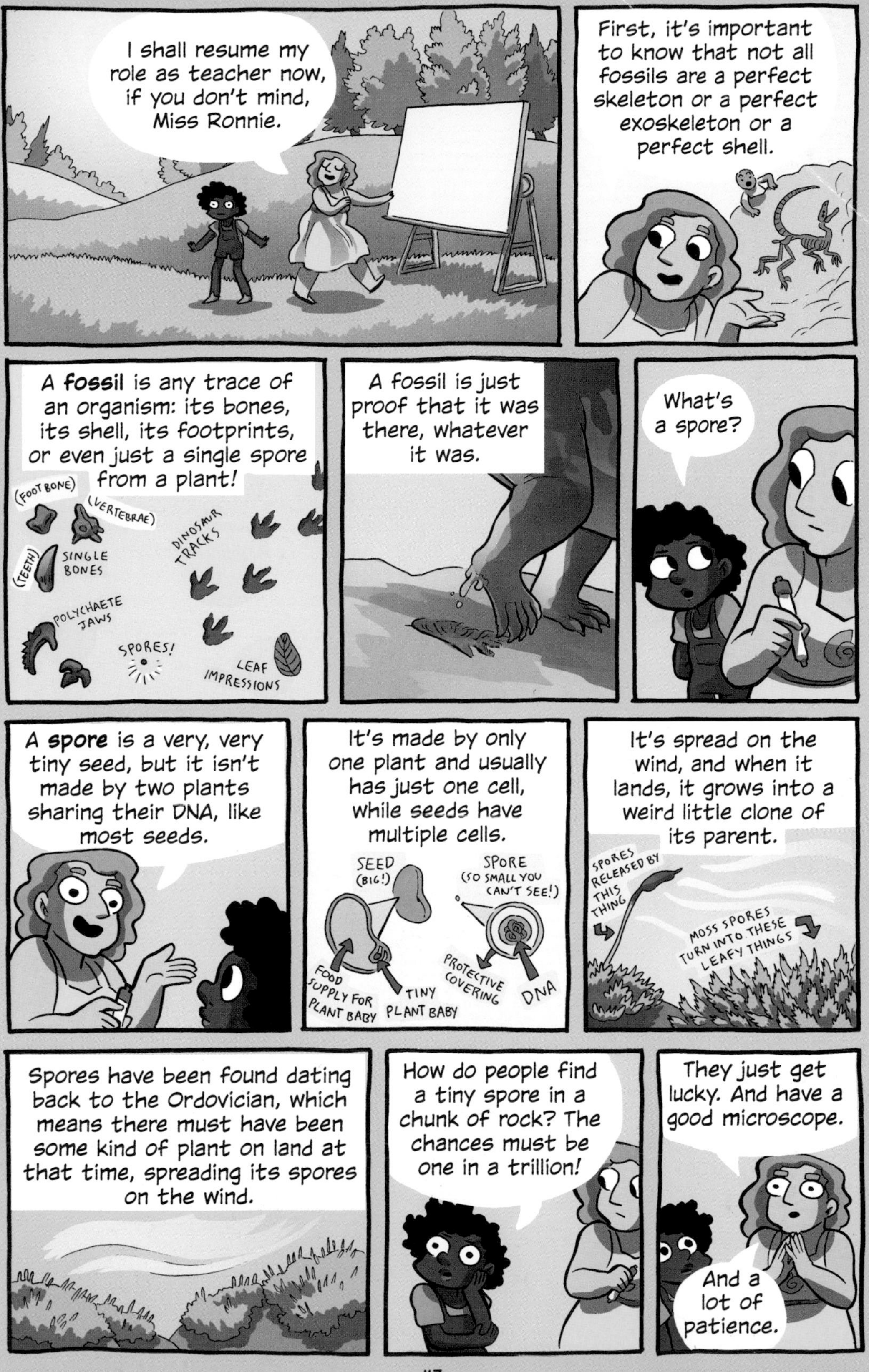
I shall resume my role as teacher now, if you don't mind, Miss Ronnie.
First, it's important to know that not all fossils are a perfect skeleton or a perfect exoskeleton or a perfect shell.
A **fossil** is any trace of an organism: its bones, its shell, its footprints, or even just a single spore from a plant!
(FOOT BONE)
(VERTEBRAE)
(TEETH)
SINGLE BONES
DINOSAUR TRACKS
POLYCHAETE JAWS
SPORES!
LEAF IMPRESSIONS
A fossil is just proof that it was there, whatever it was.
What's a spore?
A **spore** is a very, very tiny seed, but it isn't made by two plants sharing their DNA, like most seeds.
It's made by only one plant and usually has just one cell, while seeds have multiple cells.
SEED (BIG!)
SPORE (SO SMALL YOU CAN'T SEE!)
FOOD SUPPLY FOR PLANT BABY
TINY PLANT BABY
PROTECTIVE COVERING
DNA
It's spread on the wind, and when it lands, it grows into a weird little clone of its parent.
SPORES RELEASED BY THIS THING
MOSS SPORES TURN INTO THESE LEAFY THINGS
Spores have been found dating back to the Ordovician, which means there must have been some kind of plant on land at that time, spreading its spores on the wind.
How do people find a tiny spore in a chunk of rock? The chances must be one in a trillion!
They just get lucky. And have a good microscope.
And a lot of patience.

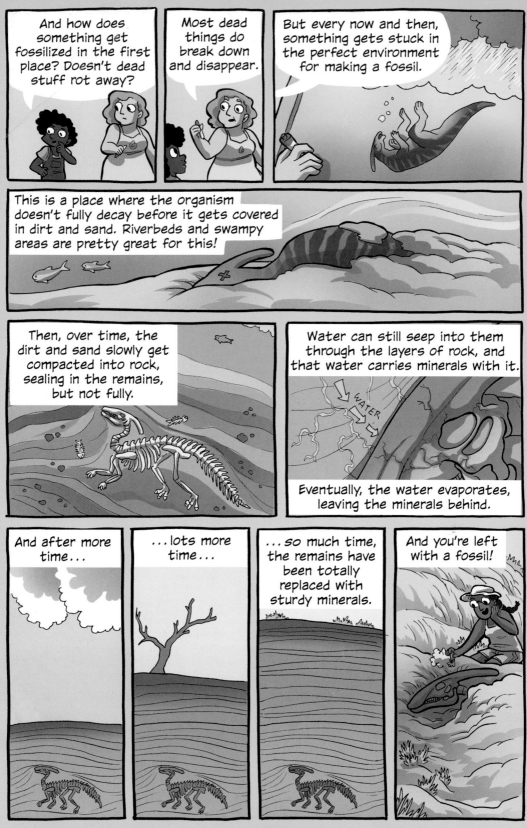

And how does something get fossilized in the first place? Doesn't dead stuff rot away?

Most dead things do break down and disappear.

But every now and then, something gets stuck in the perfect environment for making a fossil.

This is a place where the organism doesn't fully decay before it gets covered in dirt and sand. Riverbeds and swampy areas are pretty great for this!

Then, over time, the dirt and sand slowly get compacted into rock, sealing in the remains, but not fully.

Water can still seep into them through the layers of rock, and that water carries minerals with it.

WATER

Eventually, the water evaporates, leaving the minerals behind.

And after more time...

...lots more time...

...so much time, the remains have been totally replaced with sturdy minerals.

And you're left with a fossil!

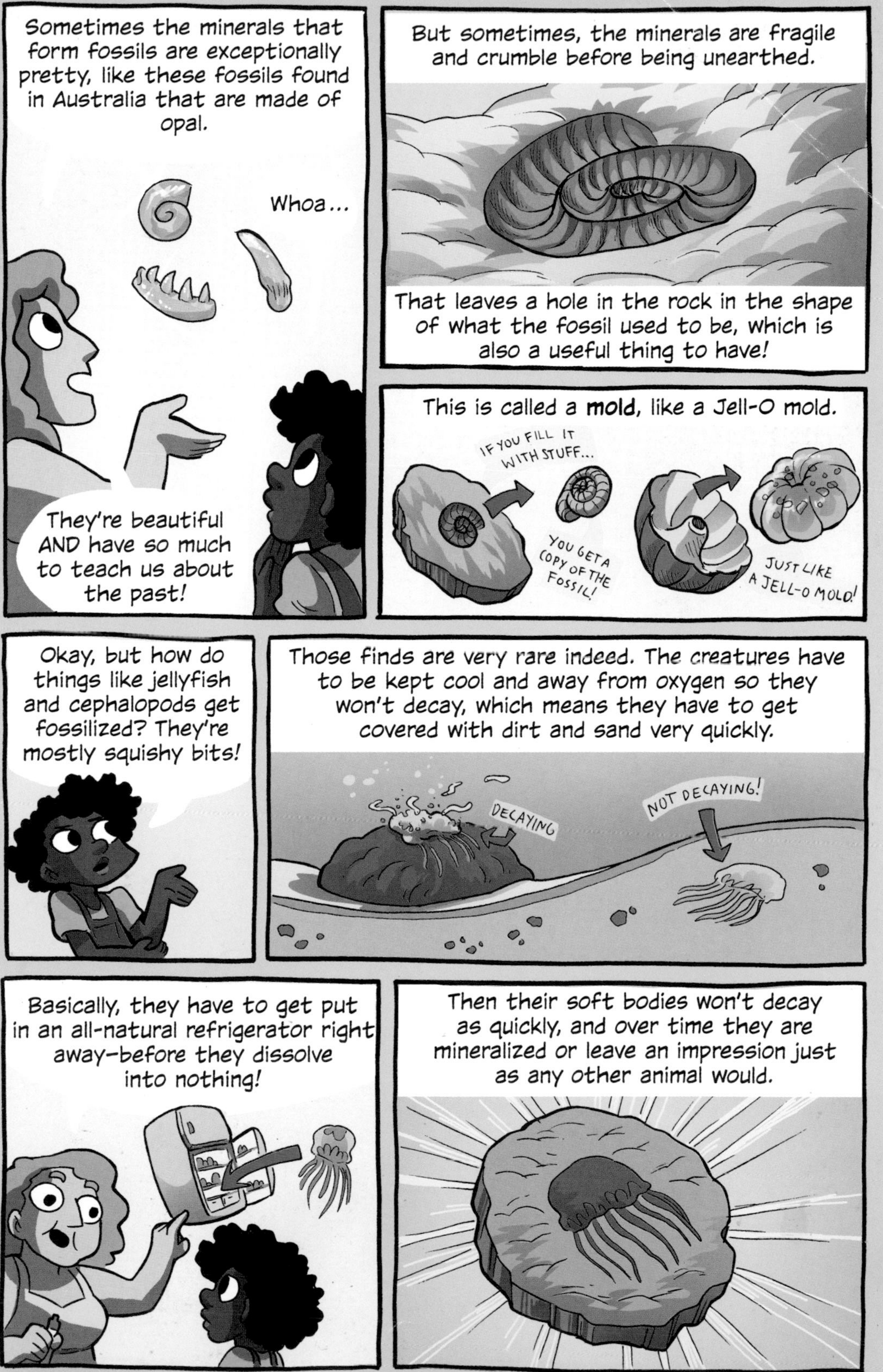
Sometimes the minerals that form fossils are exceptionally pretty, like these fossils found in Australia that are made of opal.
Whoa...
They're beautiful AND have so much to teach us about the past!
But sometimes, the minerals are fragile and crumble before being unearthed.
That leaves a hole in the rock in the shape of what the fossil used to be, which is also a useful thing to have!
This is called a **mold**, like a Jell-O mold.
IF YOU FILL IT WITH STUFF...
YOU GET A COPY OF THE FOSSIL!
JUST LIKE A JELL-O MOLD!
Okay, but how do things like jellyfish and cephalopods get fossilized? They're mostly squishy bits!
Those finds are very rare indeed. The creatures have to be kept cool and away from oxygen so they won't decay, which means they have to get covered with dirt and sand very quickly.
DECAYING
NOT DECAYING!
Basically, they have to get put in an all-natural refrigerator right away—before they dissolve into nothing!
Then their soft bodies won't decay as quickly, and over time they are mineralized or leave an impression just as any other animal would.

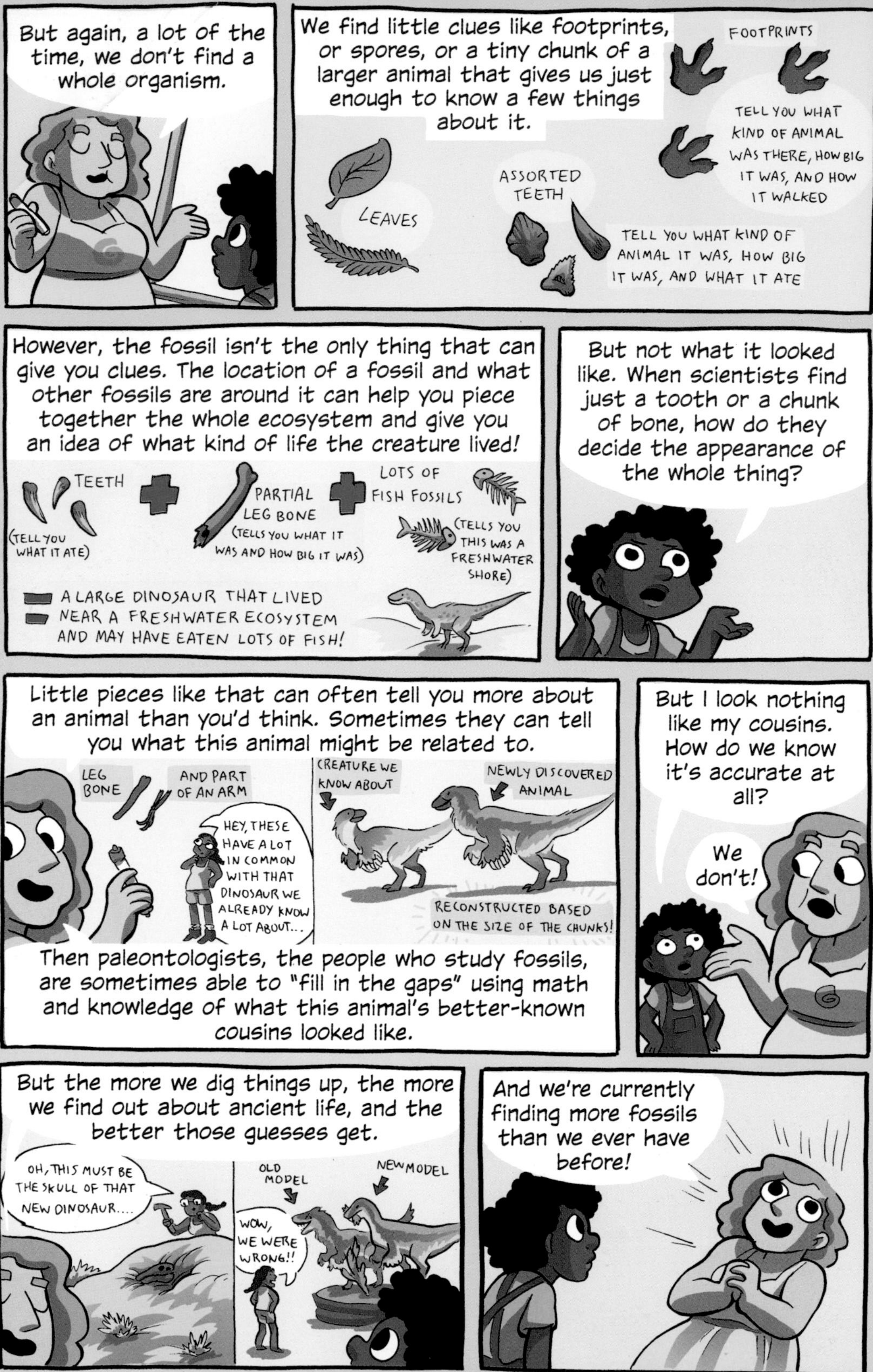

But again, a lot of the time, we don't find a whole organism.
We find little clues like footprints, or spores, or a tiny chunk of a larger animal that gives us just enough to know a few things about it.
FOOTPRINTS
TELL YOU WHAT KIND OF ANIMAL WAS THERE, HOW BIG IT WAS, AND HOW IT WALKED
LEAVES
ASSORTED TEETH
TELL YOU WHAT KIND OF ANIMAL IT WAS, HOW BIG IT WAS, AND WHAT IT ATE
However, the fossil isn't the only thing that can give you clues. The location of a fossil and what other fossils are around it can help you piece together the whole ecosystem and give you an idea of what kind of life the creature lived!
TEETH
(TELL YOU WHAT IT ATE)
PARTIAL LEG BONE
(TELLS YOU WHAT IT WAS AND HOW BIG IT WAS)
LOTS OF FISH FOSSILS
(TELLS YOU THIS WAS A FRESHWATER SHORE)
A LARGE DINOSAUR THAT LIVED NEAR A FRESHWATER ECOSYSTEM AND MAY HAVE EATEN LOTS OF FISH!
But not what it looked like. When scientists find just a tooth or a chunk of bone, how do they decide the appearance of the whole thing?
Little pieces like that can often tell you more about an animal than you'd think. Sometimes they can tell you what this animal might be related to.
LEG BONE
AND PART OF AN ARM
HEY, THESE HAVE A LOT IN COMMON WITH THAT DINOSAUR WE ALREADY KNOW A LOT ABOUT...
CREATURE WE KNOW ABOUT
NEWLY DISCOVERED ANIMAL
RECONSTRUCTED BASED ON THE SIZE OF THE CHUNKS!
Then paleontologists, the people who study fossils, are sometimes able to "fill in the gaps" using math and knowledge of what this animal's better-known cousins looked like.
But I look nothing like my cousins. How do we know it's accurate at all?
We don't!
But the more we dig things up, the more we find out about ancient life, and the better those guesses get.
OH, THIS MUST BE THE SKULL OF THAT NEW DINOSAUR....
OLD MODEL
NEW MODEL
WOW, WE WERE WRONG!!
And we're currently finding more fossils than we ever have before!

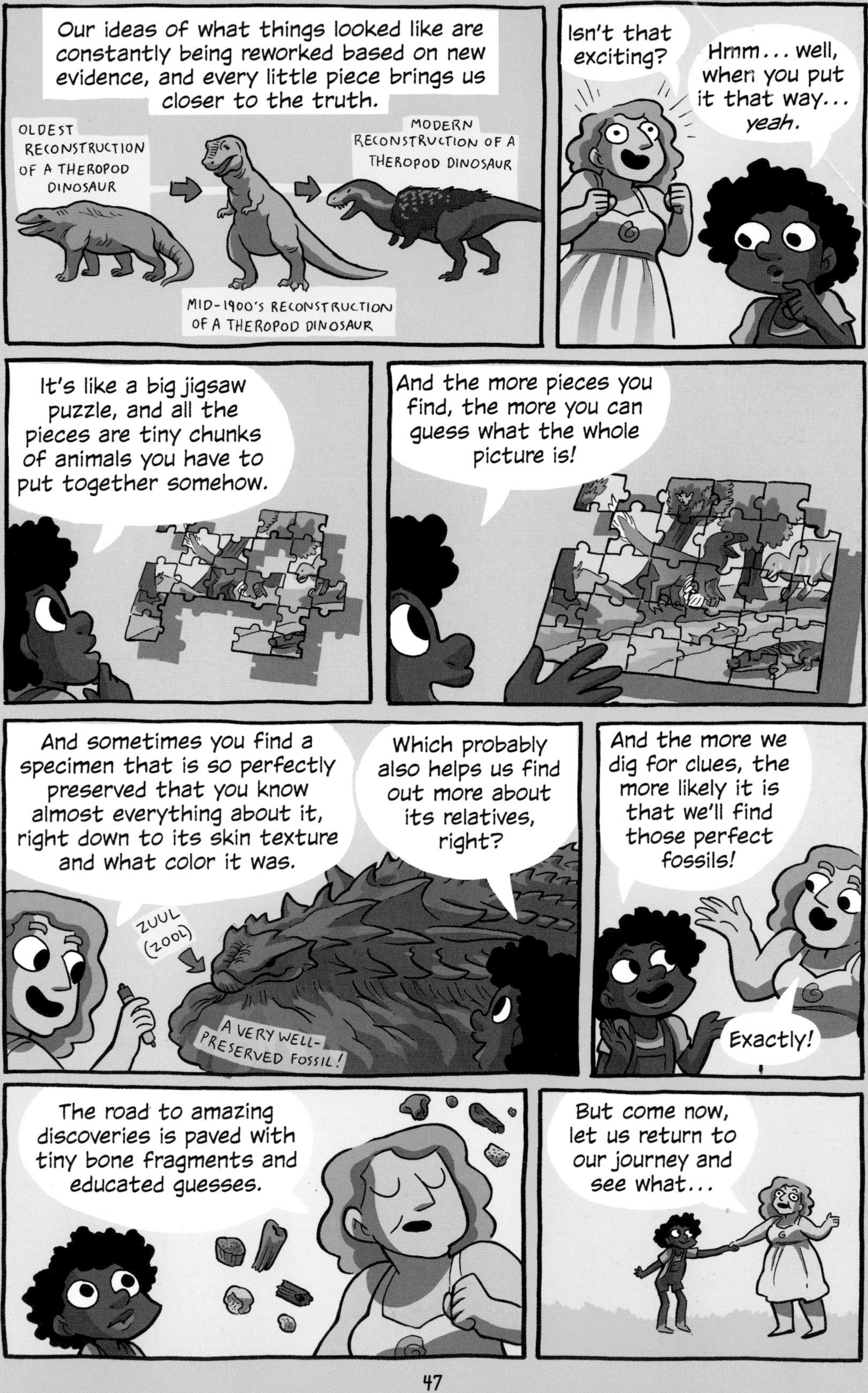

Our ideas of what things looked like are constantly being reworked based on new evidence, and every little piece brings us closer to the truth.
OLDEST RECONSTRUCTION OF A THEROPOD DINOSAUR
MID-1900'S RECONSTRUCTION OF A THEROPOD DINOSAUR
MODERN RECONSTRUCTION OF A THEROPOD DINOSAUR
Isn't that exciting?
Hmm... well, when you put it that way... *yeah.*
It's like a big jigsaw puzzle, and all the pieces are tiny chunks of animals you have to put together somehow.
And the more pieces you find, the more you can guess what the whole picture is!
And sometimes you find a specimen that is so perfectly preserved that you know almost everything about it, right down to its skin texture and what color it was.
ZUUL (ZOOL)
A VERY WELL-PRESERVED FOSSIL!
Which probably also helps us find out more about its relatives, right?
And the more we dig for clues, the more likely it is that we'll find those perfect fossils!
Exactly!
The road to amazing discoveries is paved with tiny bone fragments and educated guesses.
But come now, let us return to our journey and see what...

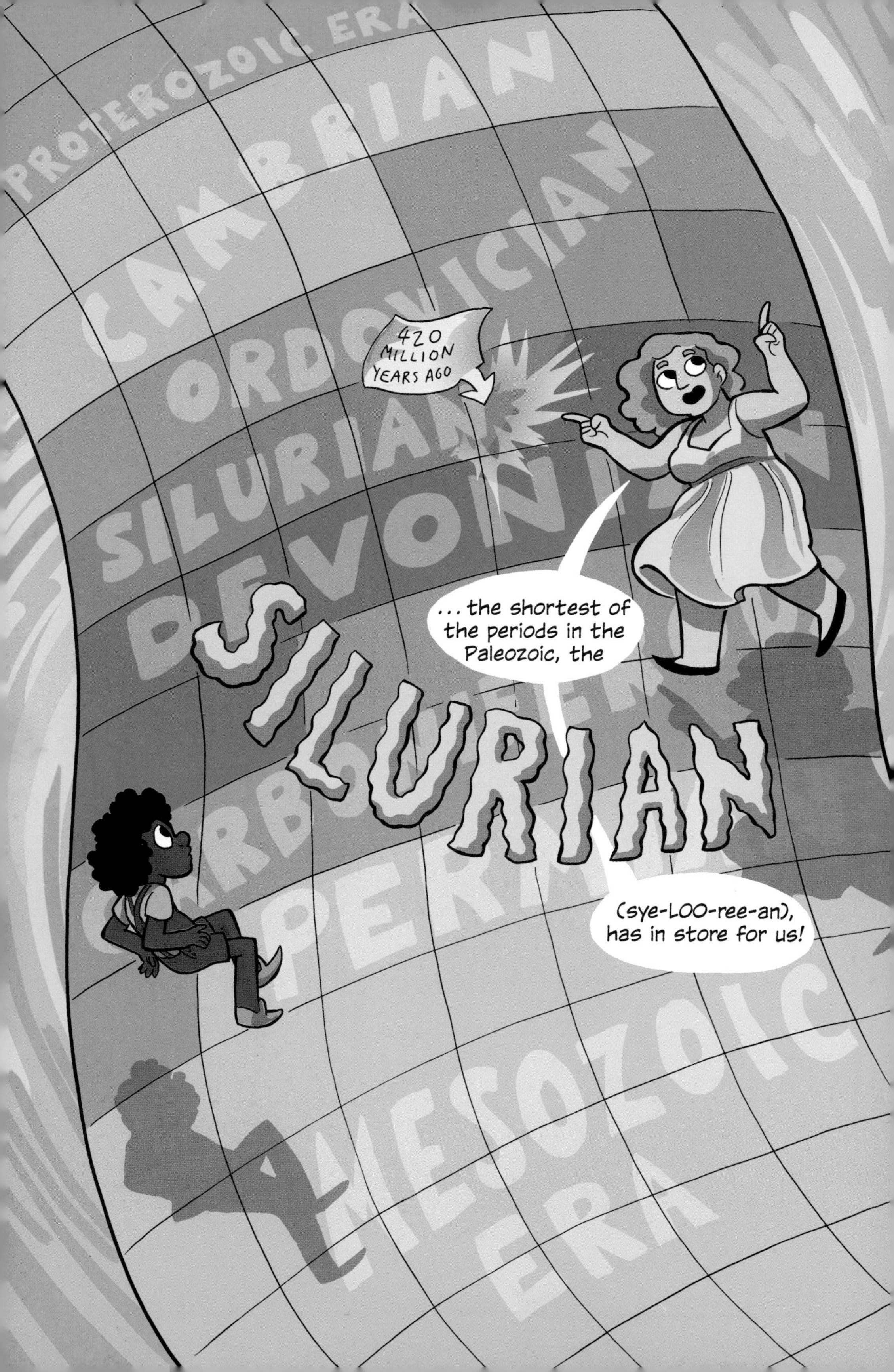
PROTEROZOIC ERA
CAMBRIAN
ORDOVICIAN
SILURIAN
DEVONIAN
420 MILLION YEARS AGO
...the shortest of the periods in the Paleozoic, the
SILURIAN
(sye-LOO-ree-an), has in store for us!
MESOZOIC ERA

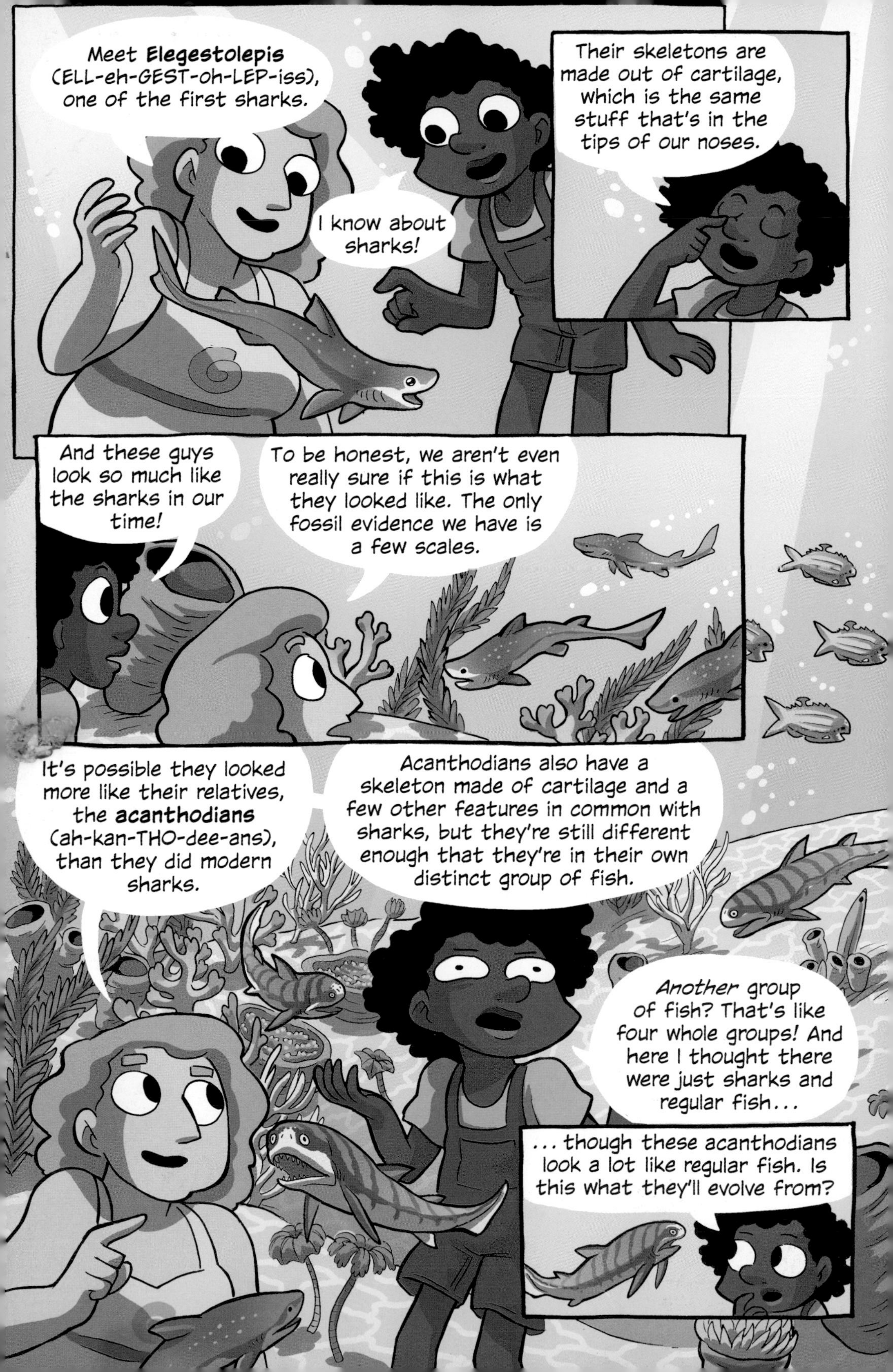

Meet **Elegestolepis** (ELL-eh-GEST-oh-LEP-iss), one of the first sharks.
I know about sharks!
Their skeletons are made out of cartilage, which is the same stuff that's in the tips of our noses.
And these guys look so much like the sharks in our time!
To be honest, we aren't even really sure if this is what they looked like. The only fossil evidence we have is a few scales.
It's possible they looked more like their relatives, the **acanthodians** (ah-kan-THO-dee-ans), than they did modern sharks.
Acanthodians also have a skeleton made of cartilage and a few other features in common with sharks, but they're still different enough that they're in their own distinct group of fish.
Another group of fish? That's like four whole groups! And here I thought there were just sharks and regular fish...
... though these acanthodians look a lot like regular fish. Is this what they'll evolve from?

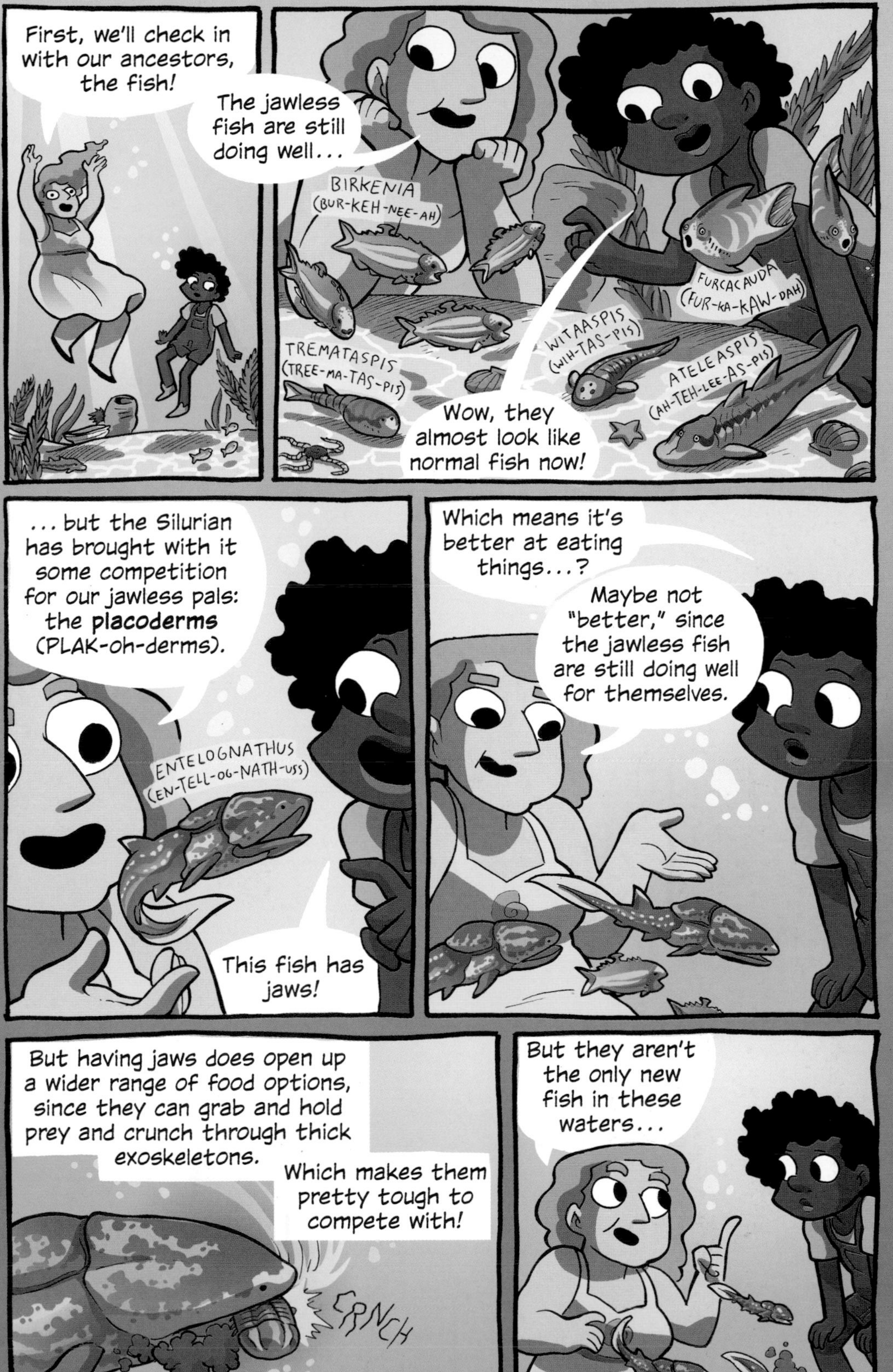
First, we'll check in with our ancestors, the fish!
The jawless fish are still doing well...
BIRKENIA (BUR-KEH-NEE-AH)
FURCACAUDA (FUR-KA-KAW-DAH)
WITAASPIS (WIH-TAS-PIS)
TREMATASPIS (TREE-MA-TAS-PIS)
ATELEASPIS (AH-TEH-LEE-AS-PIS)
Wow, they almost look like normal fish now!
... but the Silurian has brought with it some competition for our jawless pals: the **placoderms** (PLAK-oh-derms).
ENTELOGNATHUS (EN-TELL-OG-NATH-USS)
This fish has jaws!
Which means it's better at eating things...?
Maybe not "better," since the jawless fish are still doing well for themselves.
But having jaws does open up a wider range of food options, since they can grab and hold prey and crunch through thick exoskeletons.
Which makes them pretty tough to compete with!
CRNCH
But they aren't the only new fish in these waters...

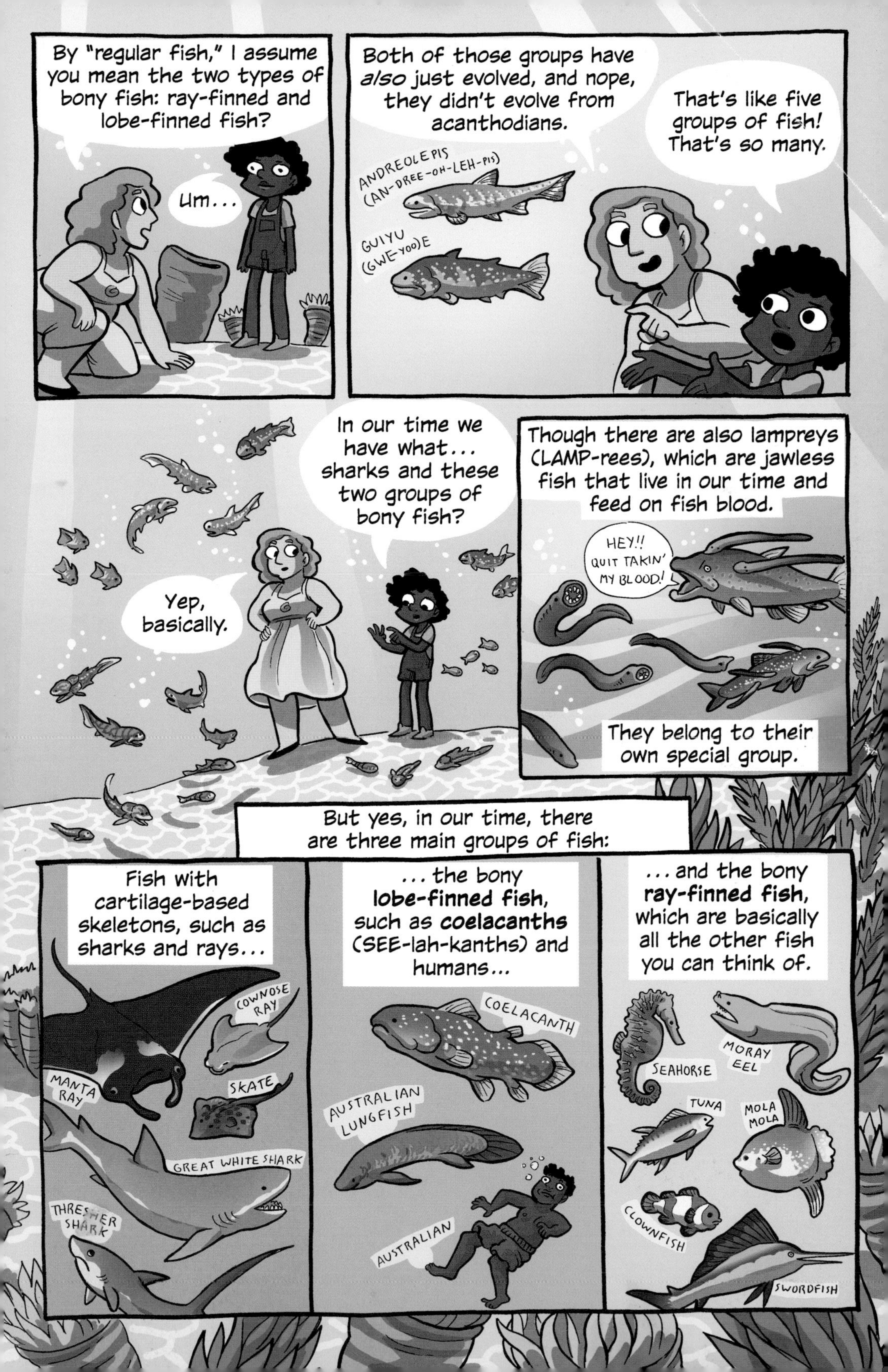

By "regular fish," I assume you mean the two types of bony fish: ray-finned and lobe-finned fish?
Um...
Both of those groups have *also* just evolved, and nope, they didn't evolve from acanthodians.
ANDREOLEPIS (AN-DREE-OH-LEH-PIS)
GUIYU (GWE-YOO)E
That's like five groups of fish! That's so many.
In our time we have what... sharks and these two groups of bony fish?
Yep, basically.
Though there are also lampreys (LAMP-rees), which are jawless fish that live in our time and feed on fish blood.
HEY!! QUIT TAKIN' MY BLOOD!
They belong to their own special group.
But yes, in our time, there are three main groups of fish:
Fish with cartilage-based skeletons, such as sharks and rays...
COWNOSE RAY
MANTA RAY
SKATE
GREAT WHITE SHARK
THRESHER SHARK
... the bony **lobe-finned fish**, such as **coelacanths** (SEE-lah-kanths) and humans...
COELACANTH
AUSTRALIAN LUNGFISH
AUSTRALIAN
... and the bony **ray-finned fish**, which are basically all the other fish you can think of.
SEAHORSE
MORAY EEL
TUNA
MOLA MOLA
CLOWNFISH
SWORDFISH

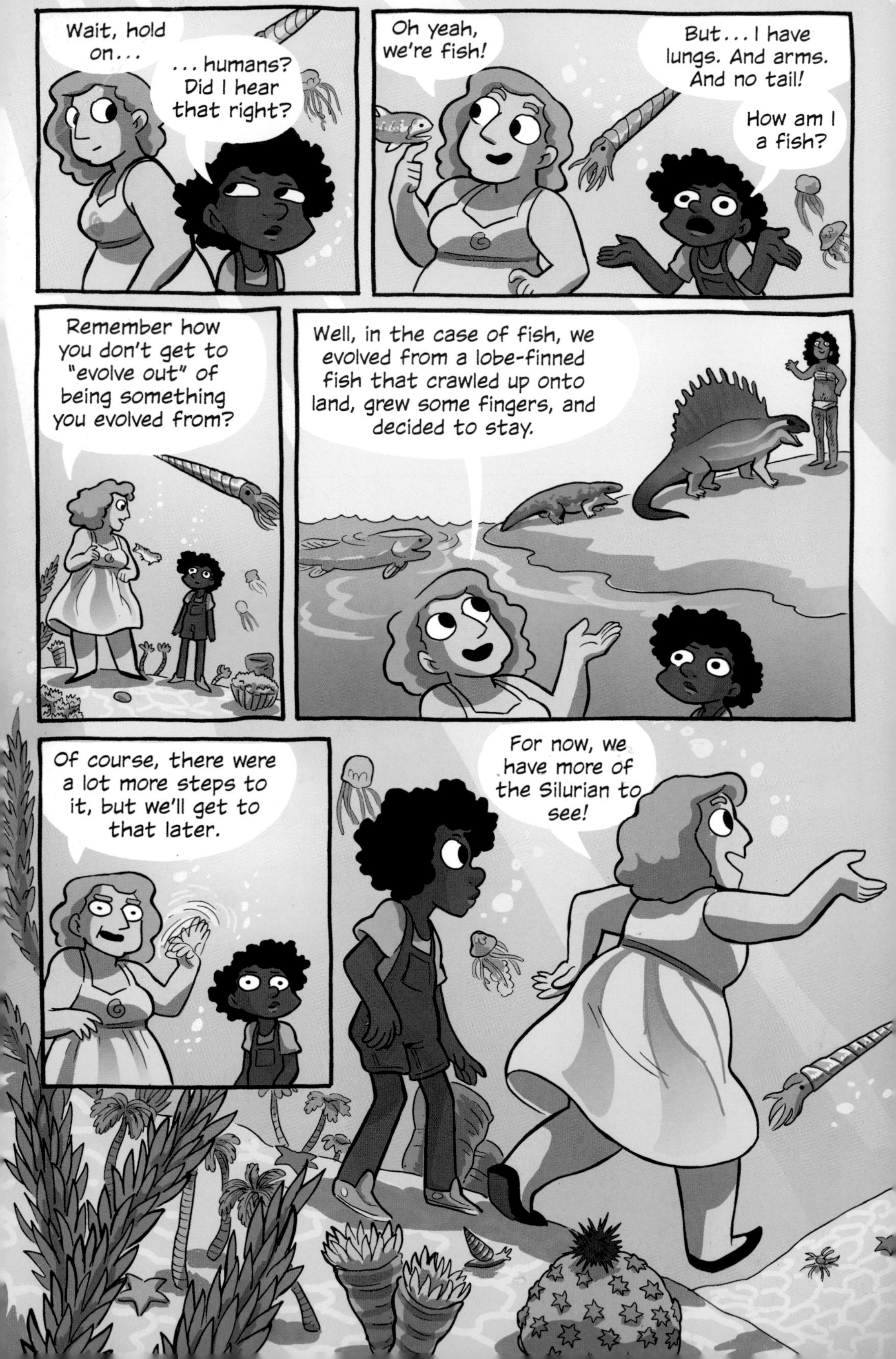
Wait, hold on...
...humans? Did I hear that right?
Oh yeah, we're fish!
But...I have lungs. And arms. And no tail!
How am I a fish?
Remember how you don't get to "evolve out" of being something you evolved from?
Well, in the case of fish, we evolved from a lobe-finned fish that crawled up onto land, grew some fingers, and decided to stay.
Of course, there were a lot more steps to it, but we'll get to that later.
For now, we have more of the Silurian to see!

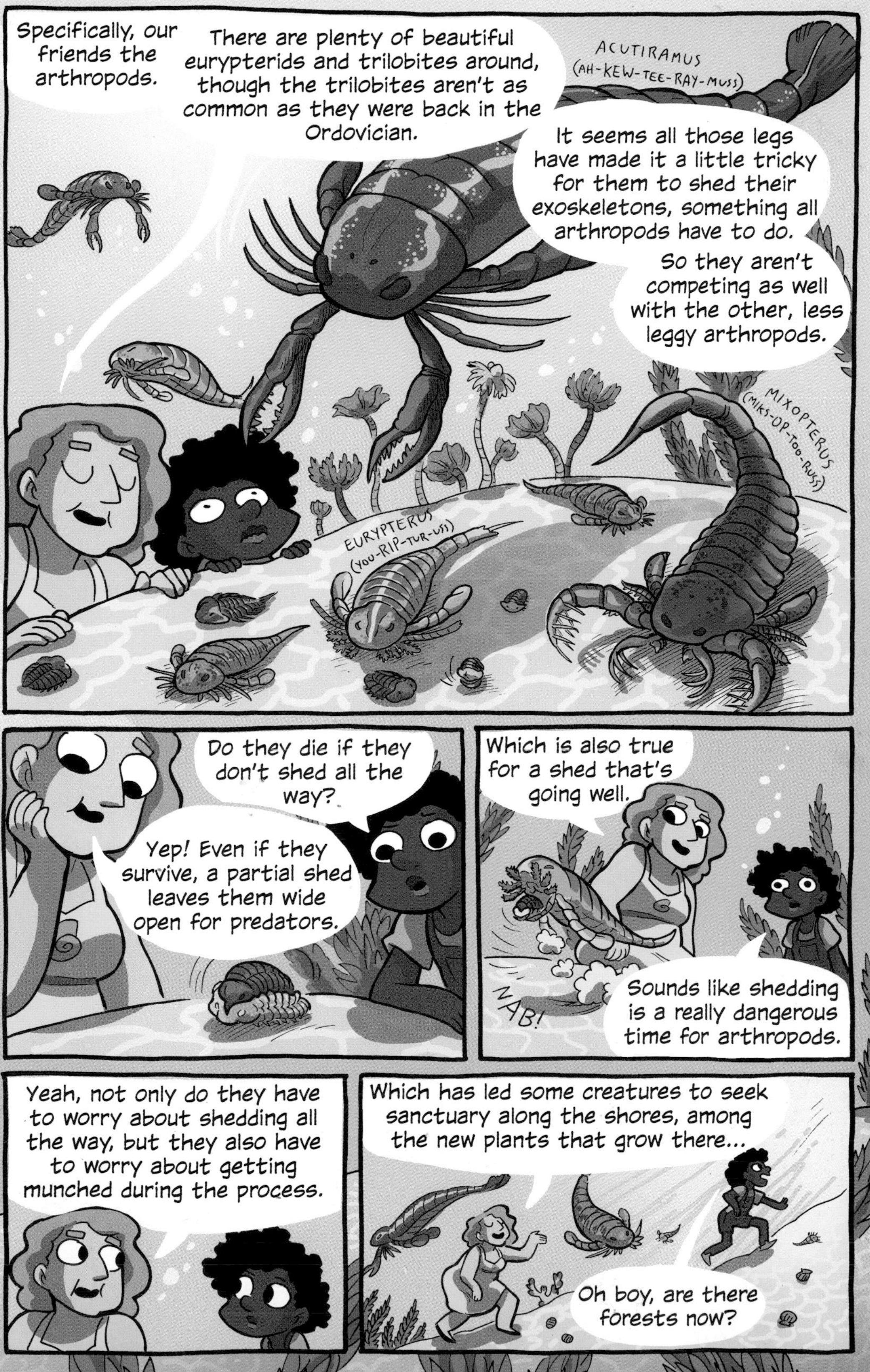
Specifically, our friends the arthropods.
There are plenty of beautiful eurypterids and trilobites around, though the trilobites aren't as common as they were back in the Ordovician.
ACUTIRAMUS (AH-KEW-TEE-RAY-MUSS)
It seems all those legs have made it a little tricky for them to shed their exoskeletons, something all arthropods have to do.
So they aren't competing as well with the other, less leggy arthropods.
MIXOPTERUS (MIKS-OP-TOO-RUSS)
EURYPTERUS (YOU-RIP-TUR-USS)
Do they die if they don't shed all the way?
Yep! Even if they survive, a partial shed leaves them wide open for predators.
Which is also true for a shed that's going well.
NAB!
Sounds like shedding is a really dangerous time for arthropods.
Yeah, not only do they have to worry about shedding all the way, but they also have to worry about getting munched during the process.
Which has led some creatures to seek sanctuary along the shores, among the new plants that grow there...
Oh boy, are there forests now?

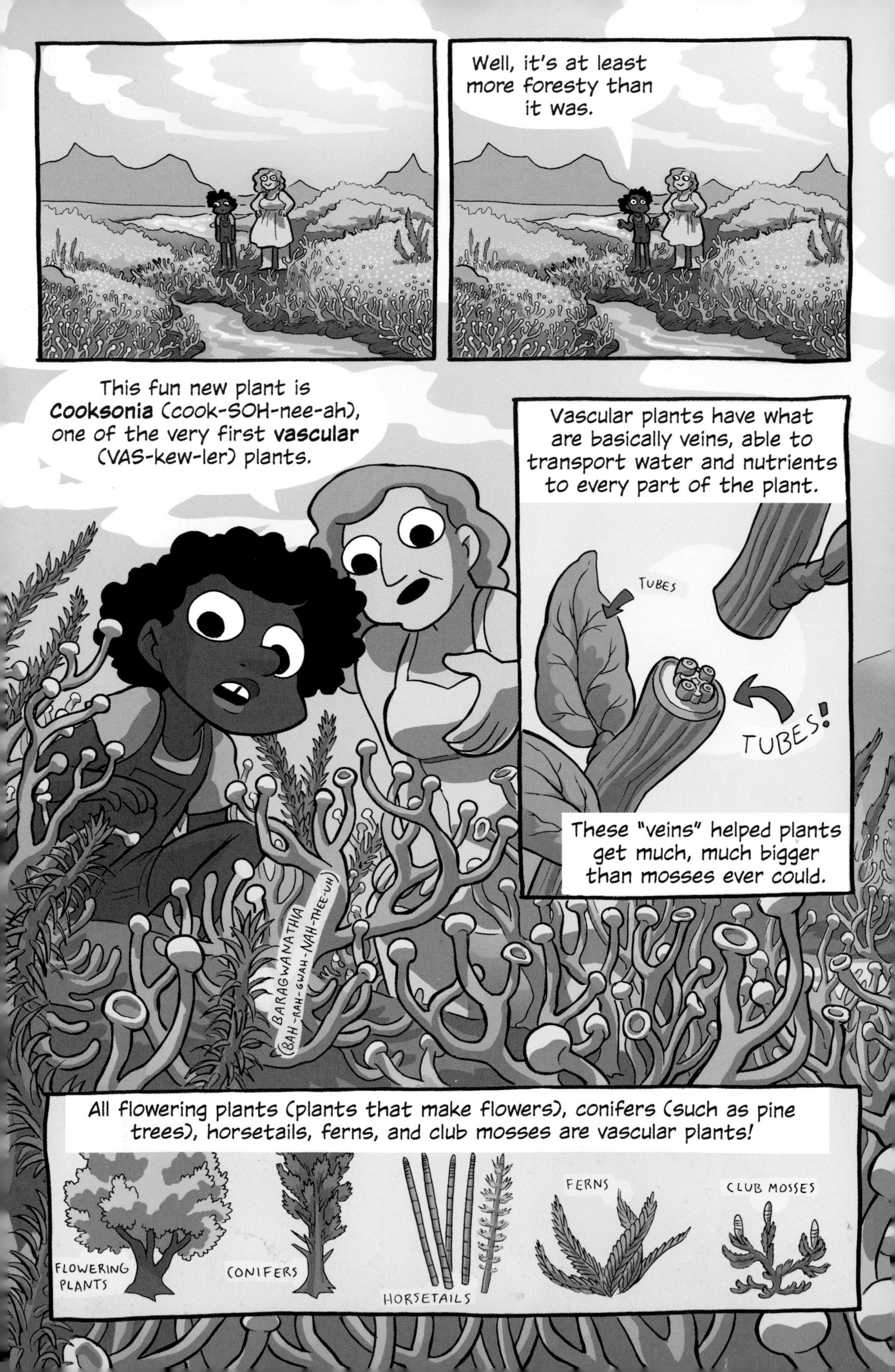

Well, it's at least more foresty than it was.
This fun new plant is **Cooksonia** (cook-SOH-nee-ah), one of the very first **vascular** (VAS-kew-ler) plants.
Vascular plants have what are basically veins, able to transport water and nutrients to every part of the plant.
TUBES
TUBES!
These "veins" helped plants get much, much bigger than mosses ever could.
BARAGWANATHIA (BAH-RAH-GWAH-NAH-THEE-UH)
All flowering plants (plants that make flowers), conifers (such as pine trees), horsetails, ferns, and club mosses are vascular plants!
FLOWERING PLANTS
CONIFERS
HORSETAILS
FERNS
CLUB MOSSES

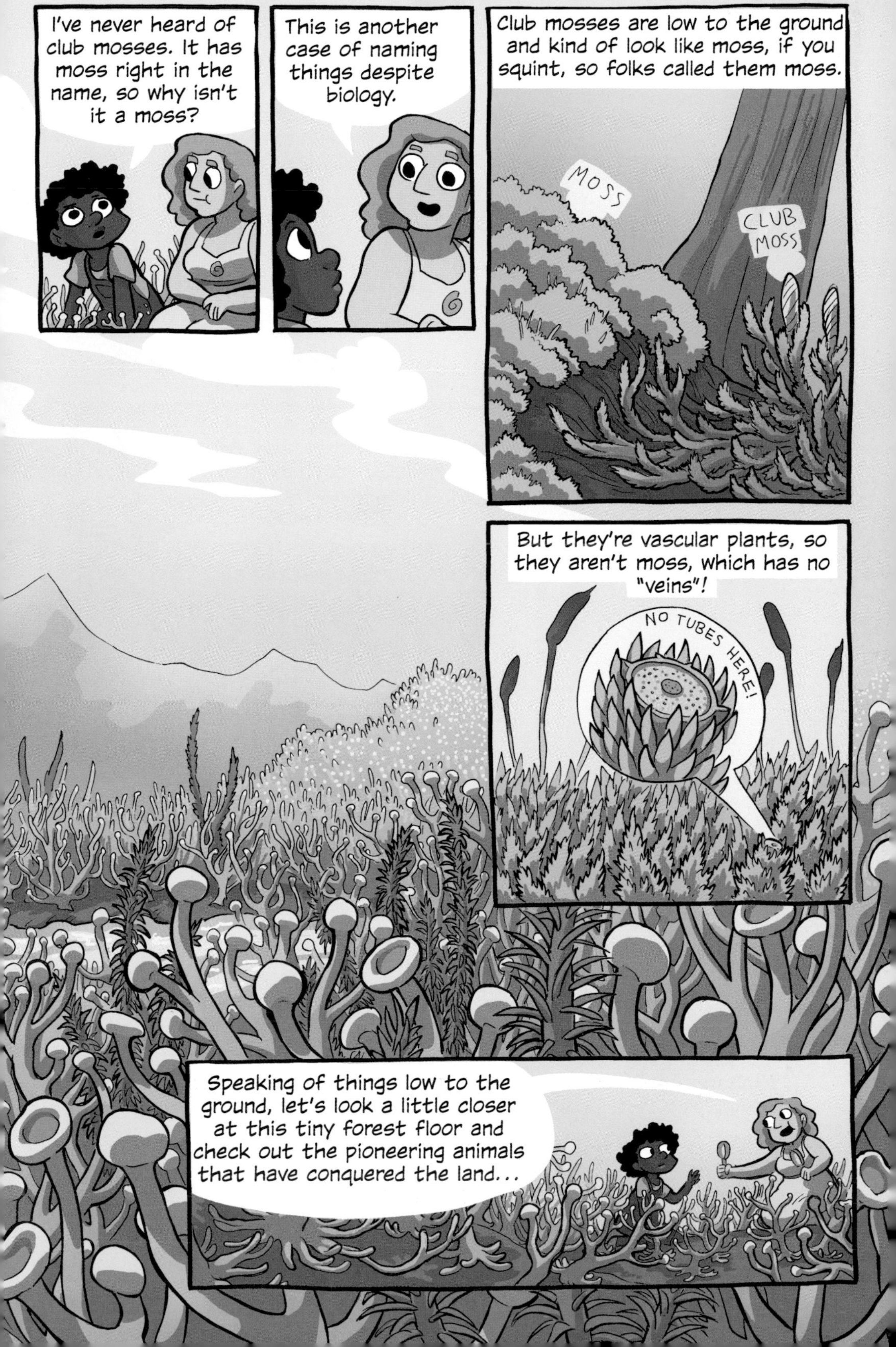

I've never heard of club mosses. It has moss right in the name, so why isn't it a moss?
This is another case of naming things despite biology.
Club mosses are low to the ground and kind of look like moss, if you squint, so folks called them moss.
MOSS
CLUB MOSS
But they're vascular plants, so they aren't moss, which has no "veins"!
NO TUBES HERE!
Speaking of things low to the ground, let's look a little closer at this tiny forest floor and check out the pioneering animals that have conquered the land...

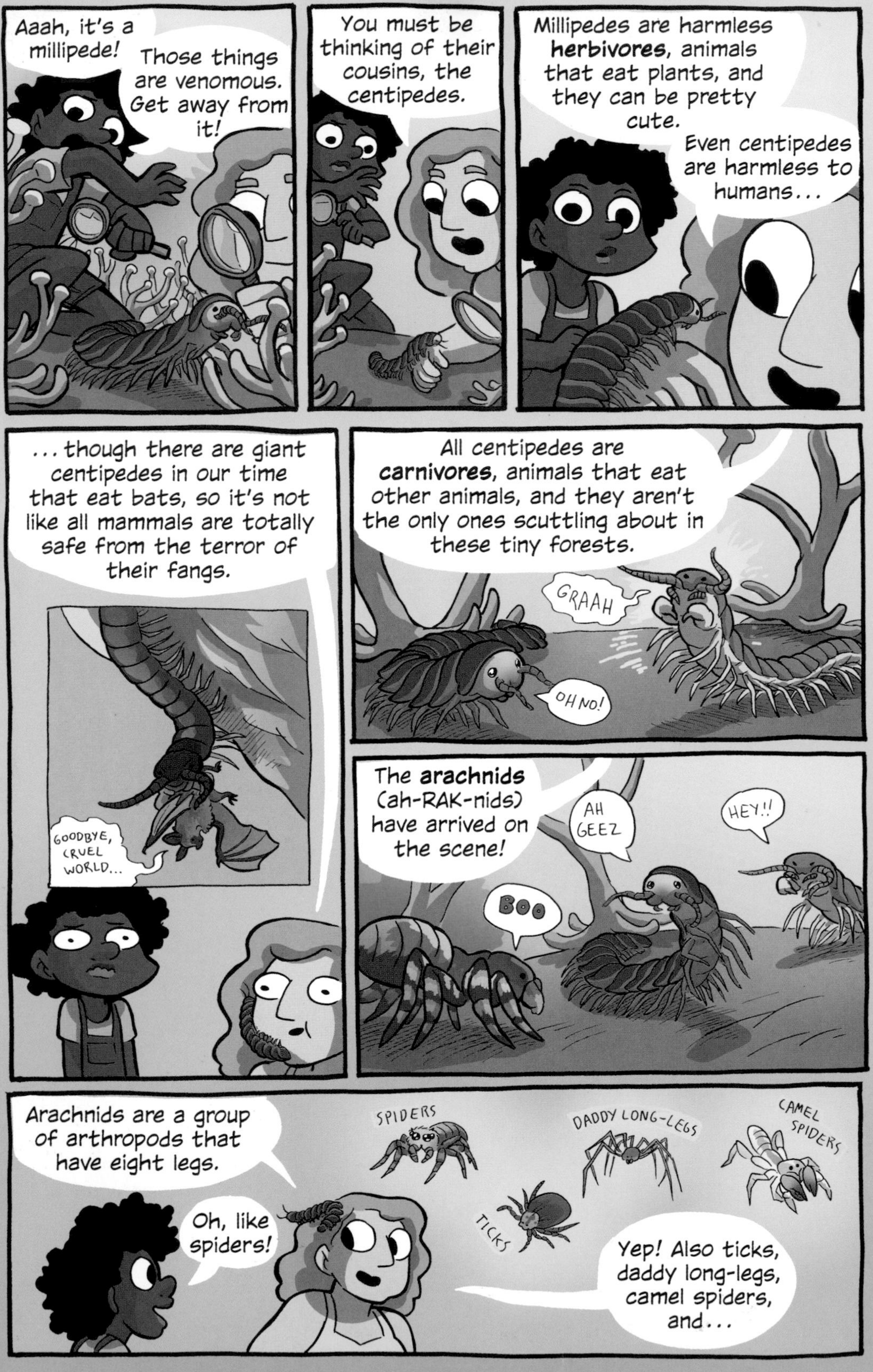
Aaah, it's a millipede!
Those things are venomous. Get away from it!
You must be thinking of their cousins, the centipedes.
Millipedes are harmless **herbivores**, animals that eat plants, and they can be pretty cute.
Even centipedes are harmless to humans...
...though there are giant centipedes in our time that eat bats, so it's not like all mammals are totally safe from the terror of their fangs.
GOODBYE, CRUEL WORLD...
All centipedes are **carnivores**, animals that eat other animals, and they aren't the only ones scuttling about in these tiny forests.
GRAAH
OH NO!
The **arachnids** (ah-RAK-nids) have arrived on the scene!
AH GEEZ
HEY!!
BOO
Arachnids are a group of arthropods that have eight legs.
SPIDERS
DADDY LONG-LEGS
CAMEL SPIDERS
TICKS
Oh, like spiders!
Yep! Also ticks, daddy long-legs, camel spiders, and...

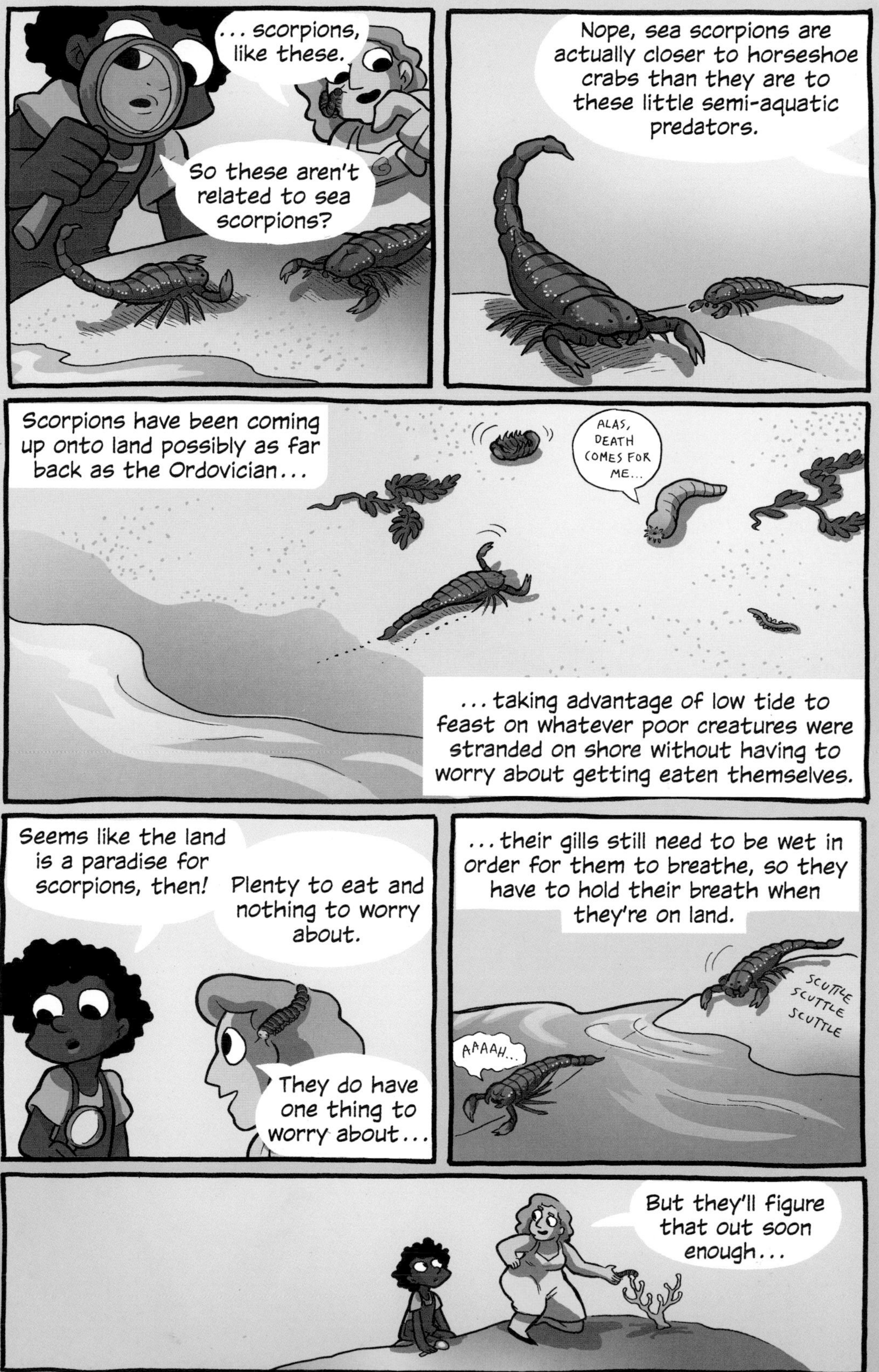

. . . scorpions, like these.
So these aren't related to sea scorpions?
Nope, sea scorpions are actually closer to horseshoe crabs than they are to these little semi-aquatic predators.
Scorpions have been coming up onto land possibly as far back as the Ordovician . . .
ALAS, DEATH COMES FOR ME...
. . . taking advantage of low tide to feast on whatever poor creatures were stranded on shore without having to worry about getting eaten themselves.
Seems like the land is a paradise for scorpions, then!
Plenty to eat and nothing to worry about.
They do have one thing to worry about . . .
. . . their gills still need to be wet in order for them to breathe, so they have to hold their breath when they're on land.
SCUTTLE SCUTTLE SCUTTLE
AAAAH...
But they'll figure that out soon enough . . .

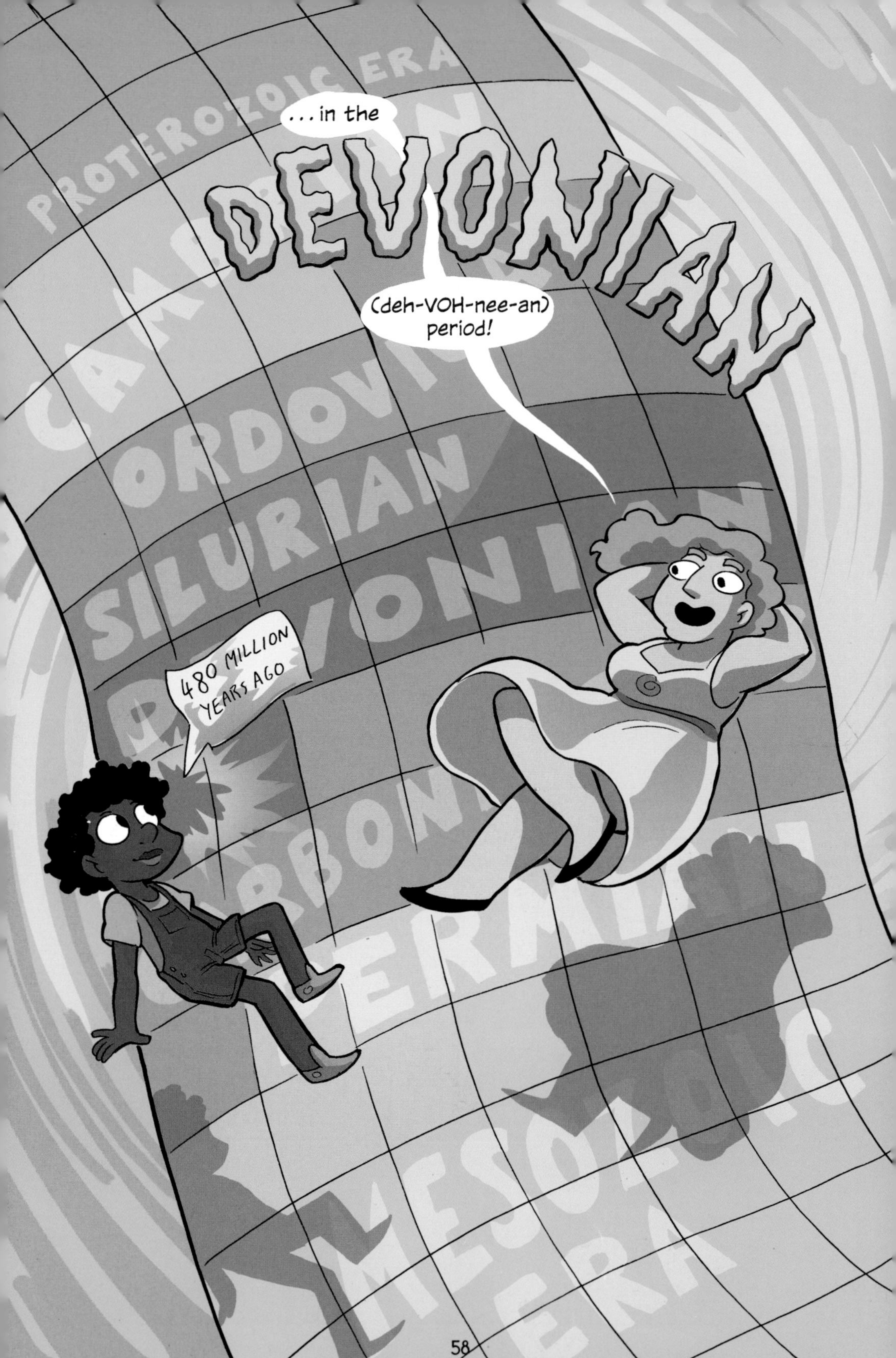
. . . in the
DEVONIAN
(deh-VOH-nee-an) period!
480 MILLION YEARS AGO
PROTEROZOIC ERA
CAMBRIAN
ORDOVICIAN
SILURIAN
DEVONIAN
CARBONIFEROUS
PERMIAN
MESOZOIC ERA

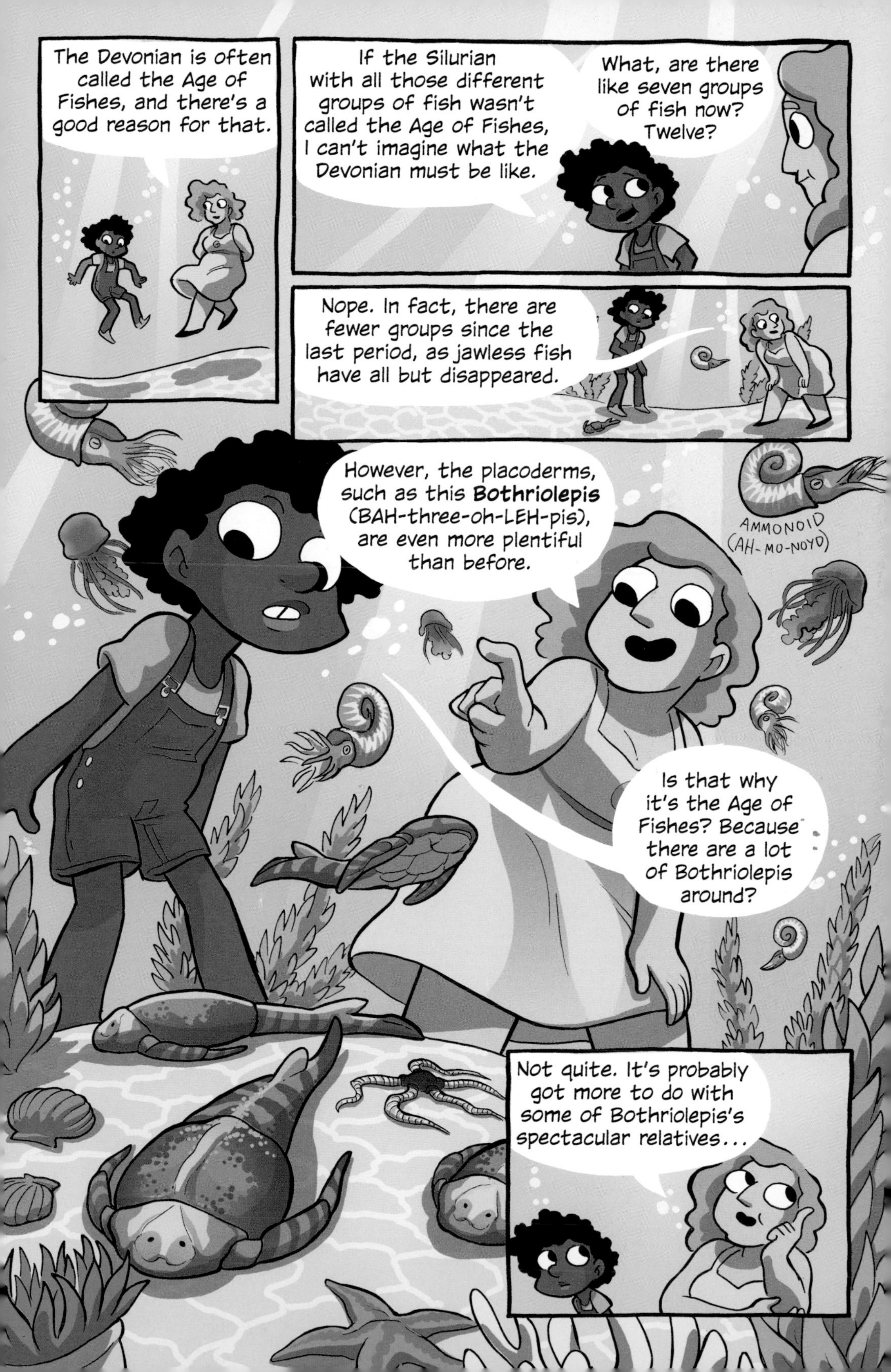
The Devonian is often called the Age of Fishes, and there's a good reason for that.
If the Silurian with all those different groups of fish wasn't called the Age of Fishes, I can't imagine what the Devonian must be like.
What, are there like seven groups of fish now? Twelve?
Nope. In fact, there are fewer groups since the last period, as jawless fish have all but disappeared.
However, the placoderms, such as this **Bothriolepis** (BAH-three-oh-LEH-pis), are even more plentiful than before.
AMMONOID (AH-MO-NOYD)
Is that why it's the Age of Fishes? Because there are a lot of Bothriolepis around?
Not quite. It's probably got more to do with some of Bothriolepis's spectacular relatives...

... such as **Dunkleosteus** (DUN-kel-OSS-tee-uss), one of the largest placoderms that's ever lived.
ASTEROLEPIS (AS-TUR-OH-LEH-PIS)
It may be able to grow up to 30 feet long, though we've only really found fossils of its head, so we aren't entirely sure how big it can get.
WOW! Check out those fangs!
And it isn't the only large placoderm swimming in the Devonian seas.

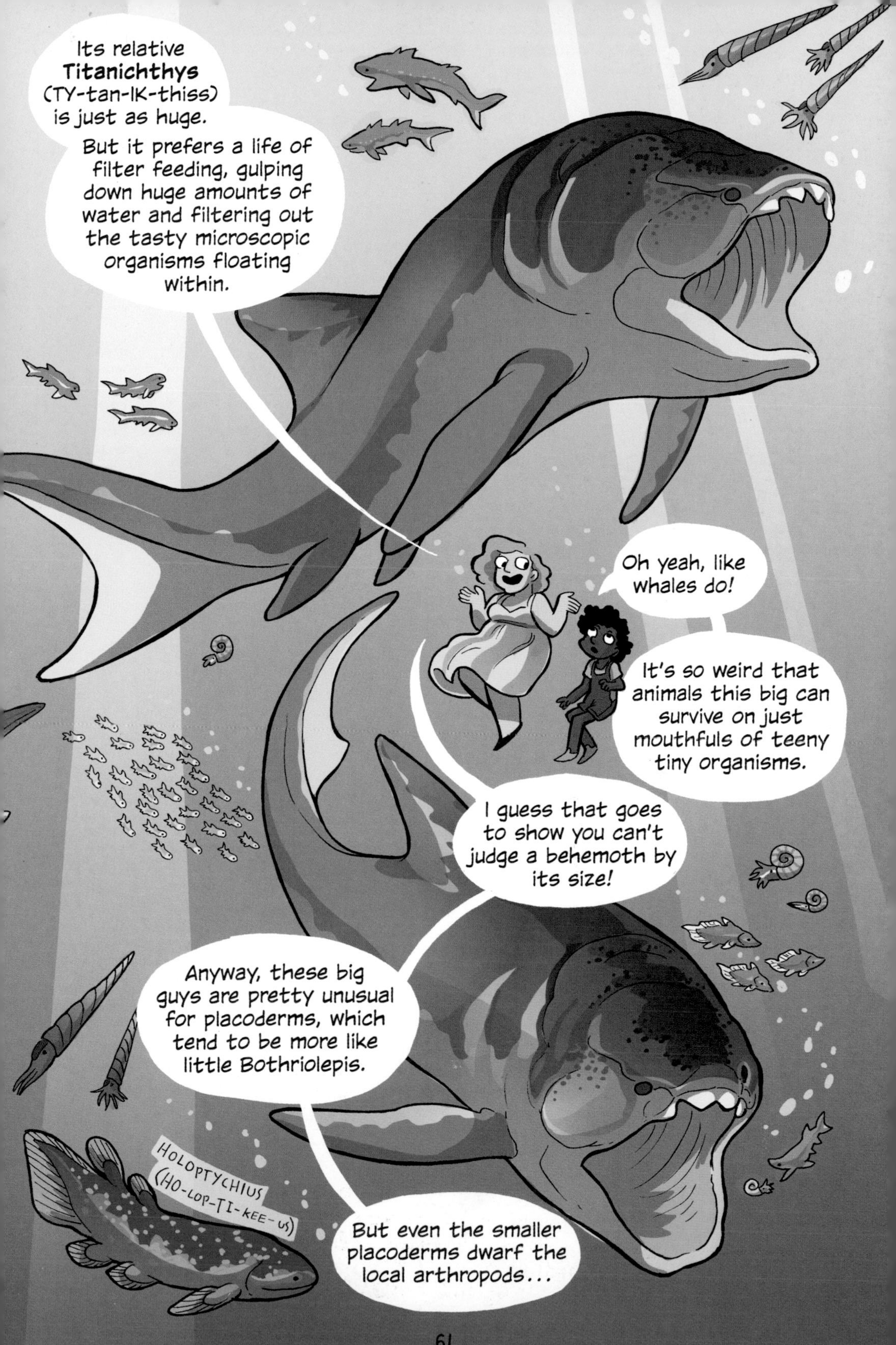
Its relative **Titanichthys** (TY-tan-IK-thiss) is just as huge.
But it prefers a life of filter feeding, gulping down huge amounts of water and filtering out the tasty microscopic organisms floating within.
Oh yeah, like whales do!
It's so weird that animals this big can survive on just mouthfuls of teeny tiny organisms.
I guess that goes to show you can't judge a behemoth by its size!
Anyway, these big guys are pretty unusual for placoderms, which tend to be more like little Bothriolepis.
HOLOPTYCHIUS (HO-LOP-TI-KEE-US)
But even the smaller placoderms dwarf the local arthropods...

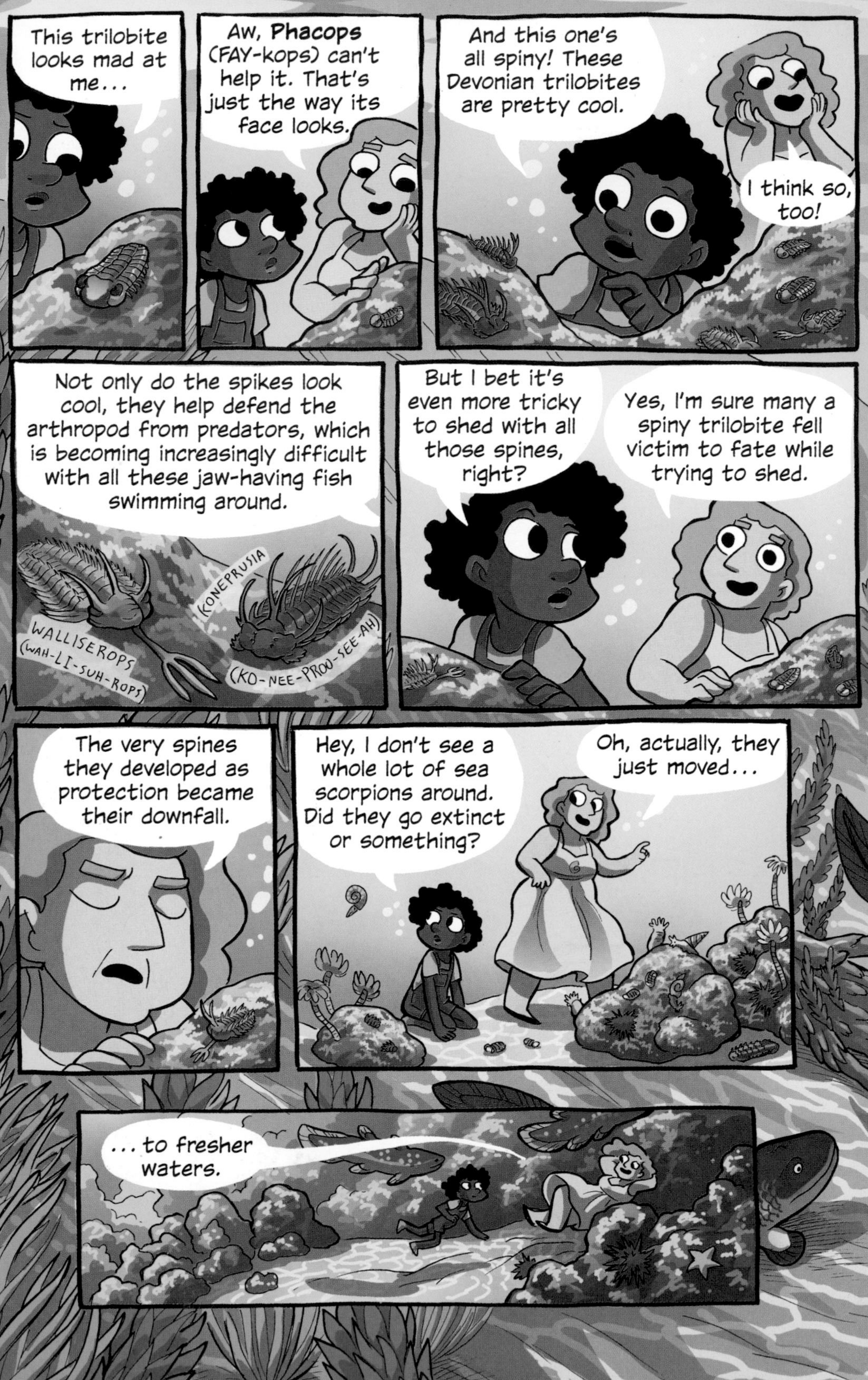
This trilobite looks mad at me...
Aw, **Phacops** (FAY-kops) can't help it. That's just the way its face looks.
And this one's all spiny! These Devonian trilobites are pretty cool.
I think so, too!
Not only do the spikes look cool, they help defend the arthropod from predators, which is becoming increasingly difficult with all these jaw-having fish swimming around.
WALLISEROPS (WAH-LI-SUH-ROPS)
KONEPRUSIA (KO-NEE-PROO-SEE-AH)
But I bet it's even more tricky to shed with all those spines, right?
Yes, I'm sure many a spiny trilobite fell victim to fate while trying to shed.
The very spines they developed as protection became their downfall.
Hey, I don't see a whole lot of sea scorpions around. Did they go extinct or something?
Oh, actually, they just moved...
...to fresher waters.

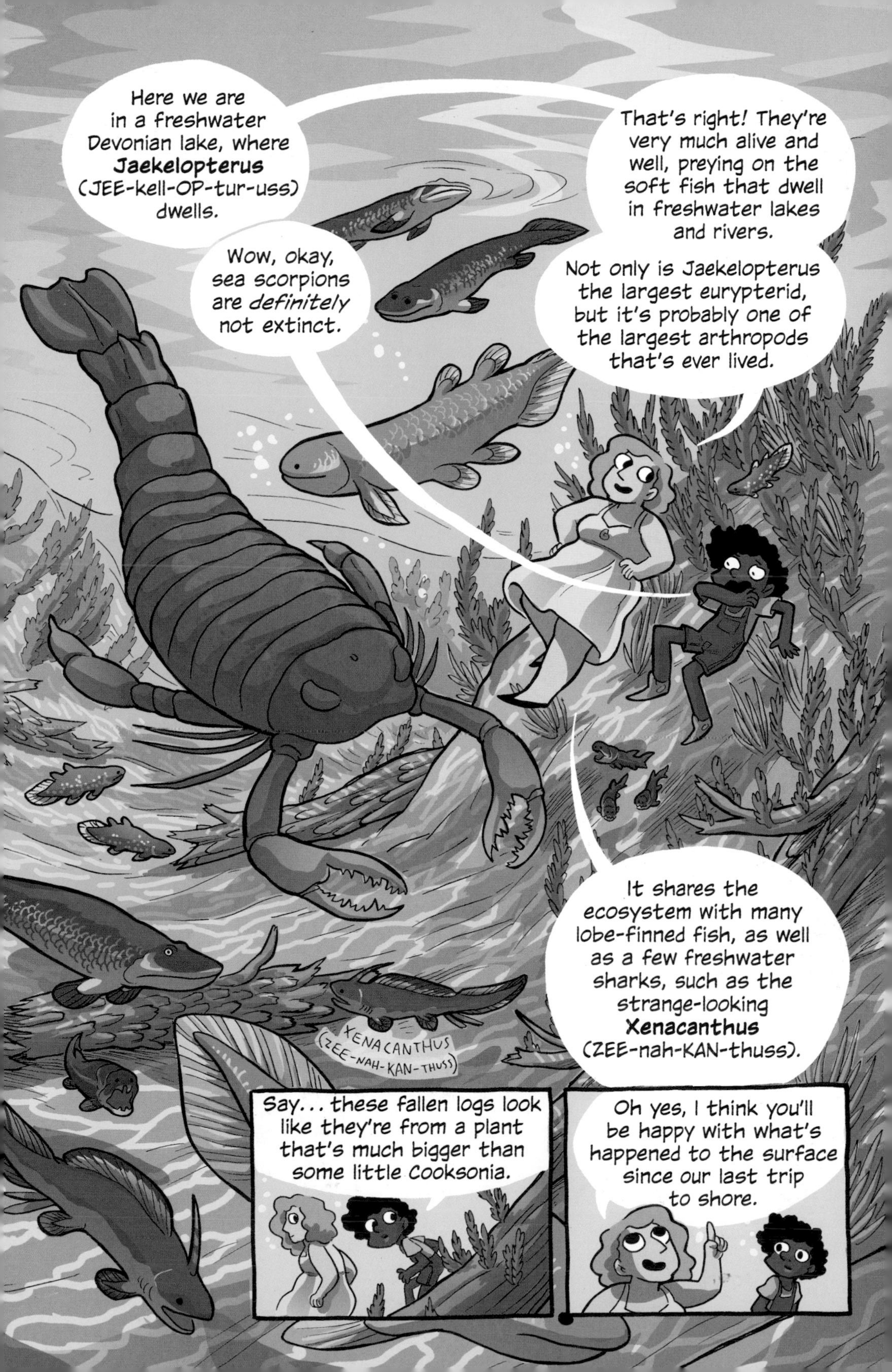
Here we are in a freshwater Devonian lake, where **Jaekelopterus** (JEE-kell-OP-tur-uss) dwells.
Wow, okay, sea scorpions are *definitely* not extinct.
That's right! They're very much alive and well, preying on the soft fish that dwell in freshwater lakes and rivers.
Not only is Jaekelopterus the largest eurypterid, but it's probably one of the largest arthropods that's ever lived.
It shares the ecosystem with many lobe-finned fish, as well as a few freshwater sharks, such as the strange-looking **Xenacanthus** (ZEE-nah-KAN-thuss).
XENACANTHUS (ZEE-NAH-KAN-THUSS)
Say... these fallen logs look like they're from a plant that's much bigger than some little Cooksonia.
Oh yes, I think you'll be happy with what's happened to the surface since our last trip to shore.

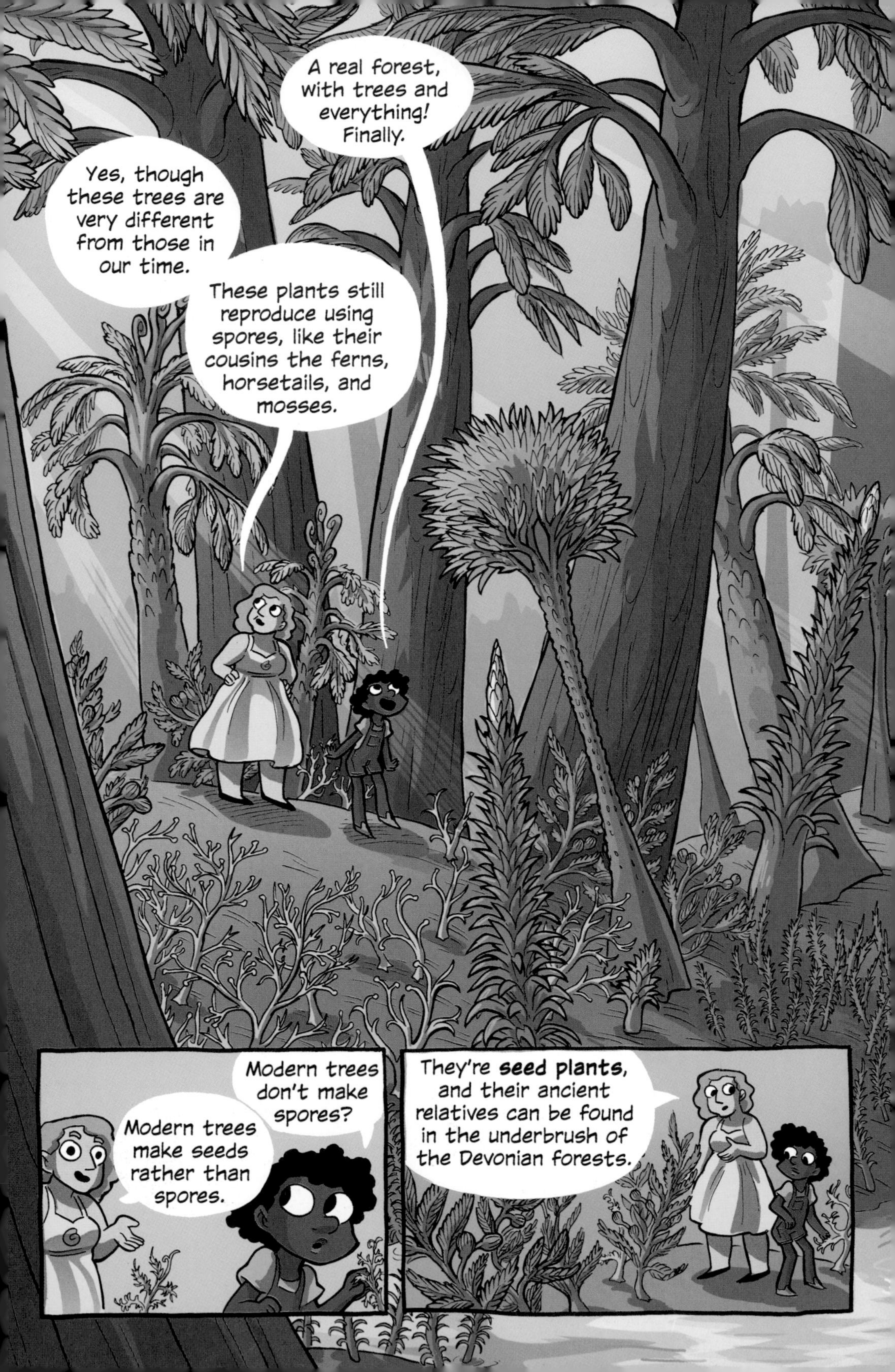
A real forest, with trees and everything! Finally.
Yes, though these trees are very different from those in our time.
These plants still reproduce using spores, like their cousins the ferns, horsetails, and mosses.
Modern trees don't make spores?
Modern trees make seeds rather than spores.
They're **seed plants**, and their ancient relatives can be found in the underbrush of the Devonian forests.

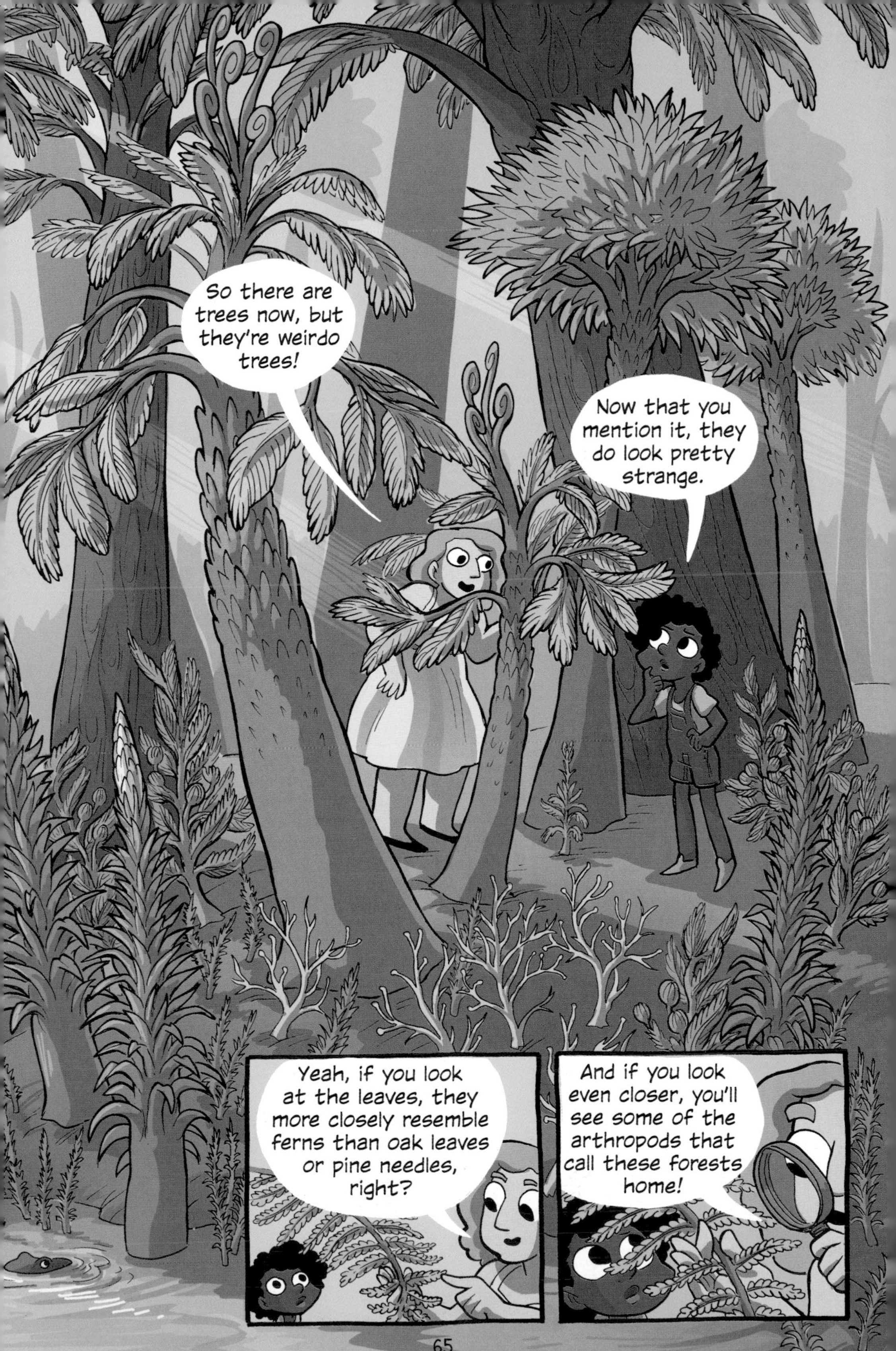
So there are trees now, but they're weirdo trees!
Now that you mention it, they do look pretty strange.
Yeah, if you look at the leaves, they more closely resemble ferns than oak leaves or pine needles, right?
And if you look even closer, you'll see some of the arthropods that call these forests home!

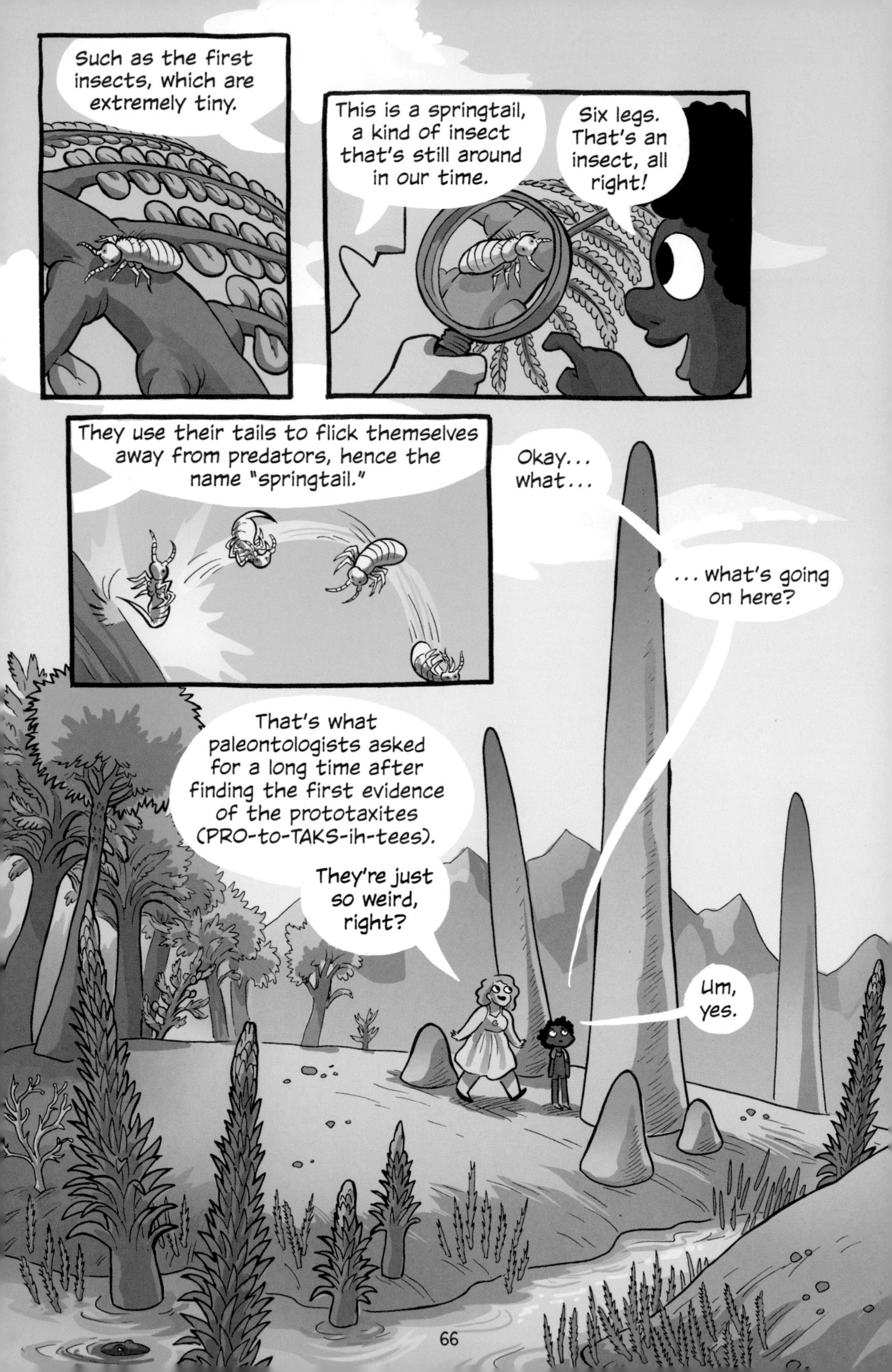
Such as the first insects, which are extremely tiny.
This is a springtail, a kind of insect that's still around in our time.
Six legs. That's an insect, all right!
They use their tails to flick themselves away from predators, hence the name "springtail."
Okay... what...
... what's going on here?
That's what paleontologists asked for a long time after finding the first evidence of the prototaxites (PRO-to-TAKS-ih-tees).
They're just so weird, right?
Um, yes.

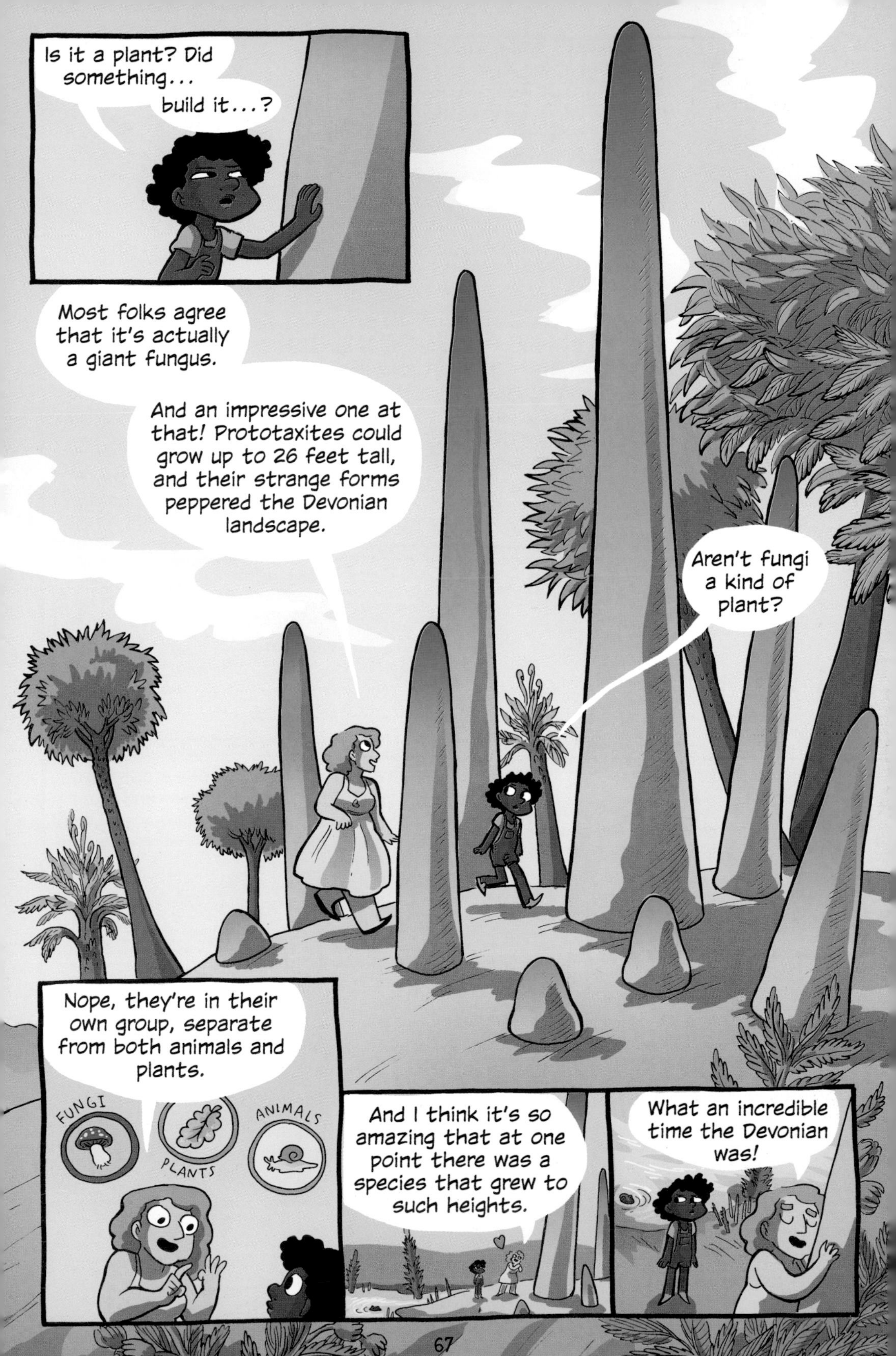

Is it a plant? Did something... build it...?
Most folks agree that it's actually a giant fungus.
And an impressive one at that! Prototaxites could grow up to 26 feet tall, and their strange forms peppered the Devonian landscape.
Aren't fungi a kind of plant?
Nope, they're in their own group, separate from both animals and plants.
FUNGI
PLANTS
ANIMALS
And I think it's so amazing that at one point there was a species that grew to such heights.
What an incredible time the Devonian was!

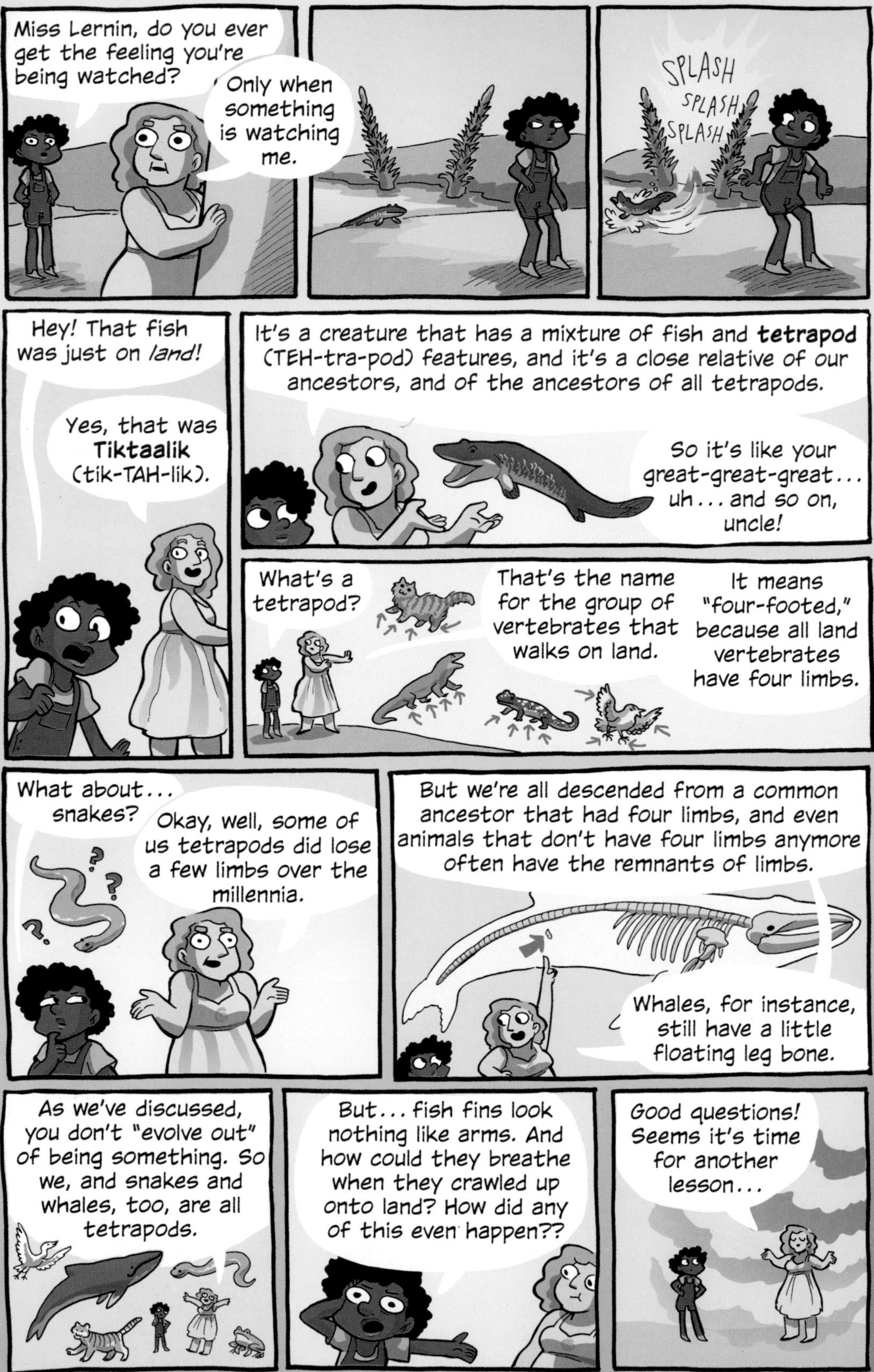
Miss Lernin, do you ever get the feeling you're being watched?
Only when something is watching me.
SPLASH
SPLASH
SPLASH
Hey! That fish was just on *land*!
Yes, that was **Tiktaalik** (tik-TAH-lik).
It's a creature that has a mixture of fish and **tetrapod** (TEH-tra-pod) features, and it's a close relative of our ancestors, and of the ancestors of all tetrapods.
So it's like your great-great-great... uh... and so on, uncle!
What's a tetrapod?
That's the name for the group of vertebrates that walks on land.
It means "four-footed," because all land vertebrates have four limbs.
What about... snakes?
Okay, well, some of us tetrapods did lose a few limbs over the millennia.
But we're all descended from a common ancestor that had four limbs, and even animals that don't have four limbs anymore often have the remnants of limbs.
Whales, for instance, still have a little floating leg bone.
As we've discussed, you don't "evolve out" of being something. So we, and snakes and whales, too, are all tetrapods.
But... fish fins look nothing like arms. And how could they breathe when they crawled up onto land? How did any of this even happen??
Good questions! Seems it's time for another lesson...

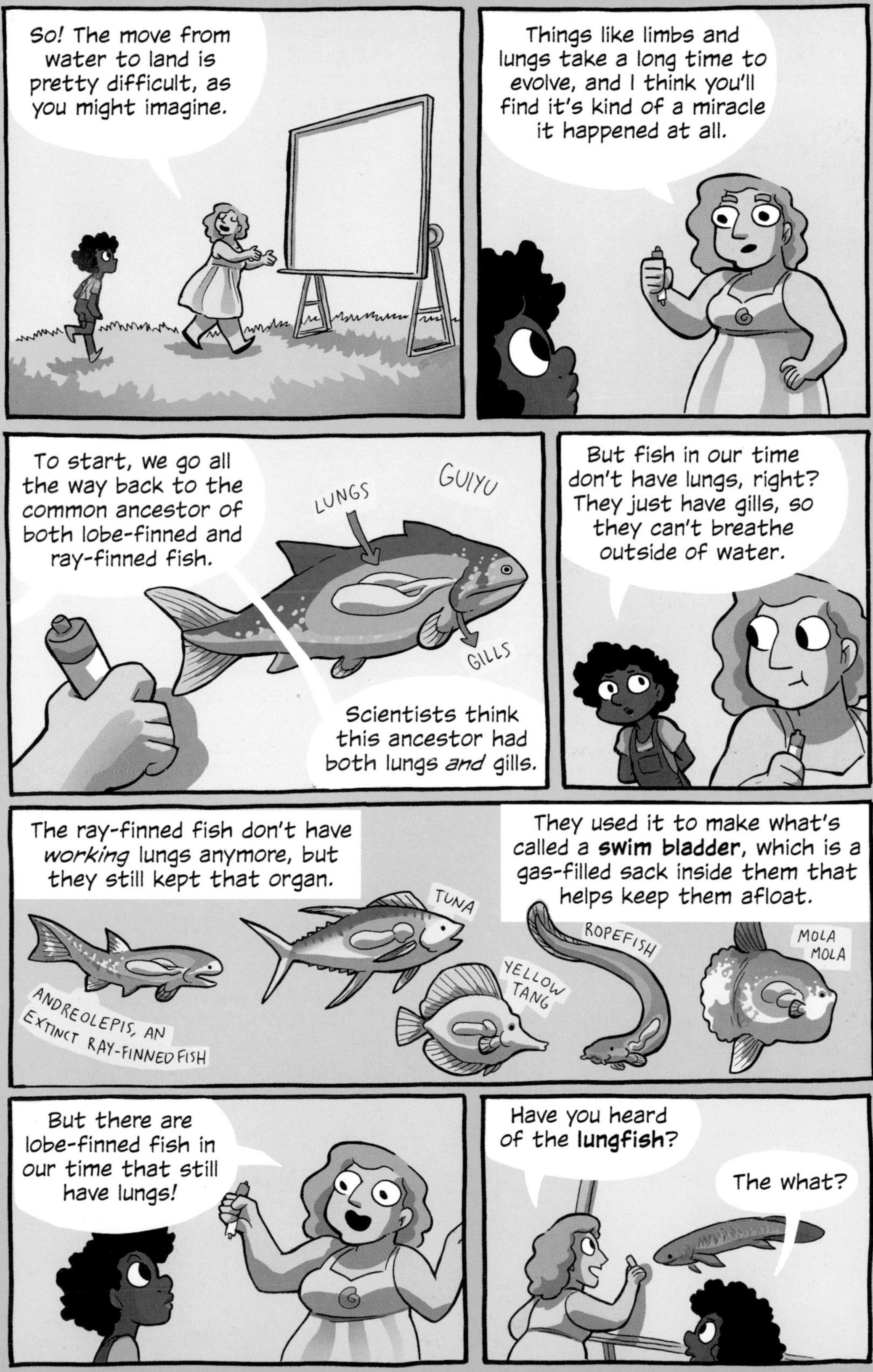

So! The move from water to land is pretty difficult, as you might imagine.
Things like limbs and lungs take a long time to evolve, and I think you'll find it's kind of a miracle it happened at all.
To start, we go all the way back to the common ancestor of both lobe-finned and ray-finned fish.
GUIYU
LUNGS
GILLS
Scientists think this ancestor had both lungs *and* gills.
But fish in our time don't have lungs, right? They just have gills, so they can't breathe outside of water.
The ray-finned fish don't have *working* lungs anymore, but they still kept that organ.
They used it to make what's called a **swim bladder**, which is a gas-filled sack inside them that helps keep them afloat.
TUNA
ROPEFISH
MOLA MOLA
YELLOW TANG
ANDREOLEPIS, AN EXTINCT RAY-FINNED FISH
But there are lobe-finned fish in our time that still have lungs!
Have you heard of the **lungfish**?
The what?

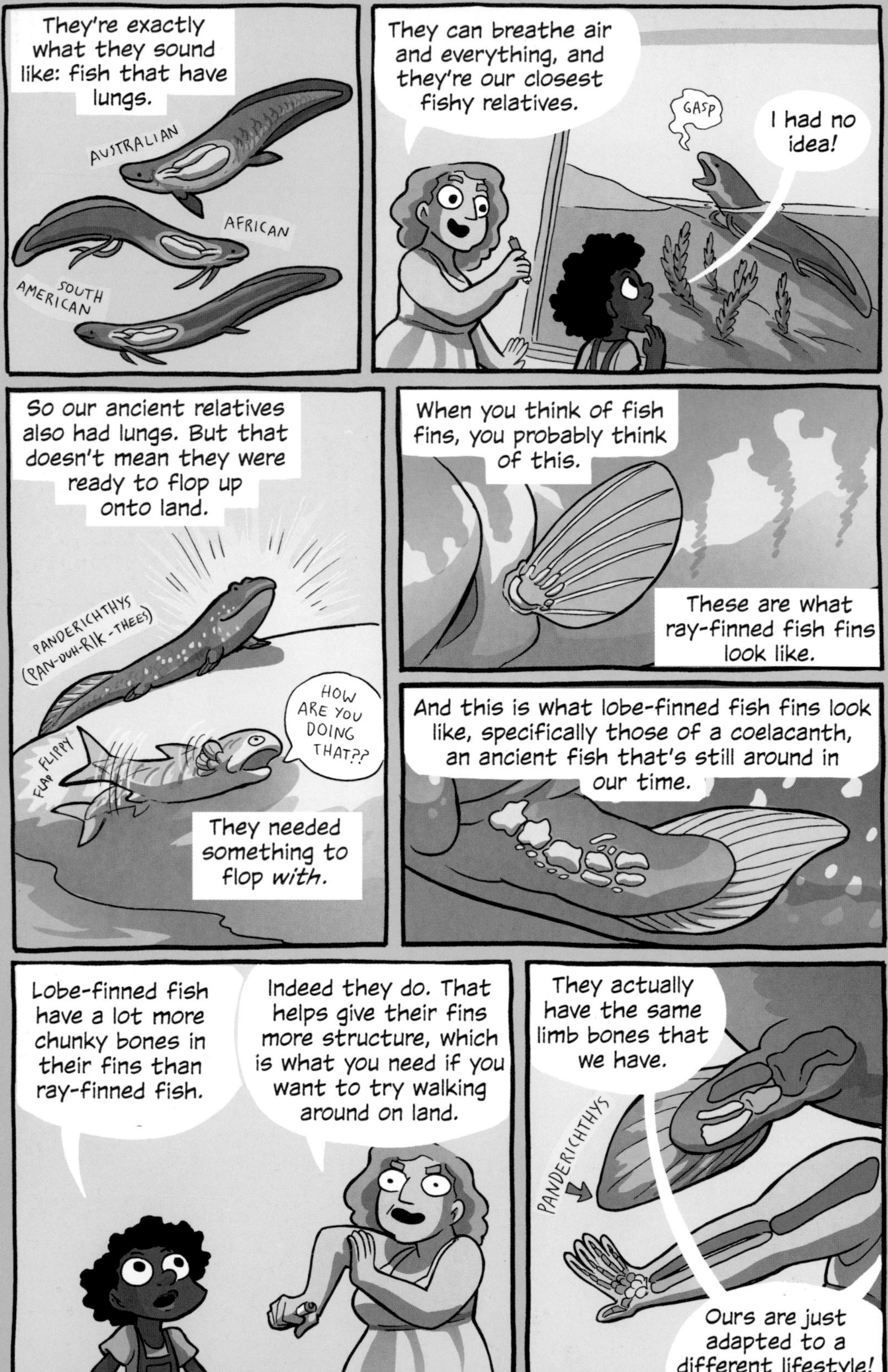

They're exactly what they sound like: fish that have lungs.
AUSTRALIAN
AFRICAN
SOUTH AMERICAN
They can breathe air and everything, and they're our closest fishy relatives.
GASP
I had no idea!
So our ancient relatives also had lungs. But that doesn't mean they were ready to flop up onto land.
PANDERICHTHYS (PAN-DUH-RIK-THEES)
FLAP FLIPPY
HOW ARE YOU DOING THAT??
They needed something to flop *with*.
When you think of fish fins, you probably think of this.
These are what ray-finned fish fins look like.
And this is what lobe-finned fish fins look like, specifically those of a coelacanth, an ancient fish that's still around in our time.
Lobe-finned fish have a lot more chunky bones in their fins than ray-finned fish.
Indeed they do. That helps give their fins more structure, which is what you need if you want to try walking around on land.
They actually have the same limb bones that we have.
PANDERICHTHYS
Ours are just adapted to a different lifestyle!

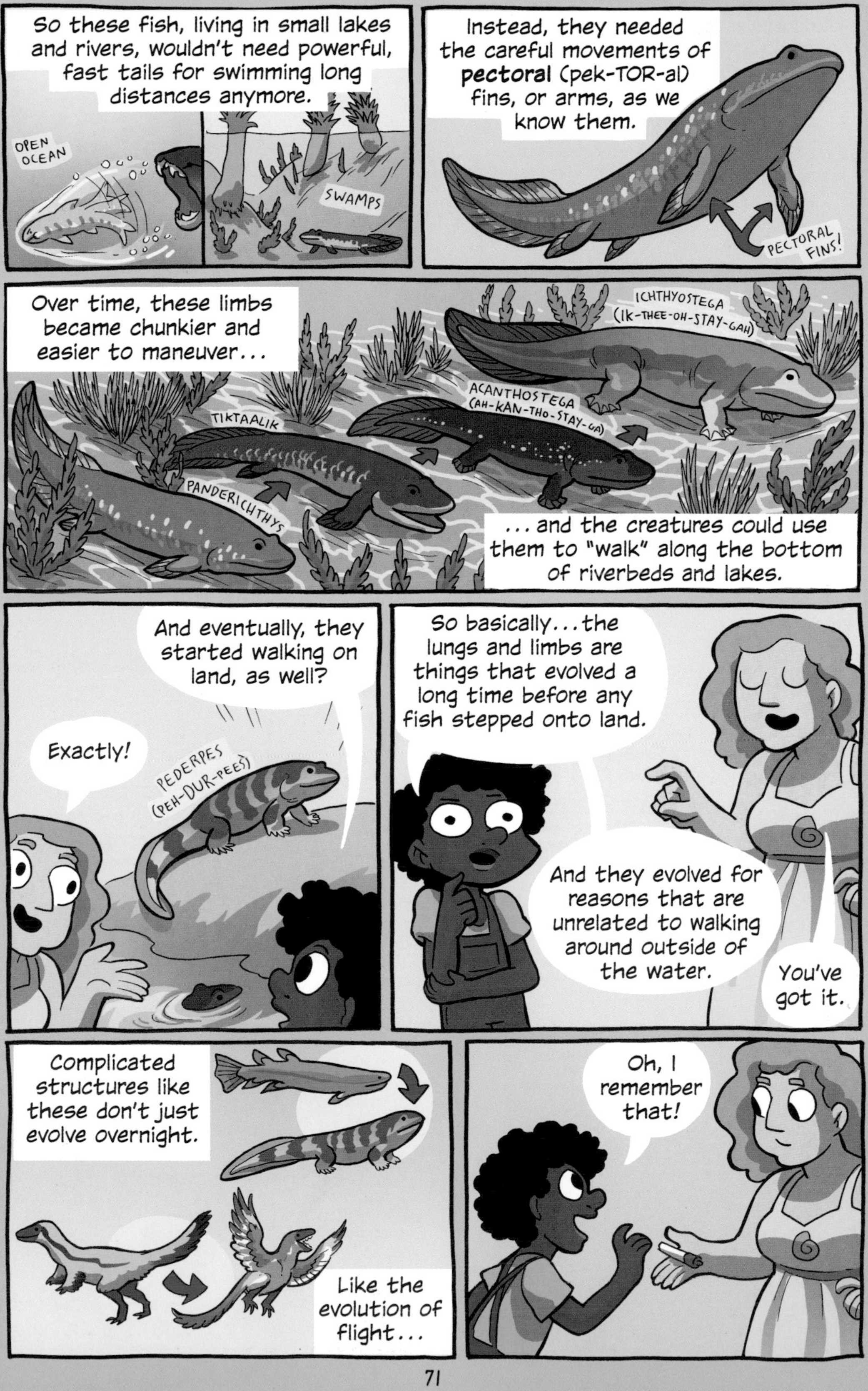

So these fish, living in small lakes and rivers, wouldn't need powerful, fast tails for swimming long distances anymore.
OPEN OCEAN
SWAMPS
Instead, they needed the careful movements of **pectoral** (pek-TOR-al) fins, or arms, as we know them.
PECTORAL FINS!
Over time, these limbs became chunkier and easier to maneuver...
ICHTHYOSTEGA (IK-THEE-OH-STAY-GAH)
ACANTHOSTEGA (AH-KAN-THO-STAY-GA)
TIKTAALIK
PANDERICHTHYS
...and the creatures could use them to "walk" along the bottom of riverbeds and lakes.
And eventually, they started walking on land, as well?
Exactly!
PEDERPES (PEH-DUR-PEES)
So basically...the lungs and limbs are things that evolved a long time before any fish stepped onto land.
And they evolved for reasons that are unrelated to walking around outside of the water.
You've got it.
Complicated structures like these don't just evolve overnight.
Like the evolution of flight...
Oh, I remember that!

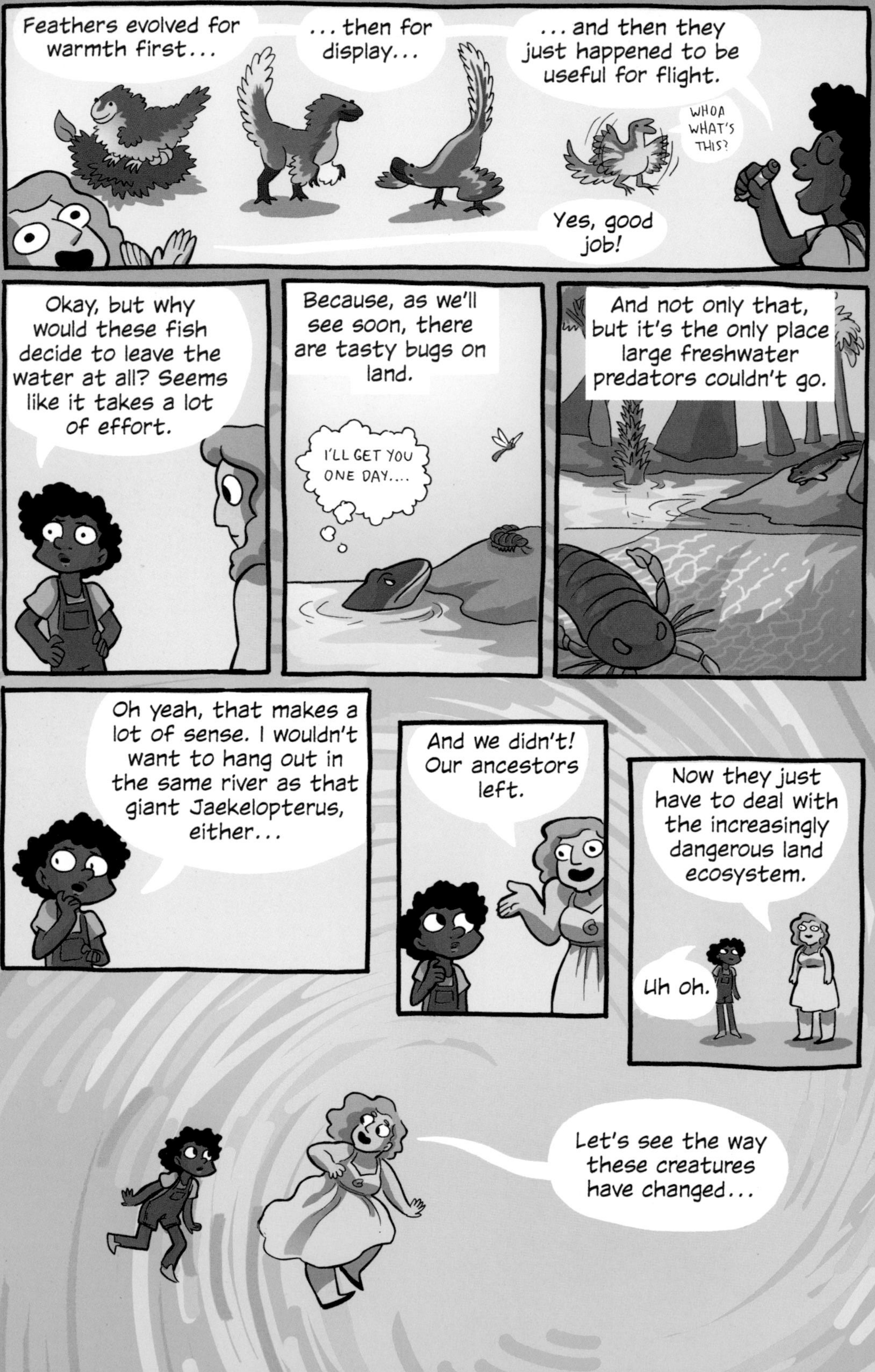
Feathers evolved for warmth first...
...then for display...
...and then they just happened to be useful for flight.
WHOA WHAT'S THIS?
Yes, good job!
Okay, but why would these fish decide to leave the water at all? Seems like it takes a lot of effort.
Because, as we'll see soon, there are tasty bugs on land.
I'LL GET YOU ONE DAY....
And not only that, but it's the only place large freshwater predators couldn't go.
Oh yeah, that makes a lot of sense. I wouldn't want to hang out in the same river as that giant Jaekelopterus, either...
And we didn't! Our ancestors left.
Now they just have to deal with the increasingly dangerous land ecosystem.
Uh oh.
Let's see the way these creatures have changed...

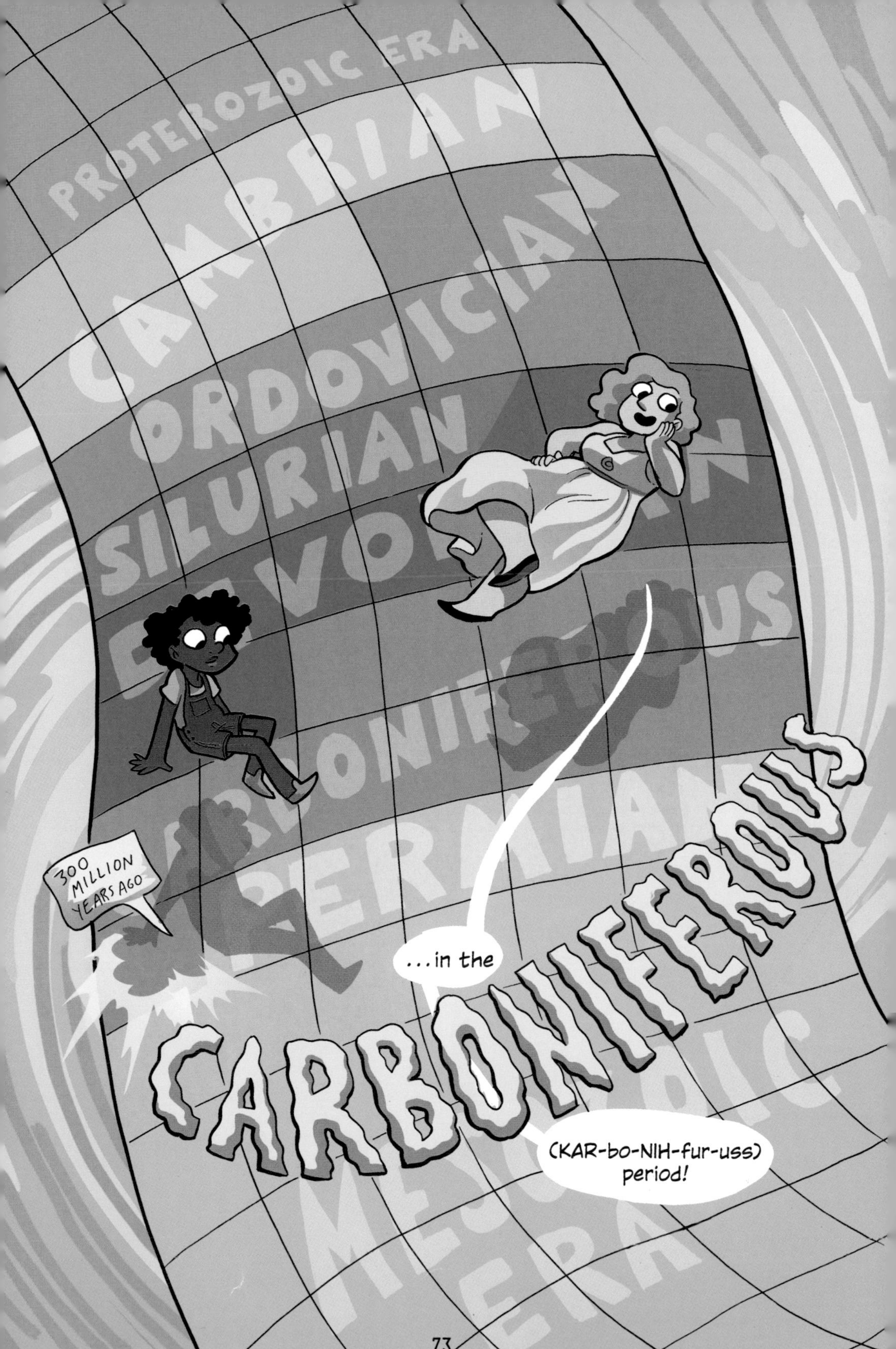
PROTEROZOIC ERA
CAMBRIAN
SILURIAN
300 MILLION YEARS AGO
...in the
CARBONIFEROUS
(KAR-bo-NIH-fur-uss) period!

The **invertebrates** (in-VER-teh-brets), any creature that isn't a vertebrate, are still as abundant as ever.

The coral reefs become more spectacular with each passing millennium...

... the echinoderms are still slowly crawling their way across the landscape, trilobites scuttling along between them...

JANASSA (JA-NAH-SAH)

That's a weird-looking trilobite.

This is actually a brand-new type of arthropod called an **isopod** (EYE-so-pod)!

You probably have a few of these in your backyard. It's a kind of **crustacean** (kruh-STAY-shun), like crabs and shrimp, and in our time, some of them live on land.

You might know them as roly-polies, or pill bugs, or wood lice, or any number of names people call these fun little bugs.

There are also some isopods in our time that live in the dark depths of the ocean, and they're *huge!*

MY CHIPS...

CRNCH CRNCH

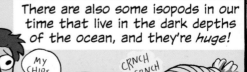

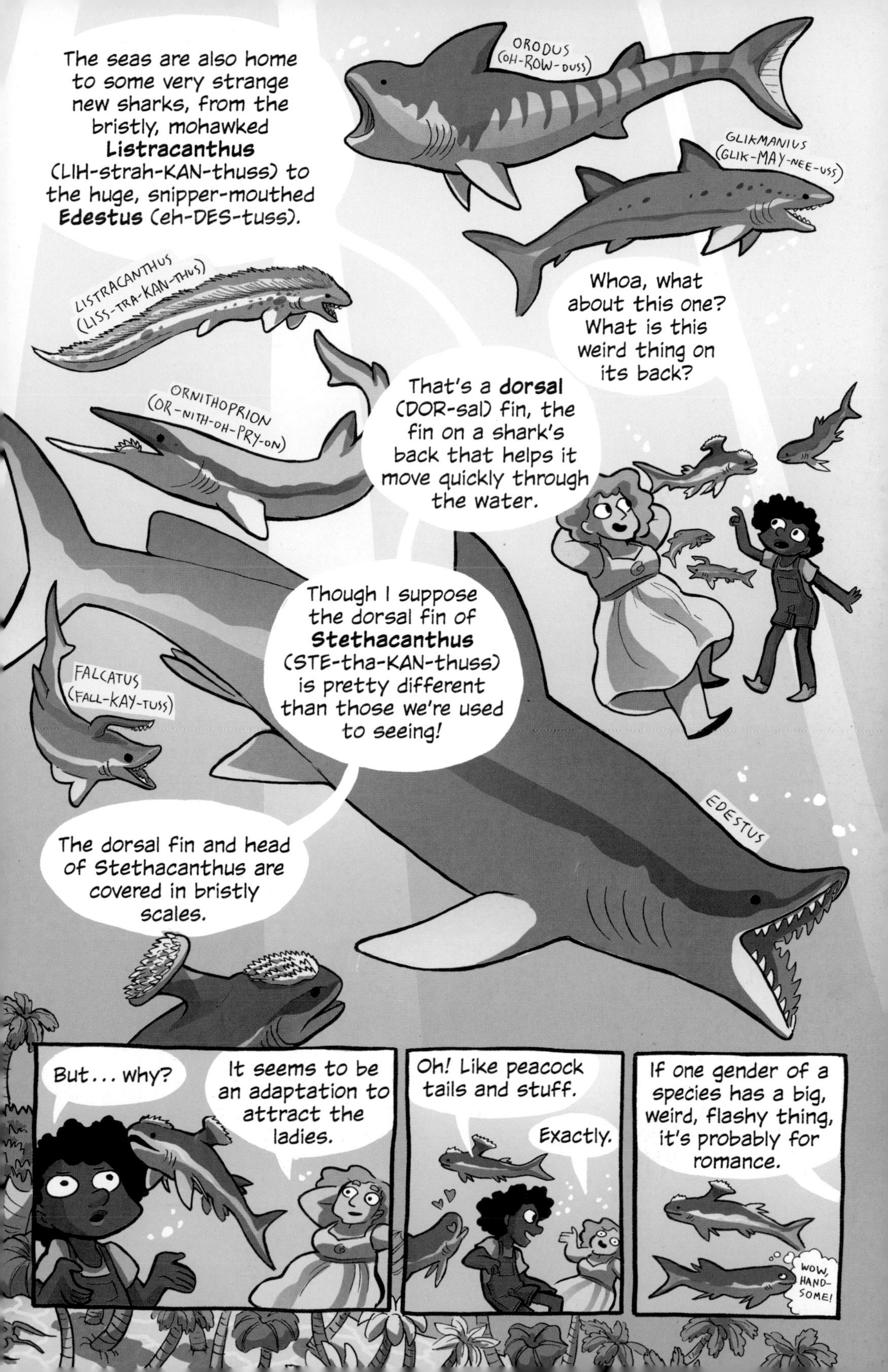

The seas are also home to some very strange new sharks, from the bristly, mohawked **Listracanthus** (LIH-strah-KAN-thuss) to the huge, snipper-mouthed **Edestus** (eh-DES-tuss).
ORODUS (OH-ROW-DUSS)
GLIKMANIUS (GLIK-MAY-NEE-USS)
LISTRACANTHUS (LISS-TRA-KAN-THUS)
Whoa, what about this one? What is this weird thing on its back?
ORNITHOPRION (OR-NITH-OH-PRY-ON)
That's a **dorsal** (DOR-sal) fin, the fin on a shark's back that helps it move quickly through the water.
Though I suppose the dorsal fin of **Stethacanthus** (STE-tha-KAN-thuss) is pretty different than those we're used to seeing!
FALCATUS (FALL-KAY-TUSS)
EDESTUS
The dorsal fin and head of Stethacanthus are covered in bristly scales.
But... why?
It seems to be an adaptation to attract the ladies.
Oh! Like peacock tails and stuff.
Exactly.
If one gender of a species has a big, weird, flashy thing, it's probably for romance.
WOW, HAND-SOME!

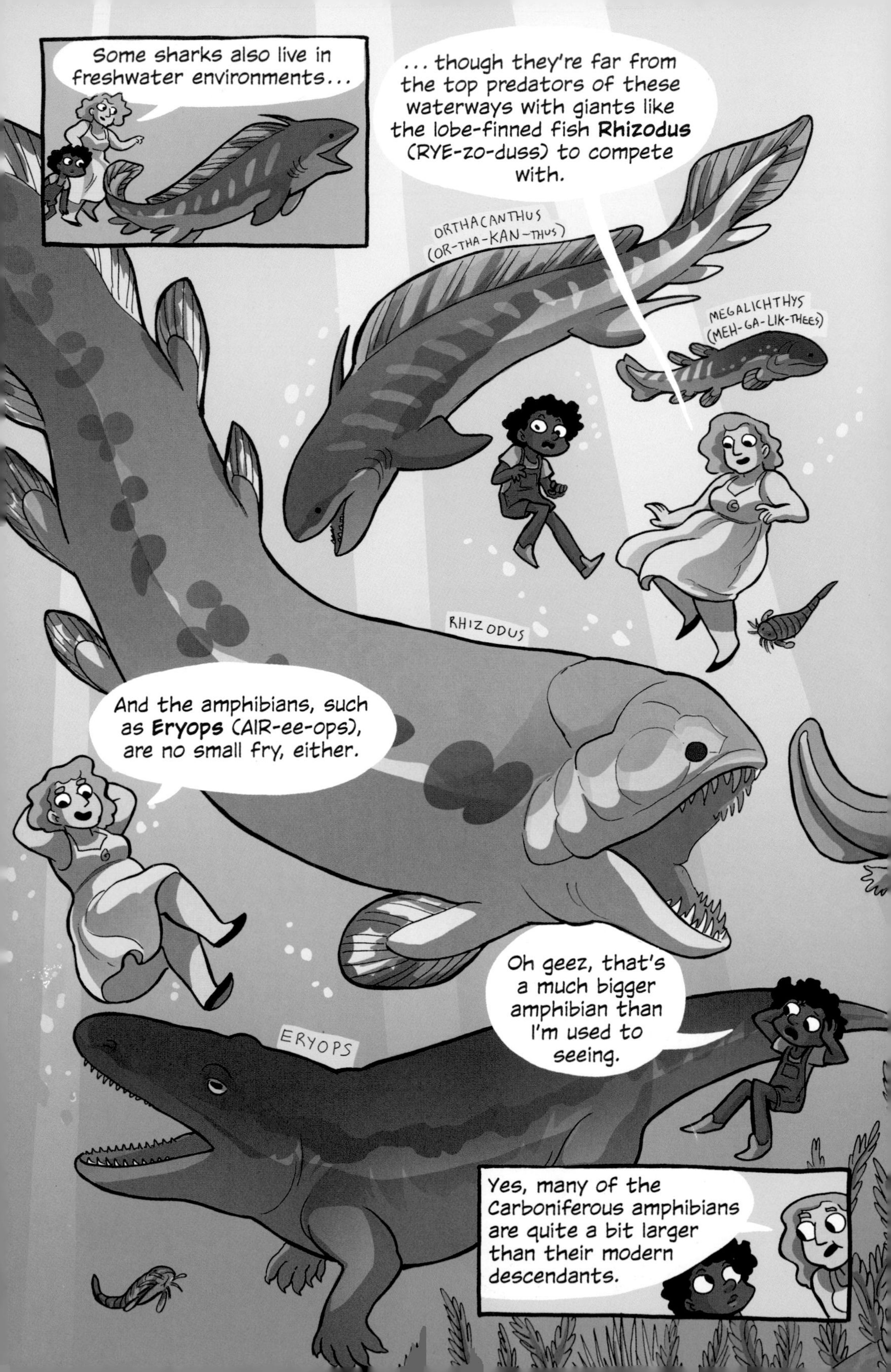
Some sharks also live in freshwater environments...
... though they're far from the top predators of these waterways with giants like the lobe-finned fish **Rhizodus** (RYE-zo-duss) to compete with.
ORTHACANTHUS (OR-THA-KAN-THUS)
MEGALICHTHYS (MEH-GA-LIK-THEES)
RHIZODUS
And the amphibians, such as **Eryops** (AIR-ee-ops), are no small fry, either.
Oh geez, that's a much bigger amphibian than I'm used to seeing.
ERYOPS
Yes, many of the Carboniferous amphibians are quite a bit larger than their modern descendants.

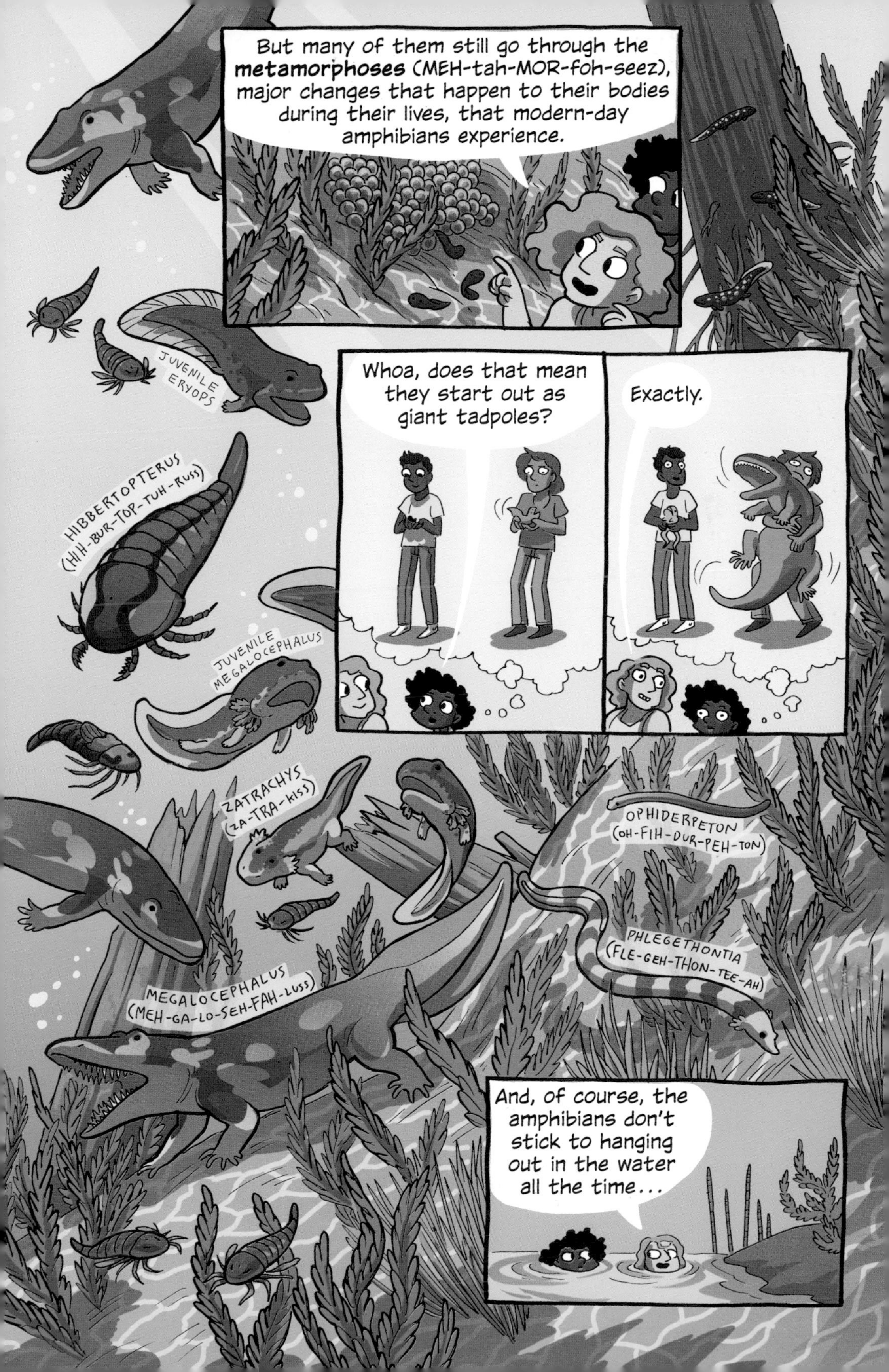
But many of them still go through the **metamorphoses** (MEH-tah-MOR-foh-seez), major changes that happen to their bodies during their lives, that modern-day amphibians experience.
JUVENILE ERYOPS
Whoa, does that mean they start out as giant tadpoles?
Exactly.
HIBBERTOPTERUS (HIH-BUR-TOP-TUH-RUSS)
JUVENILE MEGALOCEPHALUS
ZATRACHYS (ZA-TRA-KISS)
OPHIDERPETON (OH-FIH-DUR-PEH-TON)
PHLEGETHONTIA (FLE-GEH-THON-TEE-AH)
MEGALOCEPHALUS (MEH-GA-LO-SEH-FAH-LUSS)
And, of course, the amphibians don't stick to hanging out in the water all the time...

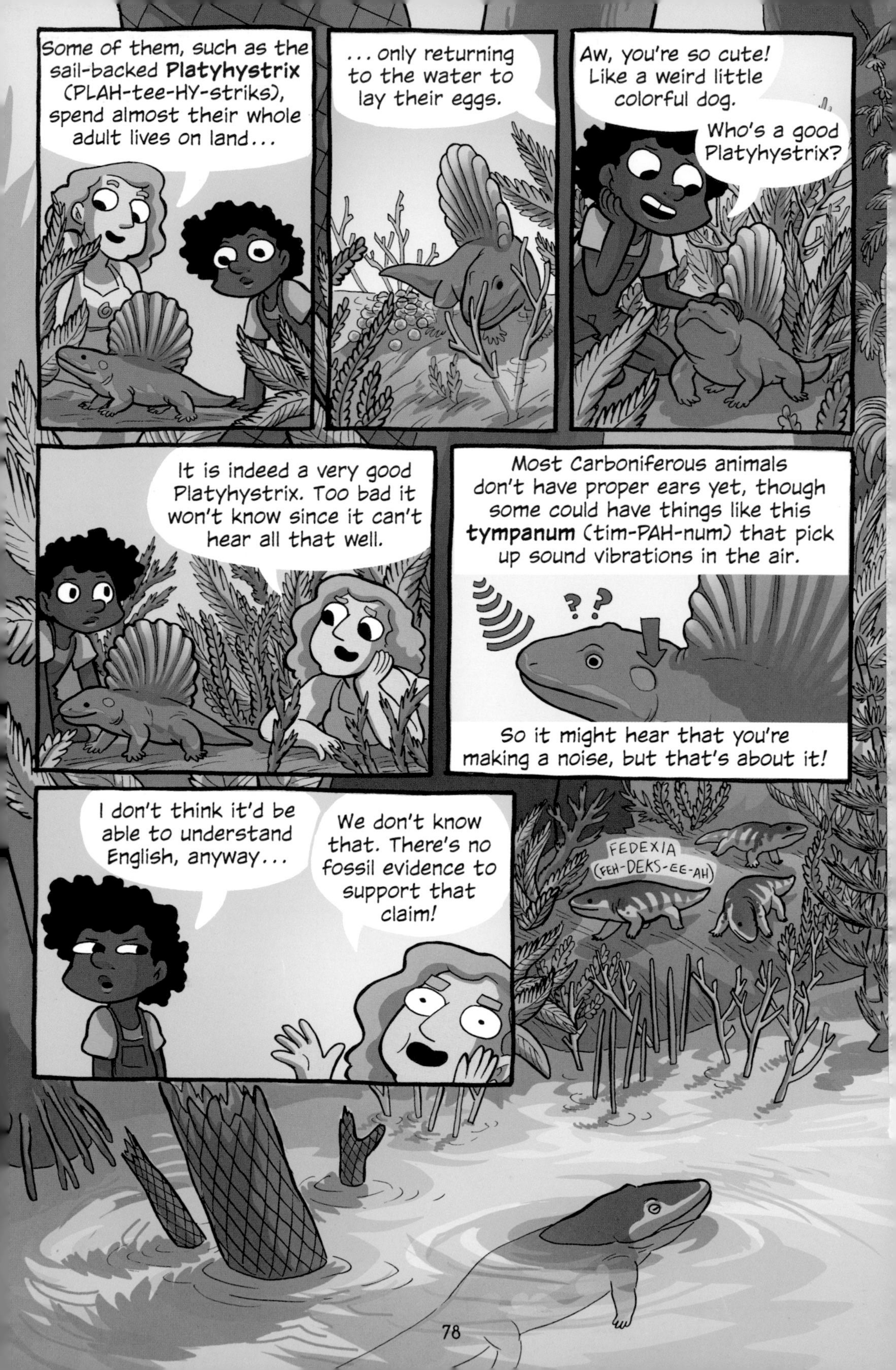

Some of them, such as the sail-backed **Platyhystrix** (PLAH-tee-HY-striks), spend almost their whole adult lives on land...
...only returning to the water to lay their eggs.
Aw, you're so cute! Like a weird little colorful dog.
Who's a good Platyhystrix?
It is indeed a very good Platyhystrix. Too bad it won't know since it can't hear all that well.
Most Carboniferous animals don't have proper ears yet, though some could have things like this **tympanum** (tim-PAH-num) that pick up sound vibrations in the air.
? ?
So it might hear that you're making a noise, but that's about it!
I don't think it'd be able to understand English, anyway...
We don't know that. There's no fossil evidence to support that claim!
FEDEXIA (FEH-DEKS-EE-AH)

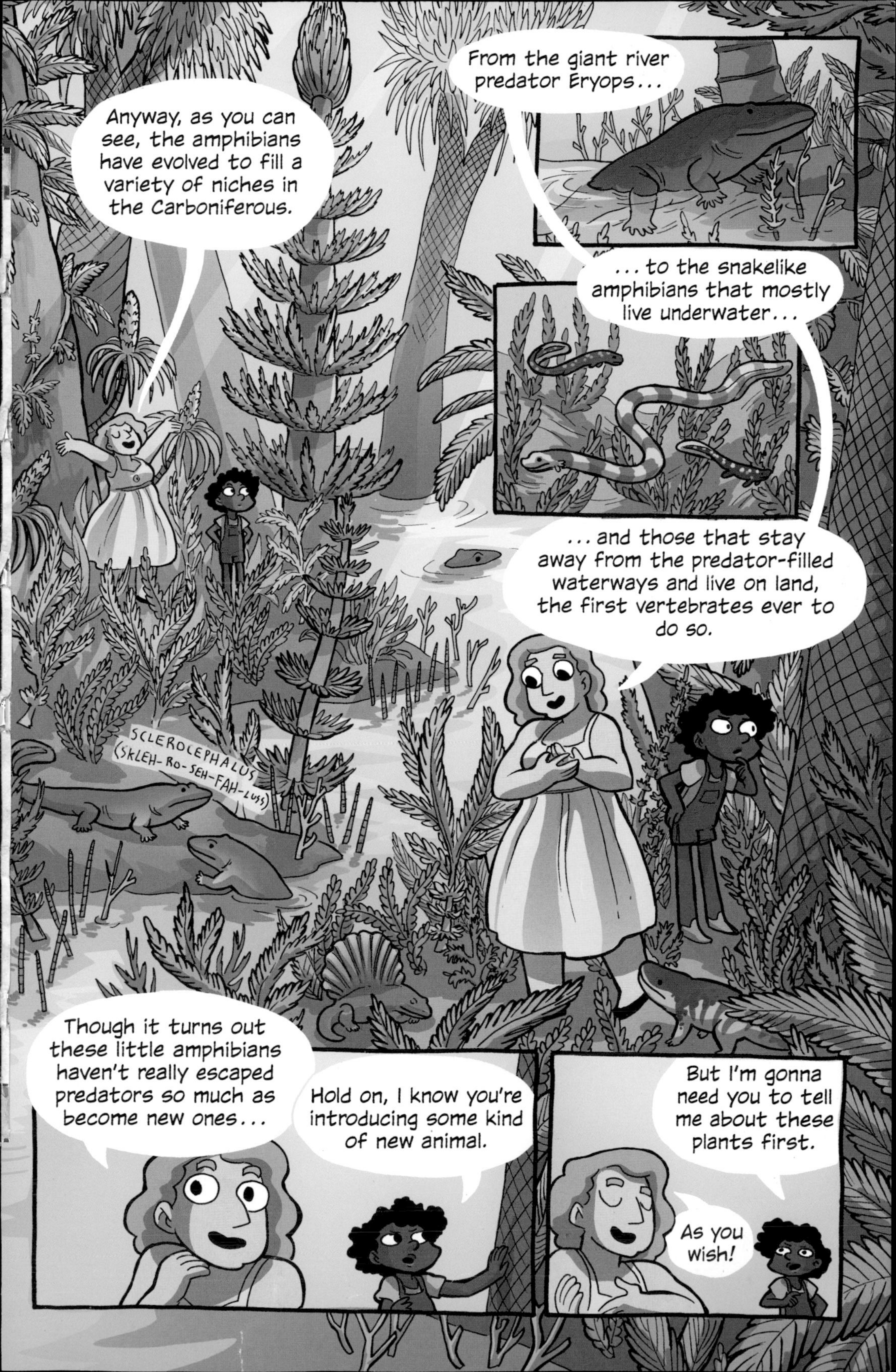

Anyway, as you can see, the amphibians have evolved to fill a variety of niches in the Carboniferous.
From the giant river predator Eryops...
...to the snakelike amphibians that mostly live underwater...
...and those that stay away from the predator-filled waterways and live on land, the first vertebrates ever to do so.
SCLEROCEPHALUS (SKLEH-RO-SEH-FAH-LUSS)
Though it turns out these little amphibians haven't really escaped predators so much as become new ones...
Hold on, I know you're introducing some kind of new animal.
But I'm gonna need you to tell me about these plants first.
As you wish!

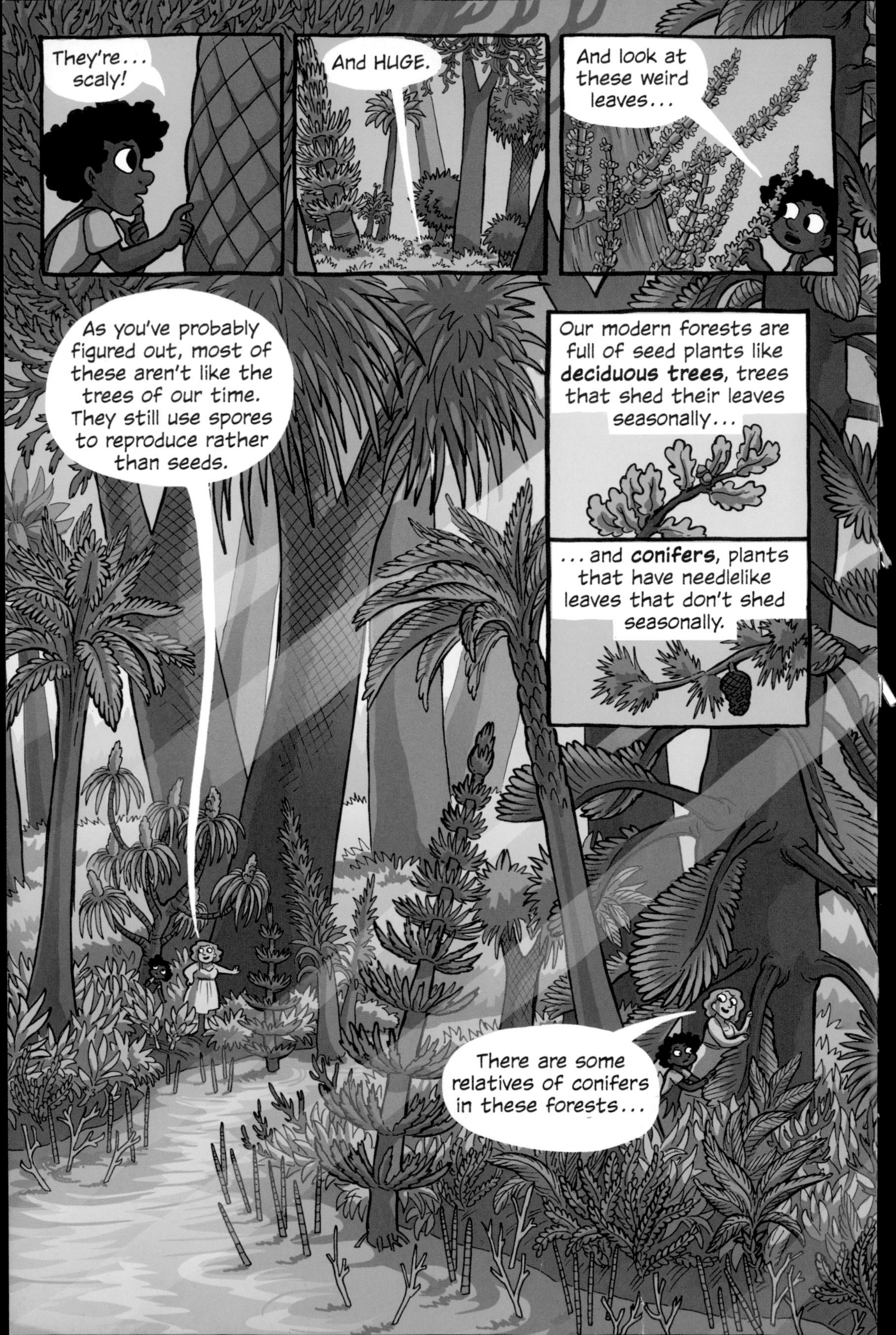
They're... scaly!
And HUGE.
And look at these weird leaves...
As you've probably figured out, most of these aren't like the trees of our time. They still use spores to reproduce rather than seeds.
Our modern forests are full of seed plants like **deciduous trees**, trees that shed their leaves seasonally...
...and **conifers**, plants that have needlelike leaves that don't shed seasonally.
There are some relatives of conifers in these forests...

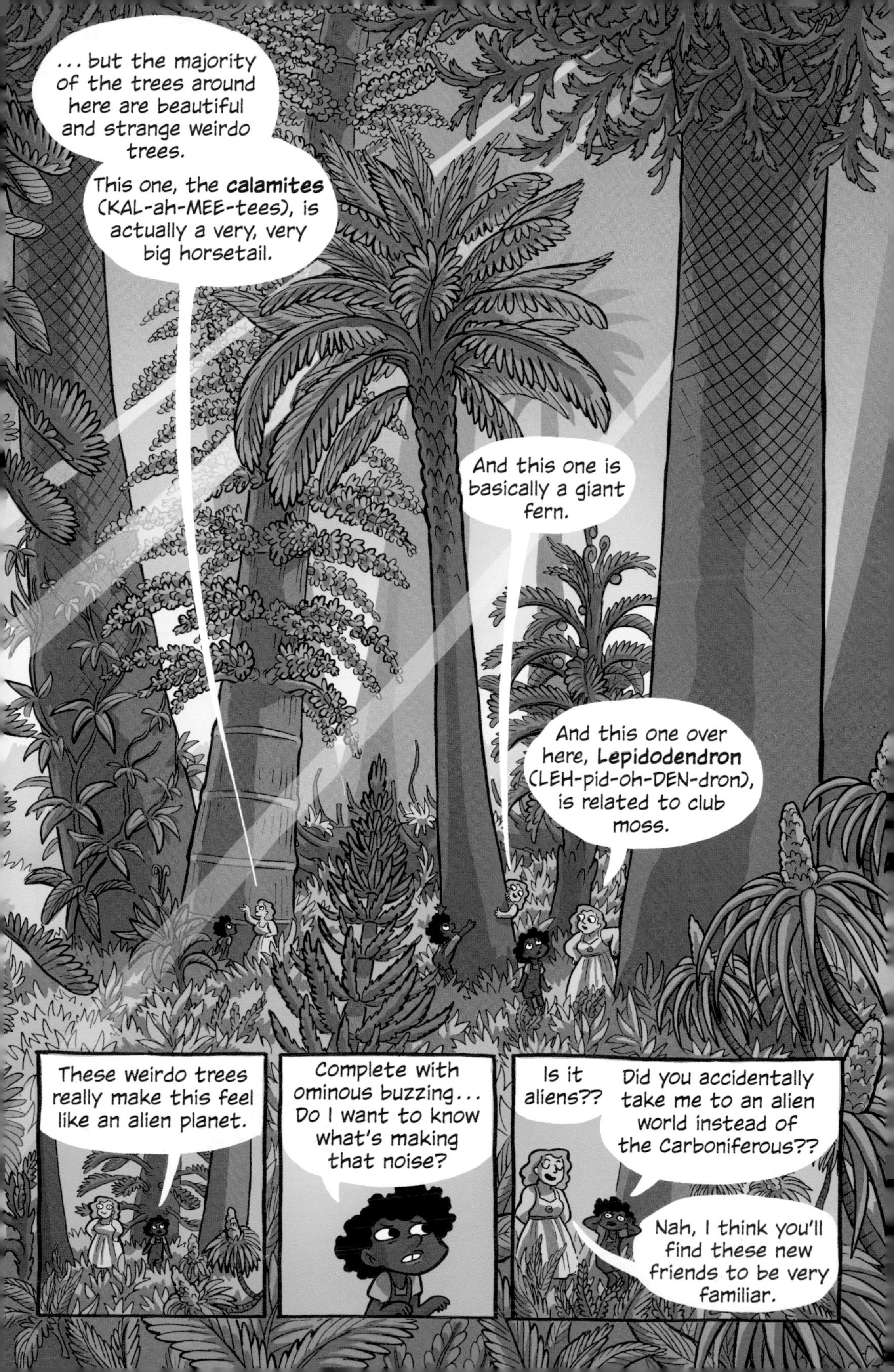

. . . but the majority of the trees around here are beautiful and strange weirdo trees.
This one, the **calamites** (KAL-ah-MEE-tees), is actually a very, very big horsetail.
And this one is basically a giant fern.
And this one over here, **Lepidodendron** (LEH-pid-oh-DEN-dron), is related to club moss.
These weirdo trees really make this feel like an alien planet.
Complete with ominous buzzing . . . Do I want to know what's making that noise?
Is it aliens??
Did you accidentally take me to an alien world instead of the Carboniferous??
Nah, I think you'll find these new friends to be very familiar.

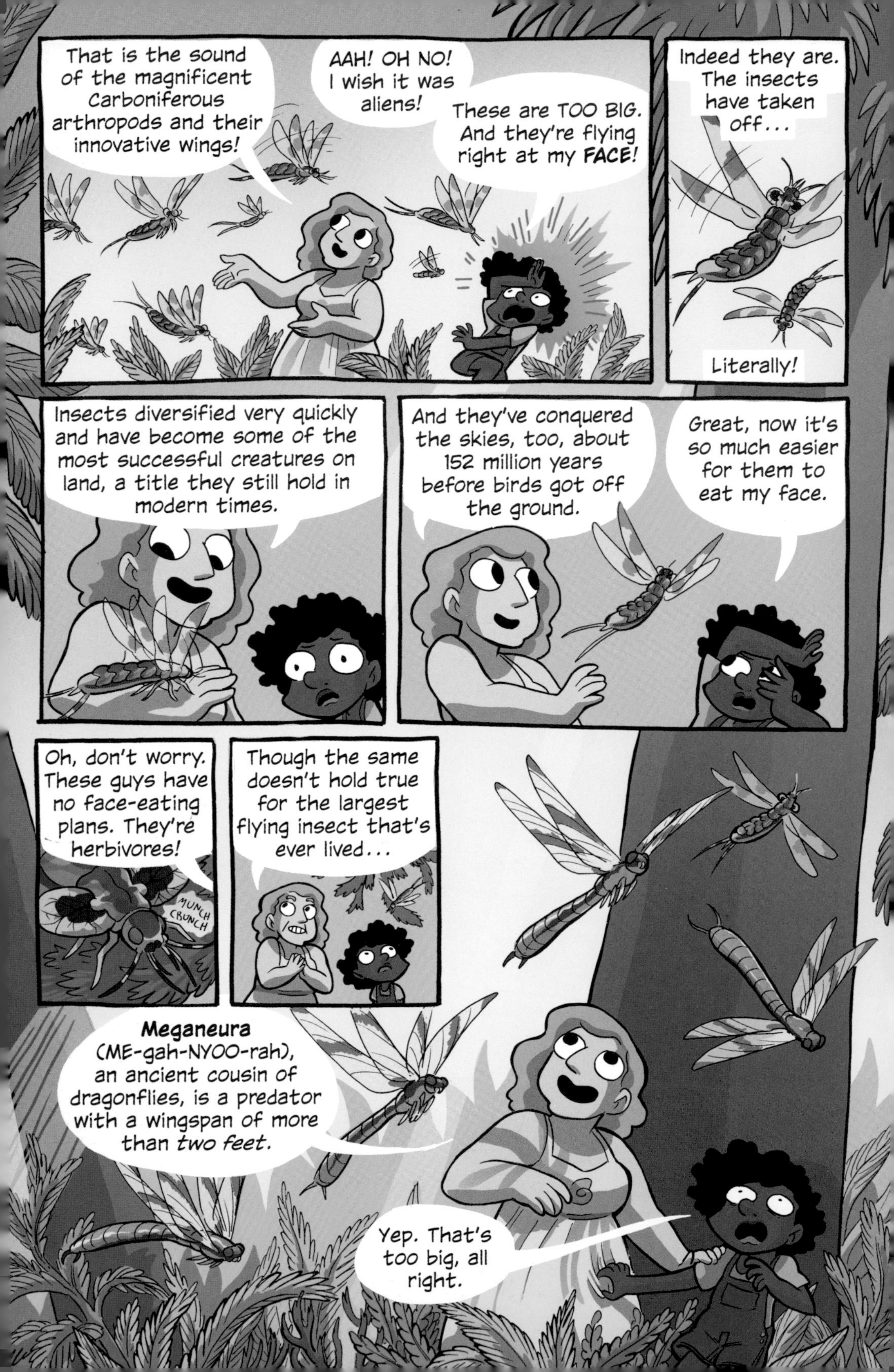
That is the sound of the magnificent Carboniferous arthropods and their innovative wings!
AAH! OH NO! I wish it was aliens!
These are TOO BIG. And they're flying right at my **FACE**!
Indeed they are. The insects have taken off...
Literally!
Insects diversified very quickly and have become some of the most successful creatures on land, a title they still hold in modern times.
And they've conquered the skies, too, about 152 million years before birds got off the ground.
Great, now it's so much easier for them to eat my face.
Oh, don't worry. These guys have no face-eating plans. They're herbivores!
MUNCH CRUNCH
Though the same doesn't hold true for the largest flying insect that's ever lived...
Meganeura (ME-gah-NYOO-rah), an ancient cousin of dragonflies, is a predator with a wingspan of more than *two feet*.
Yep. That's too big, all right.

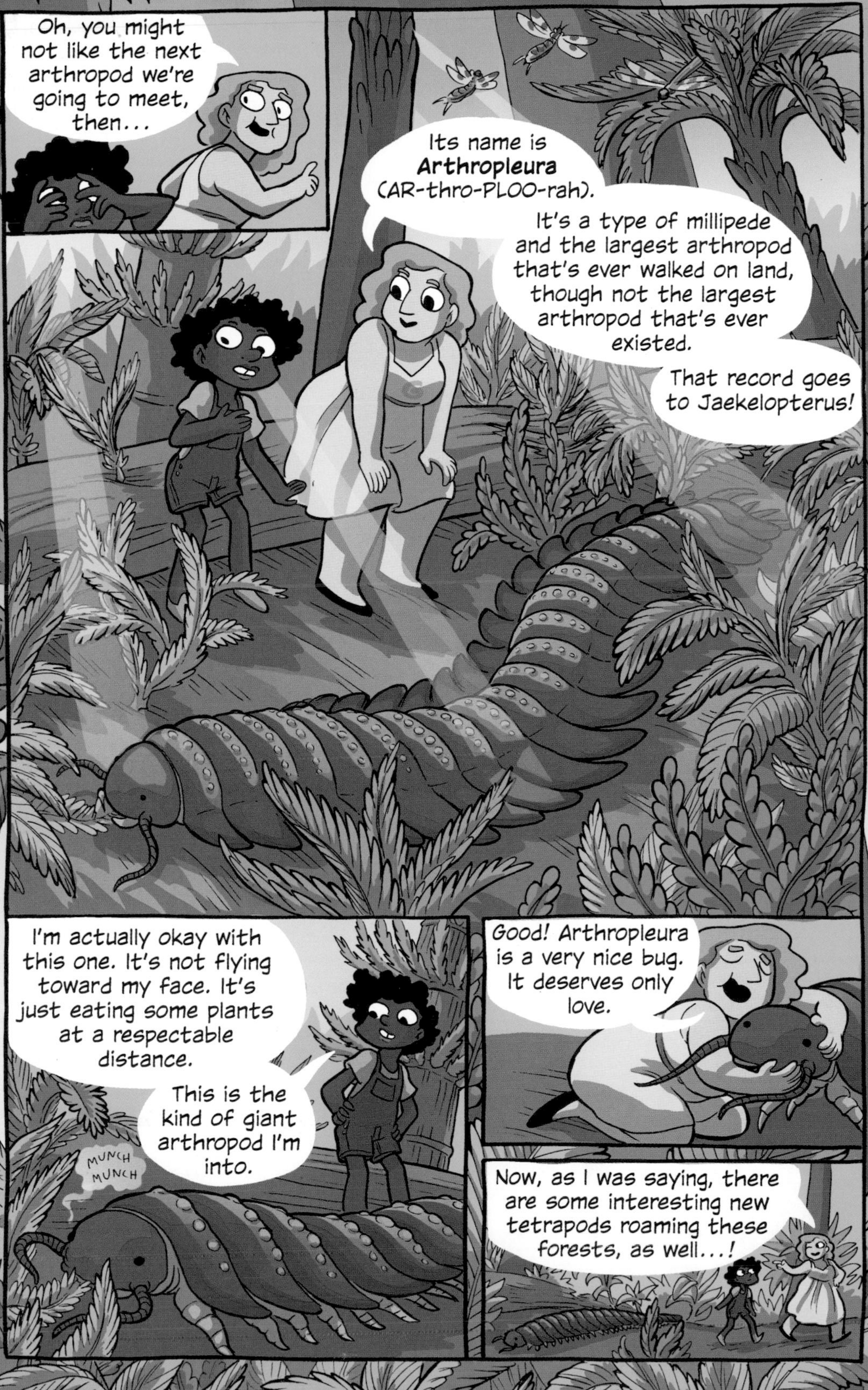

Oh, you might not like the next arthropod we're going to meet, then...
Its name is **Arthropleura** (AR-thro-PLOO-rah).
It's a type of millipede and the largest arthropod that's ever walked on land, though not the largest arthropod that's ever existed.
That record goes to Jaekelopterus!
I'm actually okay with this one. It's not flying toward my face. It's just eating some plants at a respectable distance.
This is the kind of giant arthropod I'm into.
MUNCH MUNCH
Good! Arthropleura is a very nice bug. It deserves only love.
Now, as I was saying, there are some interesting new tetrapods roaming these forests, as well...!

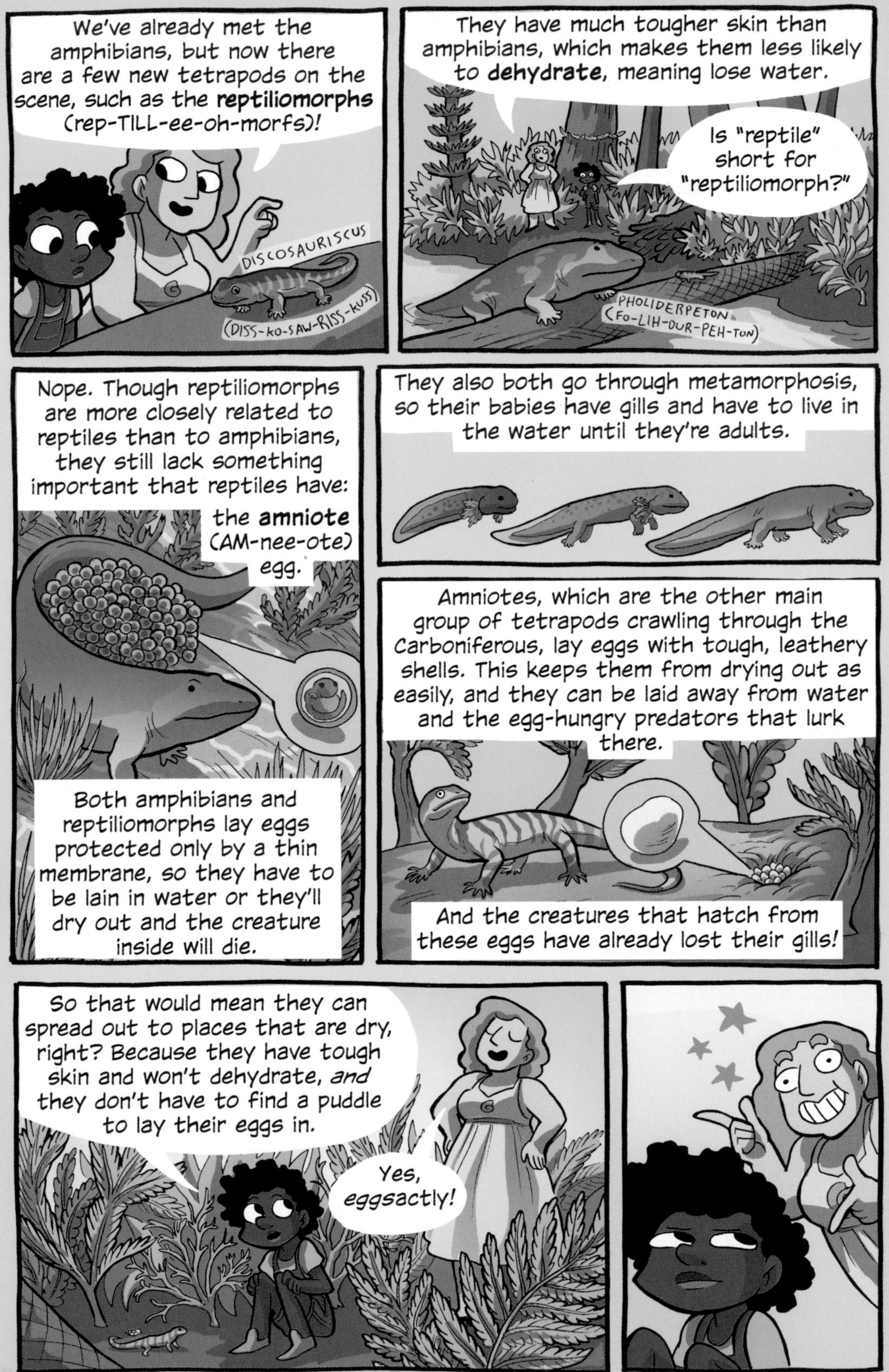
We've already met the amphibians, but now there are a few new tetrapods on the scene, such as the **reptiliomorphs** (rep-TILL-ee-oh-morfs)!
DISCOSAURISCUS
(DISS-ko-SAW-RISS-KUSS)
They have much tougher skin than amphibians, which makes them less likely to **dehydrate**, meaning lose water.
Is "reptile" short for "reptiliomorph?"
PHOLIDERPETON
(FO-LIH-DUR-PEH-TON)
Nope. Though reptiliomorphs are more closely related to reptiles than to amphibians, they still lack something important that reptiles have:
the **amniote** (AM-nee-ote) egg.
Both amphibians and reptiliomorphs lay eggs protected only by a thin membrane, so they have to be lain in water or they'll dry out and the creature inside will die.
They also both go through metamorphosis, so their babies have gills and have to live in the water until they're adults.
Amniotes, which are the other main group of tetrapods crawling through the Carboniferous, lay eggs with tough, leathery shells. This keeps them from drying out as easily, and they can be laid away from water and the egg-hungry predators that lurk there.
And the creatures that hatch from these eggs have already lost their gills!
So that would mean they can spread out to places that are dry, right? Because they have tough skin and won't dehydrate, *and* they don't have to find a puddle to lay their eggs in.
Yes, eggsactly!

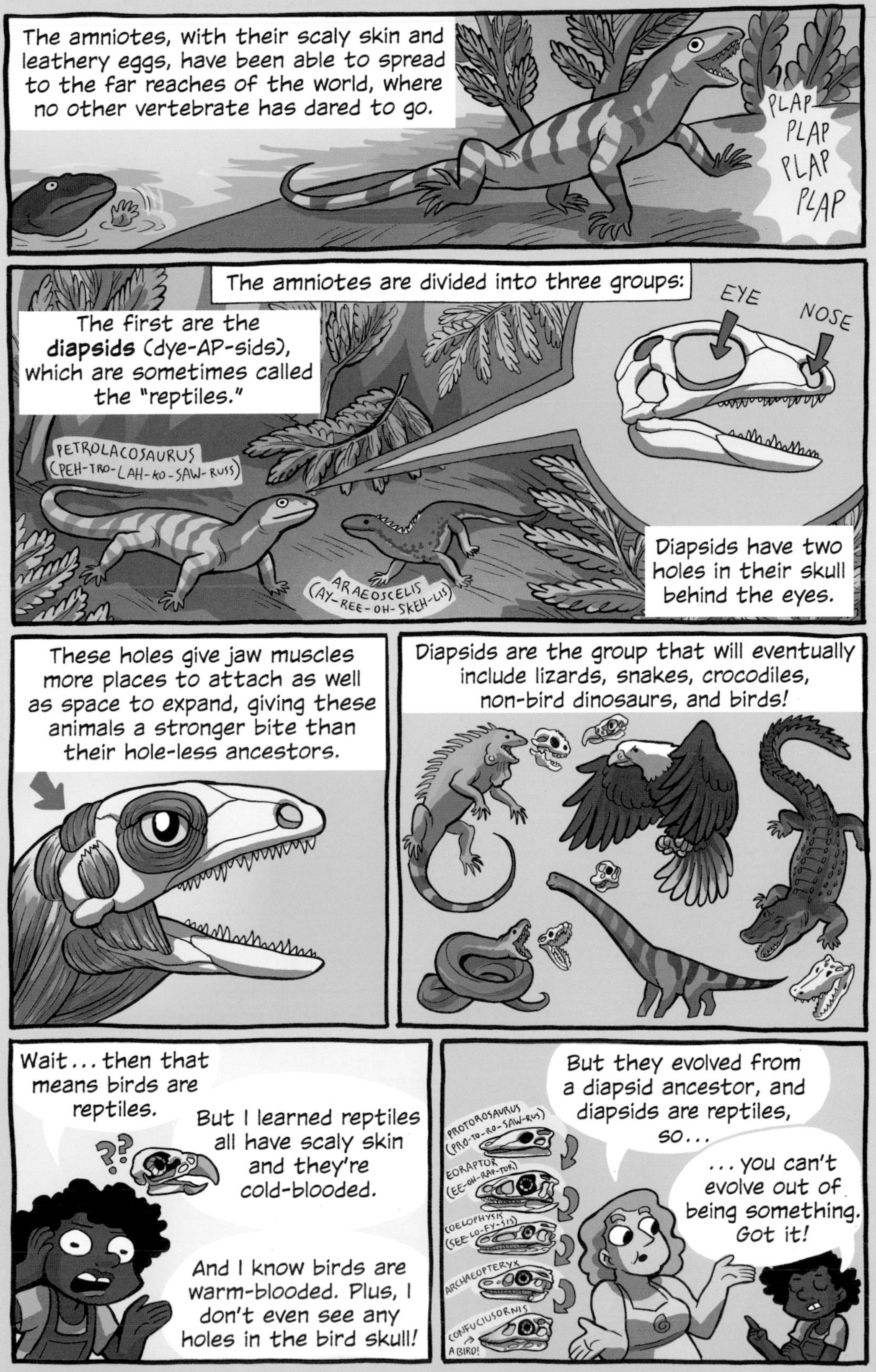
The amniotes, with their scaly skin and leathery eggs, have been able to spread to the far reaches of the world, where no other vertebrate has dared to go.
PLAP PLAP PLAP PLAP
The amniotes are divided into three groups:
The first are the **diapsids** (dye-AP-sids), which are sometimes called the "reptiles."
EYE
NOSE
PETROLACOSAURUS (PEH-TRO-LAH-KO-SAW-RUSS)
ARAEOSCELIS (AY-REE-OH-SKEH-LIS)
Diapsids have two holes in their skull behind the eyes.
These holes give jaw muscles more places to attach as well as space to expand, giving these animals a stronger bite than their hole-less ancestors.
Diapsids are the group that will eventually include lizards, snakes, crocodiles, non-bird dinosaurs, and birds!
Wait... then that means birds are reptiles.
But I learned reptiles all have scaly skin and they're cold-blooded.
??
And I know birds are warm-blooded. Plus, I don't even see any holes in the bird skull!
But they evolved from a diapsid ancestor, and diapsids are reptiles, so...
PROTOROSAURUS (PRO-TO-RO-SAW-RUS)
EORAPTOR (EE-OH-RAP-TOR)
COELOPHYSIS (SEE-LO-FY-SIS)
ARCHAEOPTERYX
CONFUCIUSORNIS
A BIRD!
...you can't evolve out of being something. Got it!

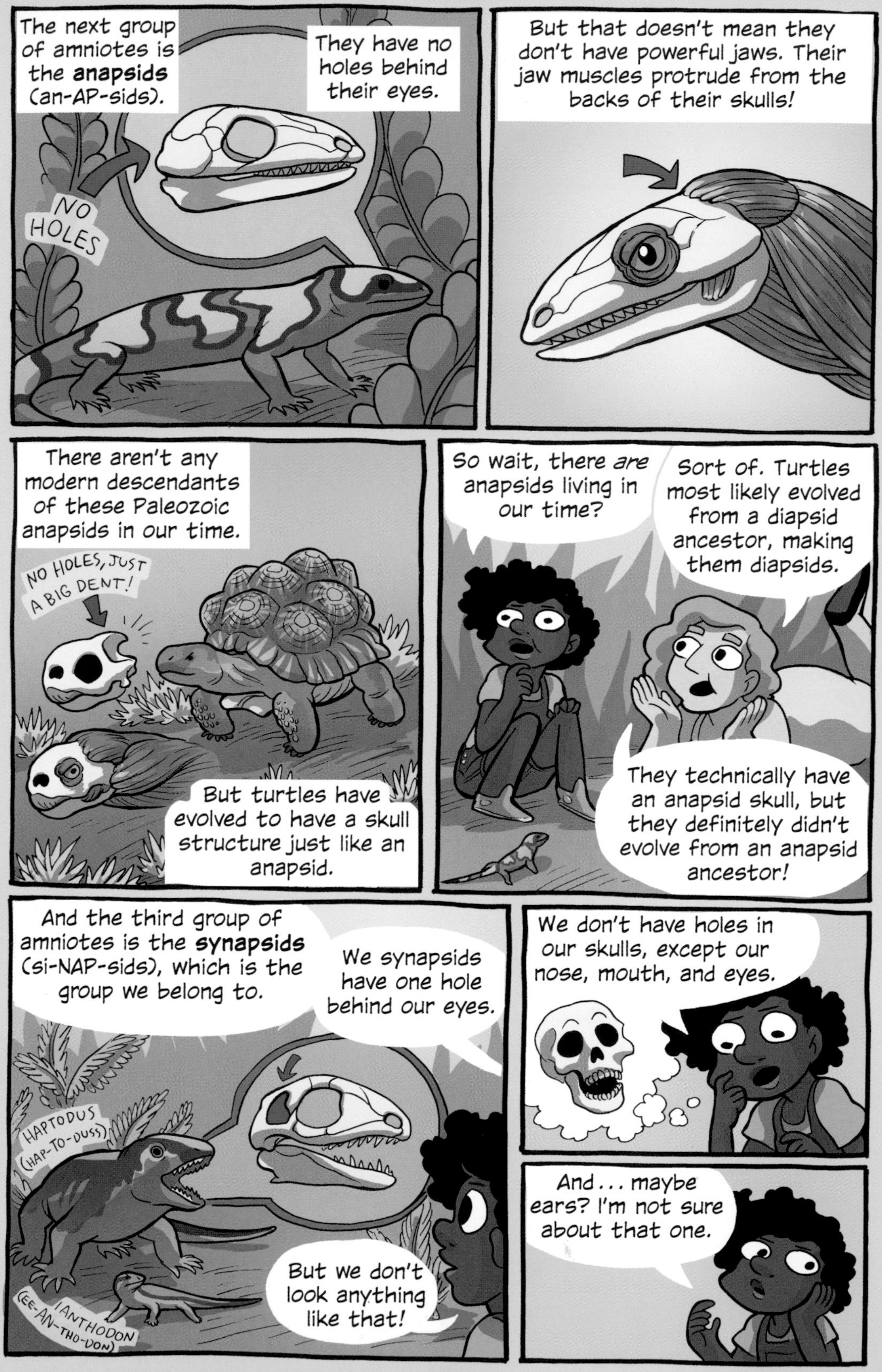
The next group of amniotes is the **anapsids** (an-AP-sids).
They have no holes behind their eyes.
NO HOLES
But that doesn't mean they don't have powerful jaws. Their jaw muscles protrude from the backs of their skulls!
There aren't any modern descendants of these Paleozoic anapsids in our time.
NO HOLES, JUST A BIG DENT!
But turtles have evolved to have a skull structure just like an anapsid.
So wait, there *are* anapsids living in our time?
Sort of. Turtles most likely evolved from a diapsid ancestor, making them diapsids.
They technically have an anapsid skull, but they definitely didn't evolve from an anapsid ancestor!
And the third group of amniotes is the **synapsids** (si-NAP-sids), which is the group we belong to.
We synapsids have one hole behind our eyes.
HAPTODUS (HAP-TO-DUSS)
IANTHODON (EE-AN-THO-DON)
But we don't look anything like that!
We don't have holes in our skulls, except our nose, mouth, and eyes.
And... maybe ears? I'm not sure about that one.

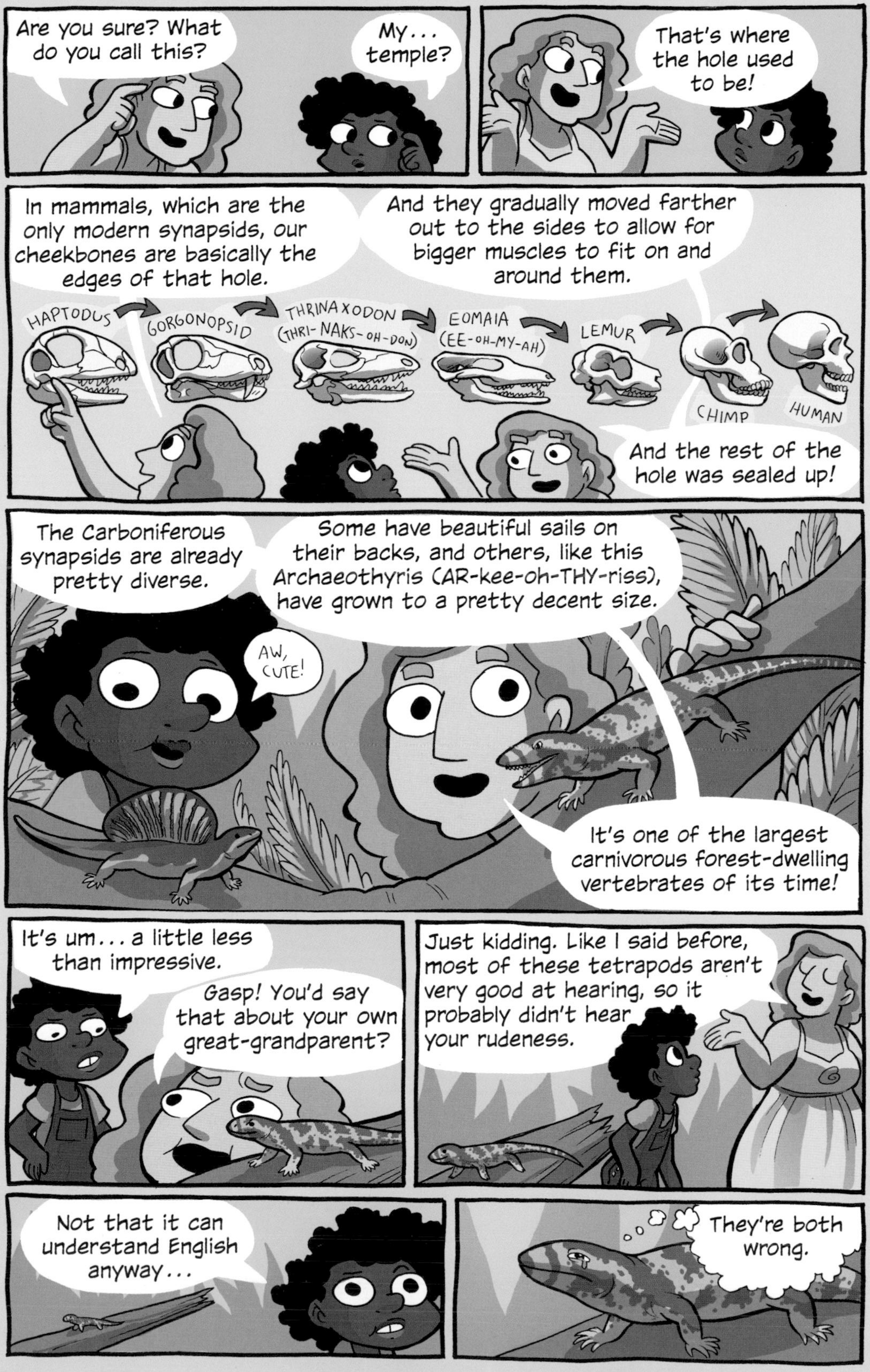

Are you sure? What do you call this?
My... temple?
That's where the hole used to be!
In mammals, which are the only modern synapsids, our cheekbones are basically the edges of that hole.
And they gradually moved farther out to the sides to allow for bigger muscles to fit on and around them.
HAPTODUS
GORGONOPSID
THRINAXODON (THRI-NAKS-OH-DON)
EOMAIA (EE-OH-MY-AH)
LEMUR
CHIMP
HUMAN
And the rest of the hole was sealed up!
The Carboniferous synapsids are already pretty diverse.
Some have beautiful sails on their backs, and others, like this Archaeothyris (AR-kee-oh-THY-riss), have grown to a pretty decent size.
AW, CUTE!
It's one of the largest carnivorous forest-dwelling vertebrates of its time!
It's um... a little less than impressive.
Gasp! You'd say that about your own great-grandparent?
Just kidding. Like I said before, most of these tetrapods aren't very good at hearing, so it probably didn't hear your rudeness.
Not that it can understand English anyway...
They're both wrong.

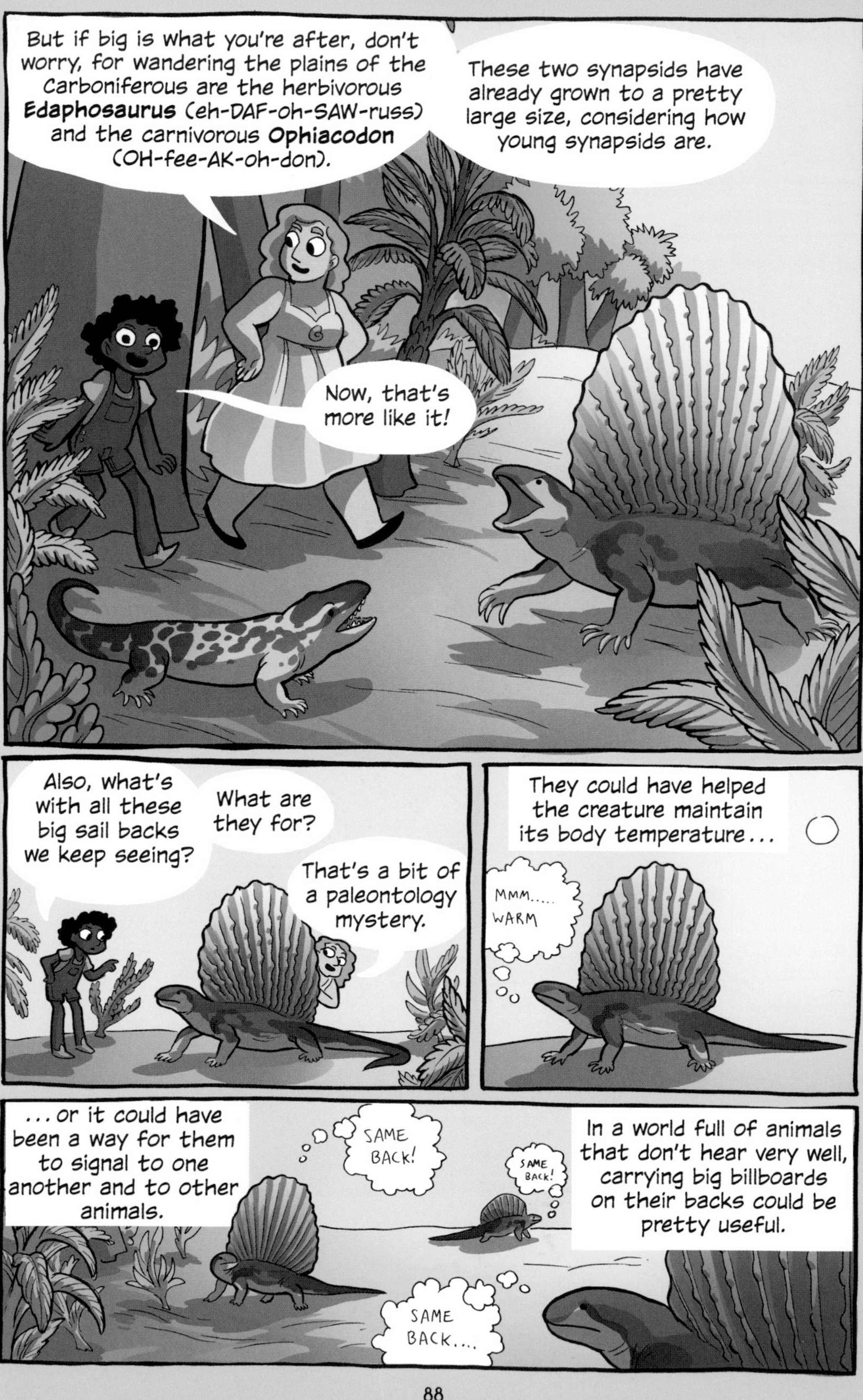
But if big is what you're after, don't worry, for wandering the plains of the Carboniferous are the herbivorous **Edaphosaurus** (eh-DAF-oh-SAW-russ) and the carnivorous **Ophiacodon** (OH-fee-AK-oh-don).
These two synapsids have already grown to a pretty large size, considering how young synapsids are.
Now, that's more like it!
Also, what's with all these big sail backs we keep seeing?
What are they for?
That's a bit of a paleontology mystery.
They could have helped the creature maintain its body temperature...
MMM..... WARM
...or it could have been a way for them to signal to one another and to other animals.
SAME BACK!
SAME BACK!
In a world full of animals that don't hear very well, carrying big billboards on their backs could be pretty useful.
SAME BACK....

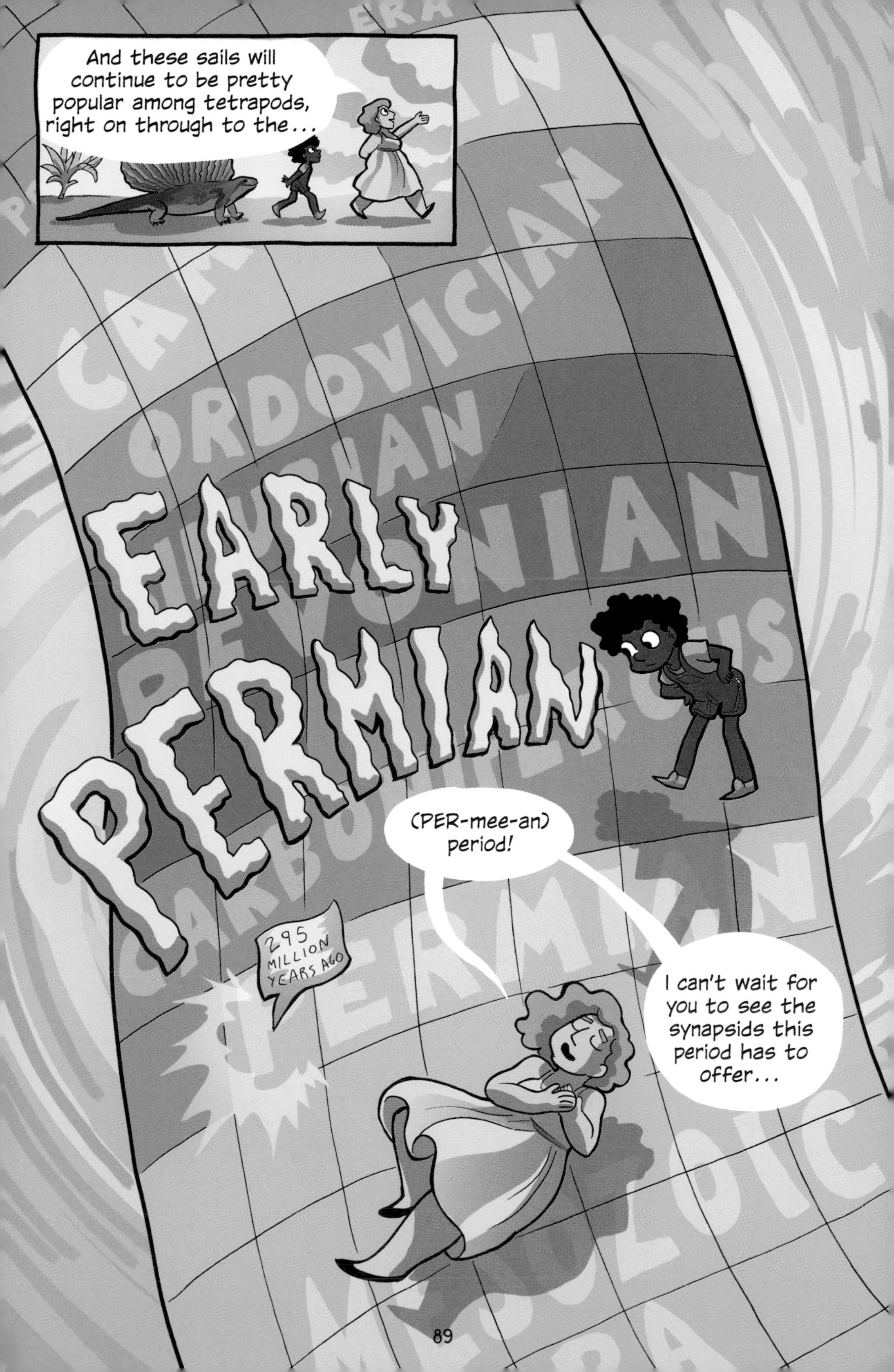
And these sails will continue to be pretty popular among tetrapods, right on through to the...
EARLY PERMIAN
(PER-mee-an) period!
295 MILLION YEARS AGO
I can't wait for you to see the synapsids this period has to offer...

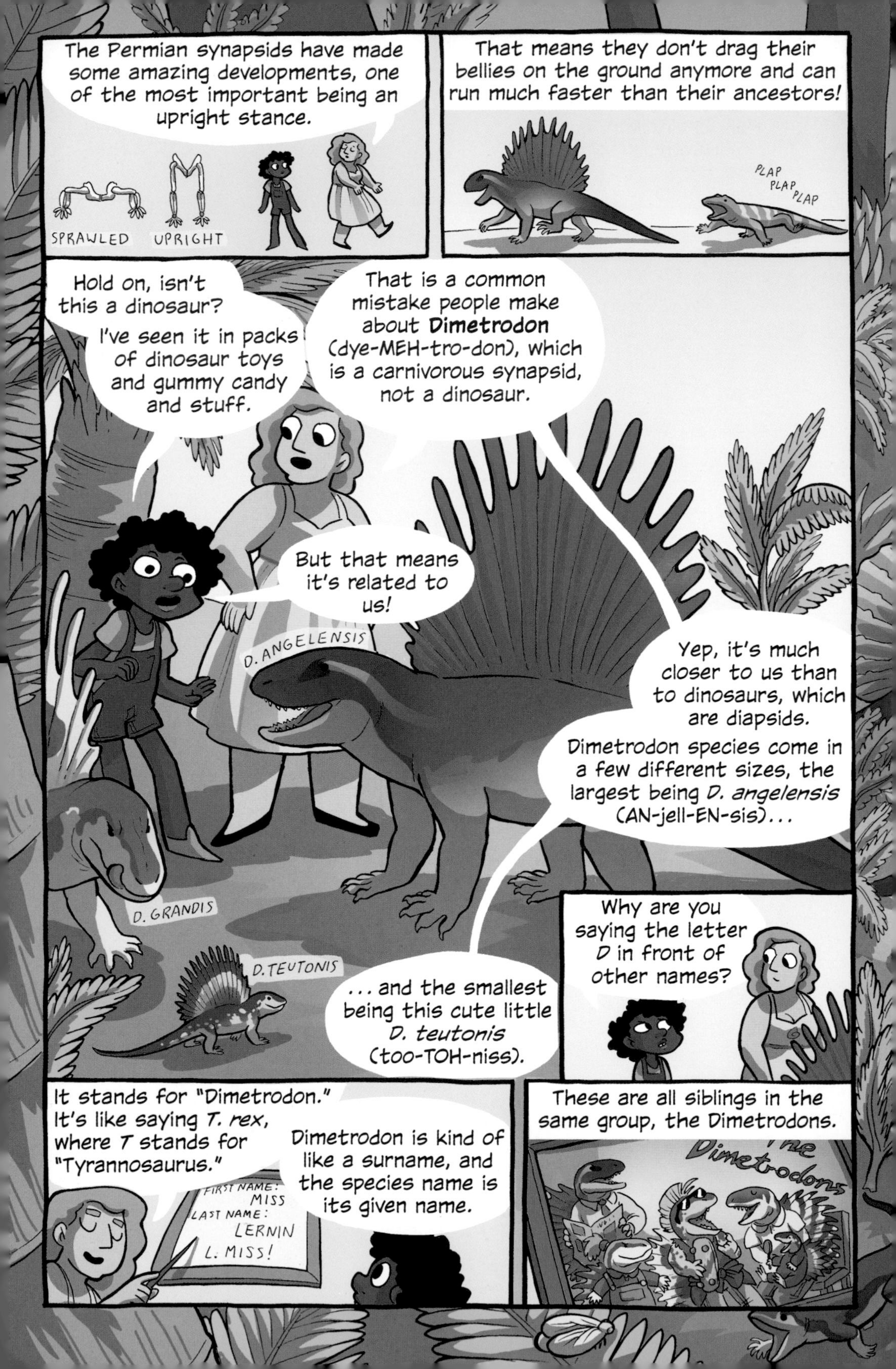
The Permian synapsids have made some amazing developments, one of the most important being an upright stance.
SPRAWLED
UPRIGHT
That means they don't drag their bellies on the ground anymore and can run much faster than their ancestors!
PLAP PLAP PLAP
Hold on, isn't this a dinosaur?
I've seen it in packs of dinosaur toys and gummy candy and stuff.
That is a common mistake people make about **Dimetrodon** (dye-MEH-tro-don), which is a carnivorous synapsid, not a dinosaur.
But that means it's related to us!
D. ANGELENSIS
Yep, it's much closer to us than to dinosaurs, which are diapsids.
Dimetrodon species come in a few different sizes, the largest being *D. angelensis* (AN-jell-EN-sis)...
D. GRANDIS
D. TEUTONIS
...and the smallest being this cute little *D. teutonis* (too-TOH-niss).
Why are you saying the letter *D* in front of other names?
It stands for "Dimetrodon." It's like saying *T. rex*, where *T* stands for "Tyrannosaurus."
Dimetrodon is kind of like a surname, and the species name is its given name.
FIRST NAME: MISS
LAST NAME: LERNIN
L. MISS!
These are all siblings in the same group, the Dimetrodons.
The Dimetrodons

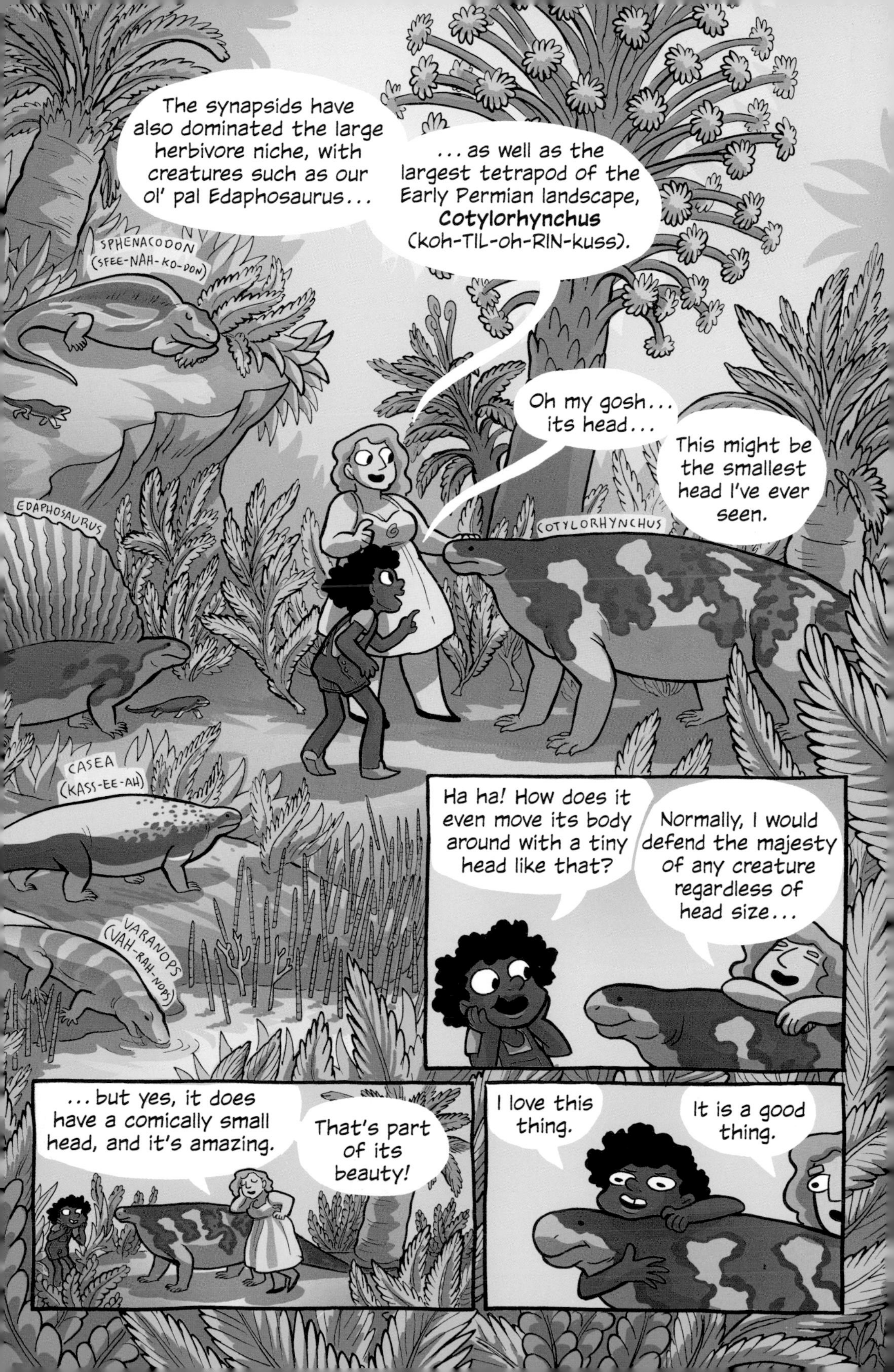
The synapsids have also dominated the large herbivore niche, with creatures such as our ol' pal Edaphosaurus...
...as well as the largest tetrapod of the Early Permian landscape, **Cotylorhynchus** (koh-TIL-oh-RIN-kuss).
SPHENACODON (SFEE-NAH-KO-DON)
EDAPHOSAURUS
COTYLORHYNCHUS
CASEA (KASS-EE-AH)
VARANOPS (VAH-RAH-NOPS)
Oh my gosh... its head...
This might be the smallest head I've ever seen.
Ha ha! How does it even move its body around with a tiny head like that?
Normally, I would defend the majesty of any creature regardless of head size...
...but yes, it does have a comically small head, and it's amazing.
That's part of its beauty!
I love this thing.
It is a good thing.

But it is not the last good thing we'll meet on our journey!
Let's head back to the forests . . .
. . . where reptiliomorphs such as this **Limnoscelis** (LIM-naw-seh-liss) prowl for their smaller cousins and any unfortunate amphibians that may be hiding in the underbrush.
Seymouria (see-MOR-ee-ah) is one such cousin, and it is well adapted to living on land even though it has to return to the water to lay its eggs.
DIADECTES (DYE-AH-DEK-TEES)
It has spread far and wide and is one of the most successful Permian reptiliomorphs.
ARCHERIA (AR-KEE-REE-AH)

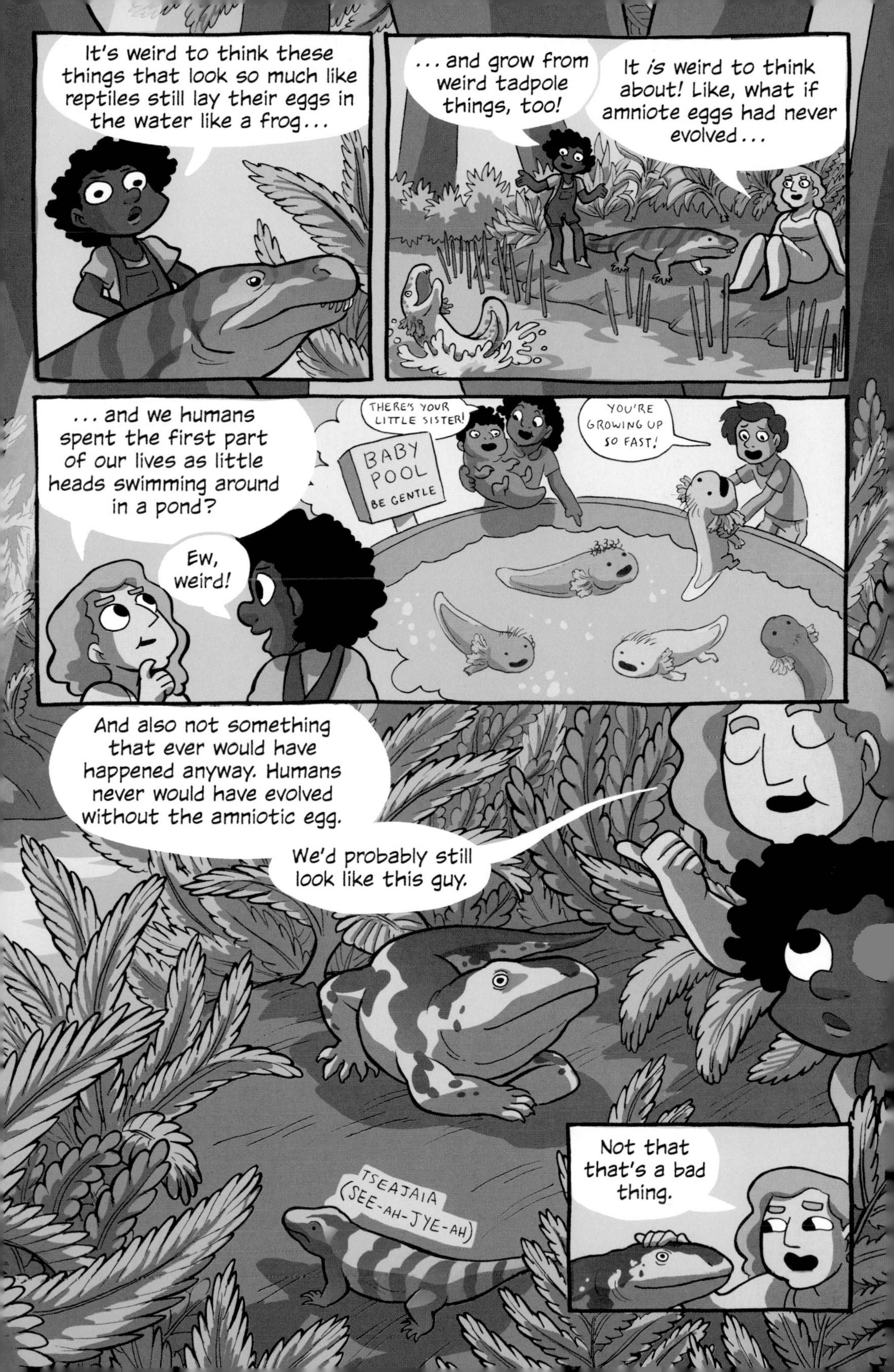
It's weird to think these things that look so much like reptiles still lay their eggs in the water like a frog...
...and grow from weird tadpole things, too!
It *is* weird to think about! Like, what if amniote eggs had never evolved...
...and we humans spent the first part of our lives as little heads swimming around in a pond?
THERE'S YOUR LITTLE SISTER!
BABY POOL BE GENTLE
YOU'RE GROWING UP SO FAST!
Ew, weird!
And also not something that ever would have happened anyway. Humans never would have evolved without the amniotic egg.
We'd probably still look like this guy.
TSEAJAIA (SEE-AH-JYE-AH)
Not that that's a bad thing.

There are still anapsids in these forests, as well, such as this cute little **Belebey** (BELL-eh-beh)...

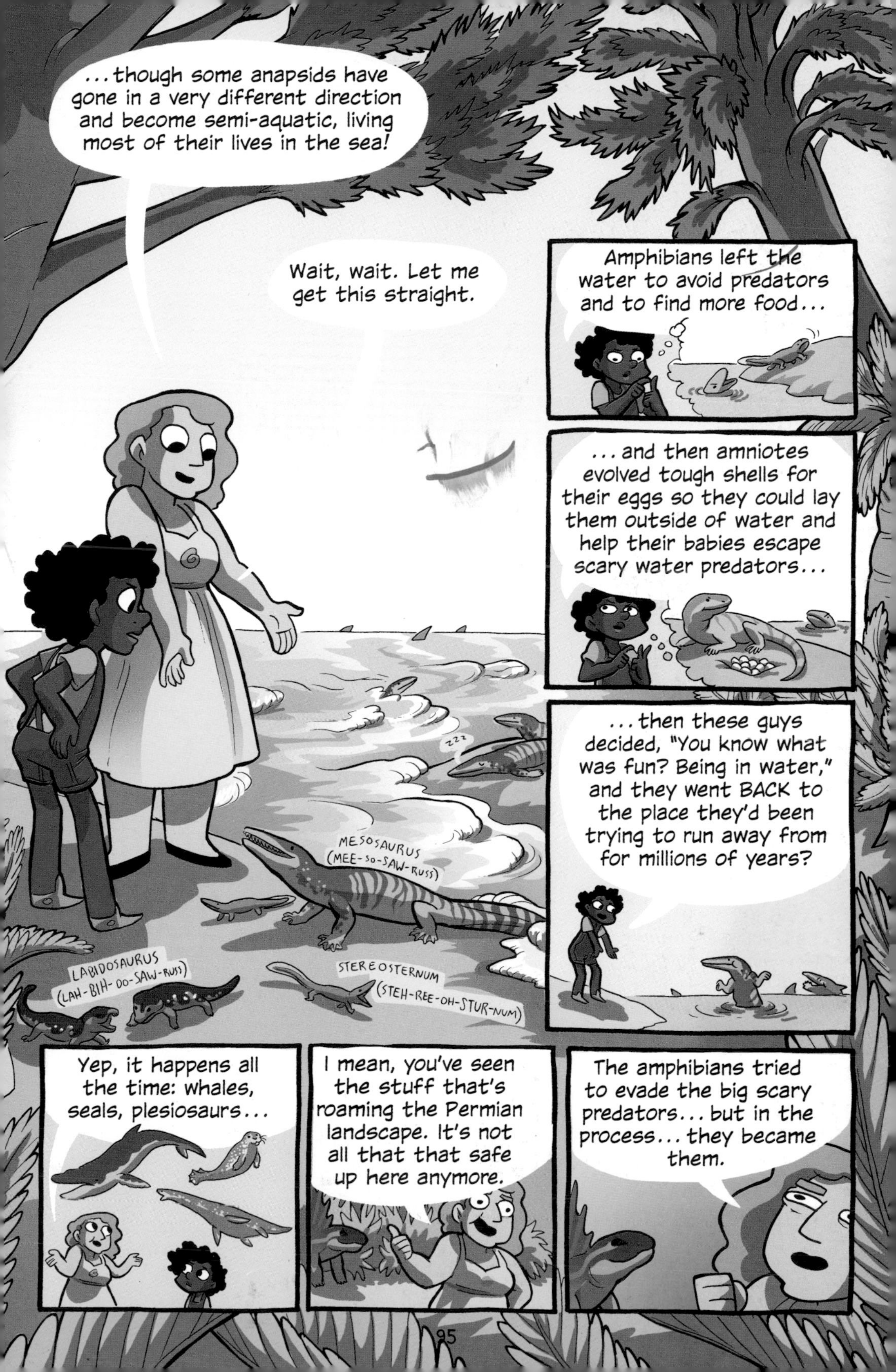

...though some anapsids have gone in a very different direction and become semi-aquatic, living most of their lives in the sea!
Wait, wait. Let me get this straight.
Amphibians left the water to avoid predators and to find more food...
...and then amniotes evolved tough shells for their eggs so they could lay them outside of water and help their babies escape scary water predators...
...then these guys decided, "You know what was fun? Being in water," and they went BACK to the place they'd been trying to run away from for millions of years?
MESOSAURUS (MEE-SO-SAW-RUSS)
LABIDOSAURUS (LAH-BIH-DO-SAW-RUSS)
STEREOSTERNUM (STEH-REE-OH-STUR-NUM)
Yep, it happens all the time: whales, seals, plesiosaurs...
I mean, you've seen the stuff that's roaming the Permian landscape. It's not all that that safe up here anymore.
The amphibians tried to evade the big scary predators... but in the process... they became them.

Such as the large predatory amphibians **Melosaurus** (MELL-oh-SAW-russ) and **Edops** (EE-dops), which stalk the Permian waterways.
These amphibians spend time both in and out of water.
But some have evolved to spend most of their time away from water, living out almost all of their lives in the underbrush.
PAT PAT
EDOPS
ZATRACHYS
There are also some amphibians that prefer the water...
...and still others, such as **Trimerorhachis** (TRY-meh-ro-RAH-kiss), that live their entire lives without stepping foot on solid ground.
TRIMERORHACHIS

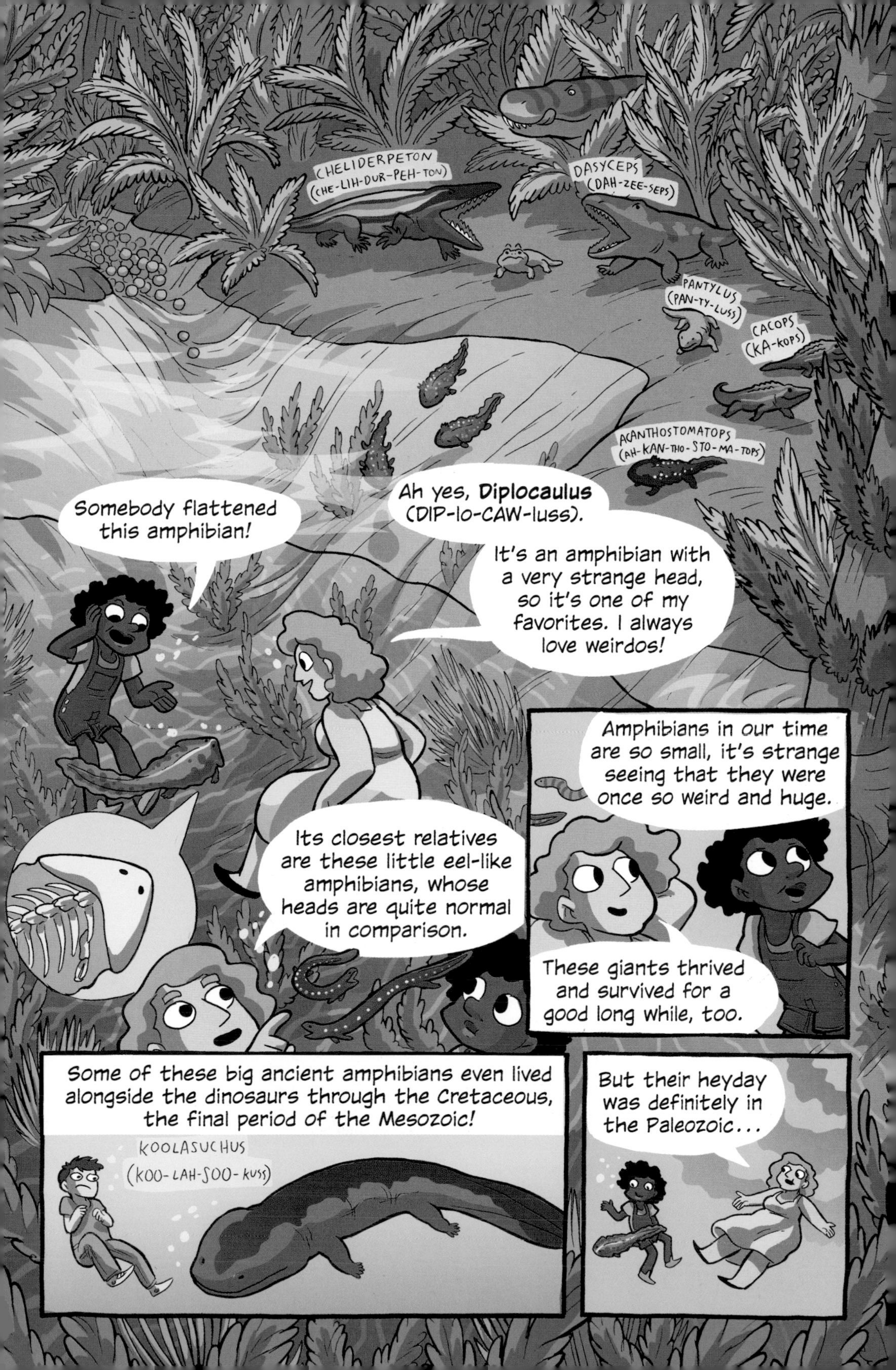
CHELIDERPETON
(CHE-LIH-DUR-PEH-TON)
DASYCEPS
(DAH-ZEE-SEPS)
PANTYLUS
(PAN-TY-LUSS)
CACOPS
(KA-KOPS)
ACANTHOSTOMATOPS
(AH-KAN-THO-STO-MA-TOPS)
Somebody flattened this amphibian!
Ah yes, **Diplocaulus** (DIP-lo-CAW-luss).
It's an amphibian with a very strange head, so it's one of my favorites. I always love weirdos!
Its closest relatives are these little eel-like amphibians, whose heads are quite normal in comparison.
Amphibians in our time are so small, it's strange seeing that they were once so weird and huge.
These giants thrived and survived for a good long while, too.
Some of these big ancient amphibians even lived alongside the dinosaurs through the Cretaceous, the final period of the Mesozoic!
KOOLASUCHUS
(KOO-LAH-SOO-KUSS)
But their heyday was definitely in the Paleozoic...

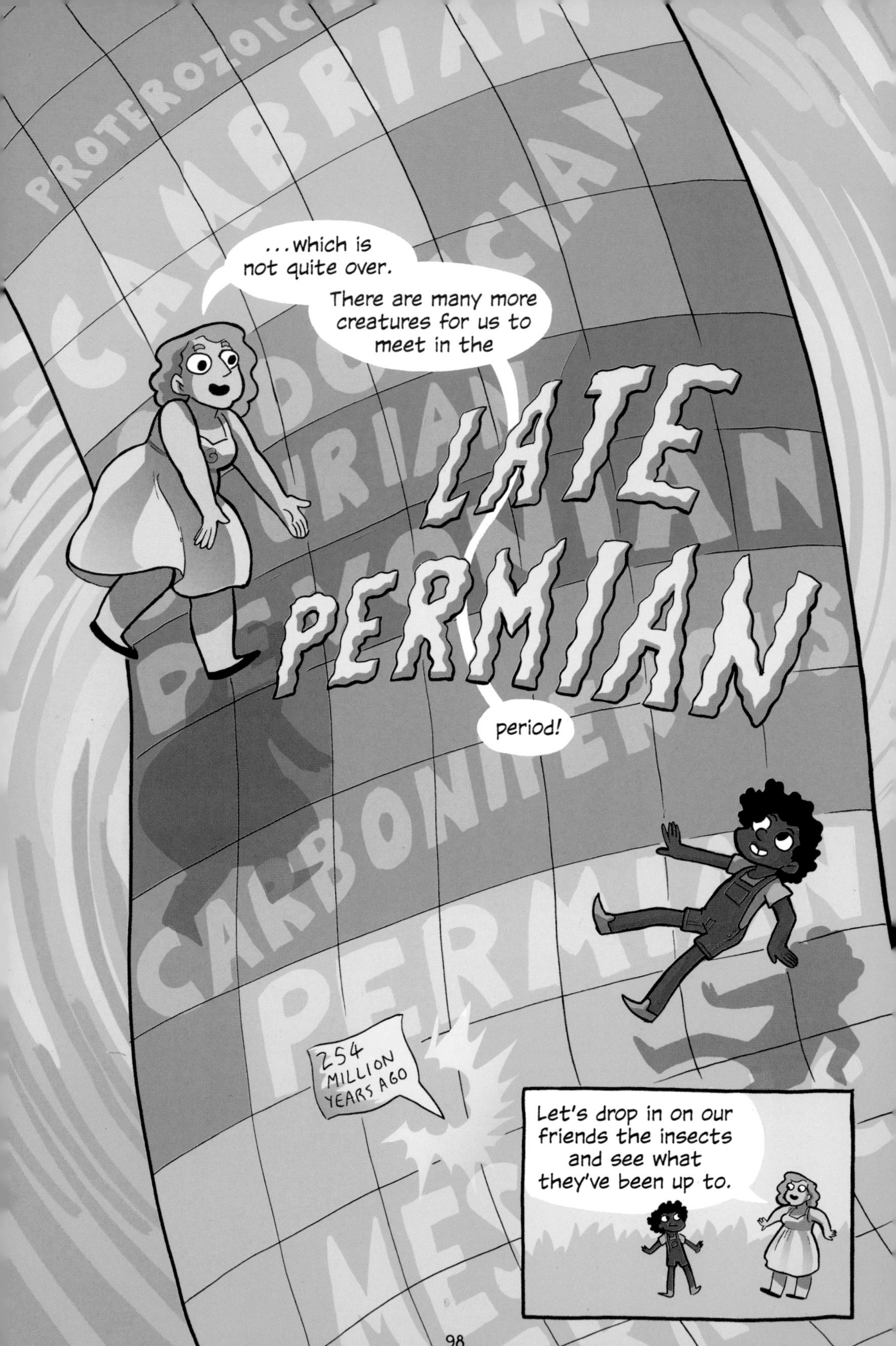
PROTEROZOIC
CAMBRIAN
...which is not quite over.
There are many more creatures for us to meet in the
LATE PERMIAN
period!
254 MILLION YEARS AGO
Let's drop in on our friends the insects and see what they've been up to.

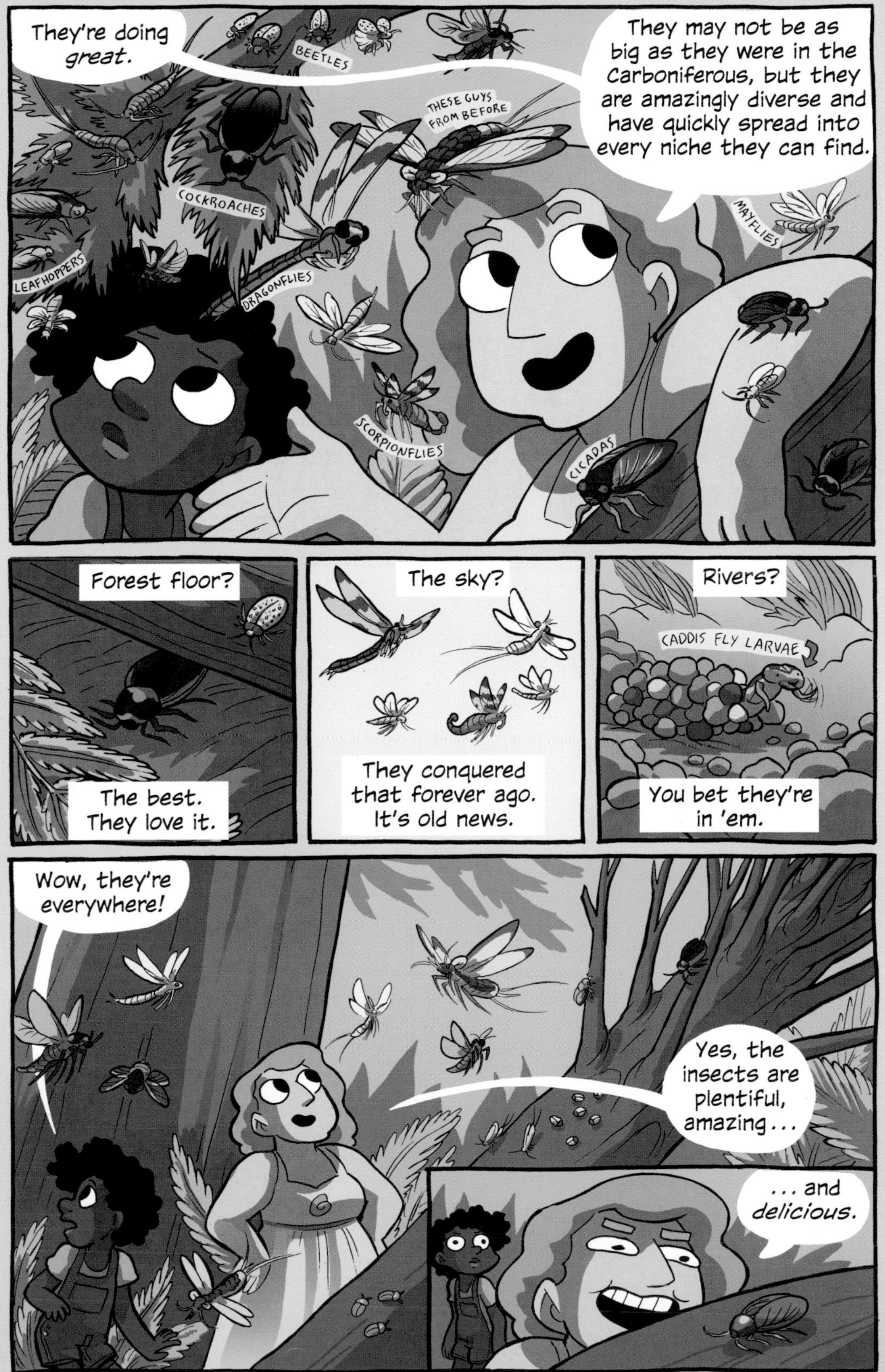
They're doing *great.*
BEETLES
They may not be as big as they were in the Carboniferous, but they are amazingly diverse and have quickly spread into every niche they can find.
THESE GUYS FROM BEFORE
COCKROACHES
MAYFLIES
LEAFHOPPERS
DRAGONFLIES
SCORPIONFLIES
CICADAS
Forest floor?
The best. They love it.
The sky?
They conquered that forever ago. It's old news.
Rivers?
CADDIS FLY LARVAE
You bet they're in 'em.
Wow, they're everywhere!
Yes, the insects are plentiful, amazing . . .
. . . and *delicious.*

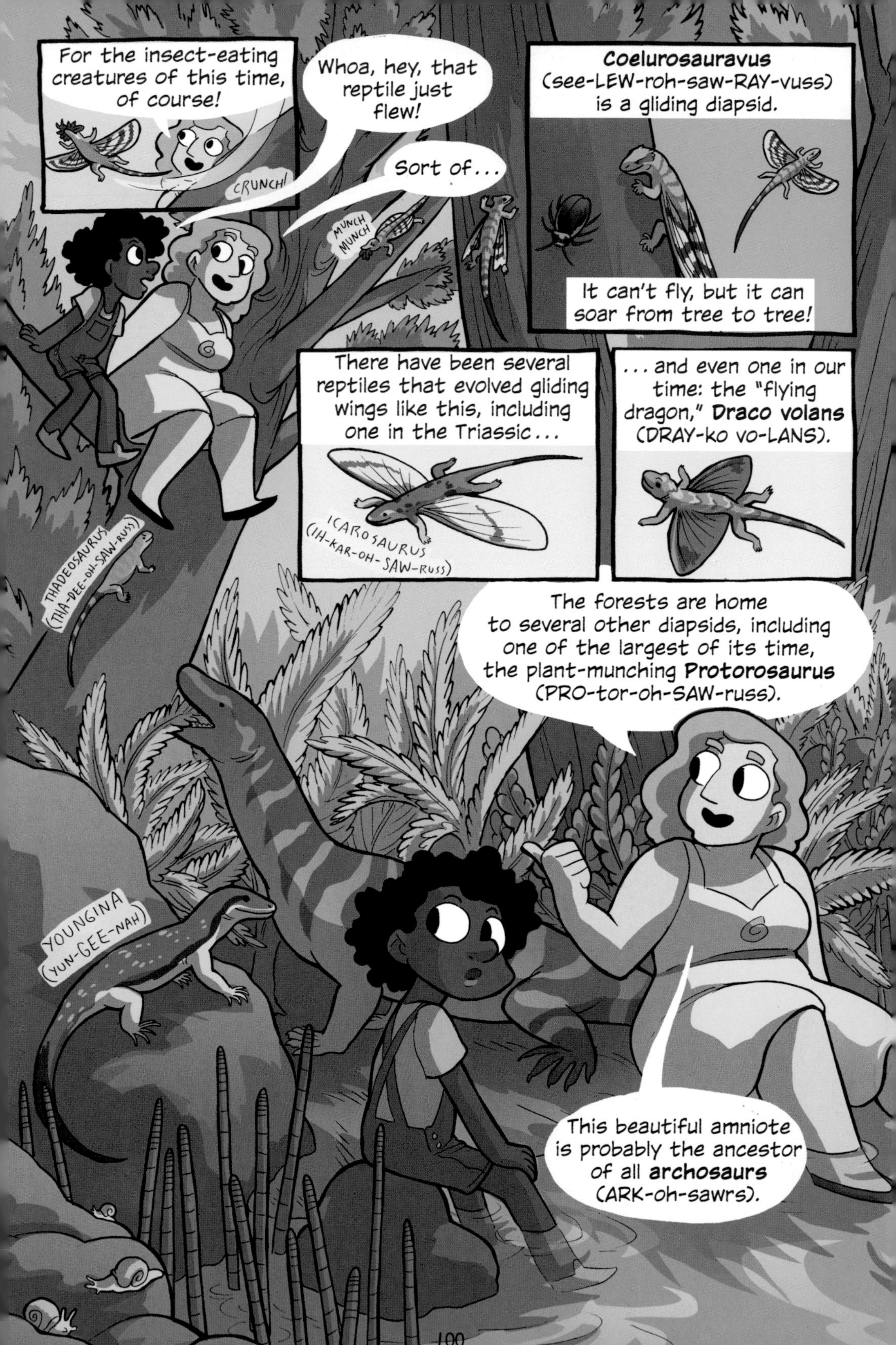

For the insect-eating creatures of this time, of course!
CRUNCH!
Whoa, hey, that reptile just flew!
Sort of...
MUNCH MUNCH
Coelurosauravus (see-LEW-roh-saw-RAY-vuss) is a gliding diapsid.
It can't fly, but it can soar from tree to tree!
There have been several reptiles that evolved gliding wings like this, including one in the Triassic...
ICAROSAURUS (IH-KAR-OH-SAW-RUSS)
...and even one in our time: the "flying dragon," **Draco volans** (DRAY-ko vo-LANS).
THADEOSAURUS (THA-DEE-OH-SAW-RUSS)
The forests are home to several other diapsids, including one of the largest of its time, the plant-munching **Protorosaurus** (PRO-tor-oh-SAW-russ).
YOUNGINA (YUN-GEE-NAH)
This beautiful amniote is probably the ancestor of all **archosaurs** (ARK-oh-sawrs).

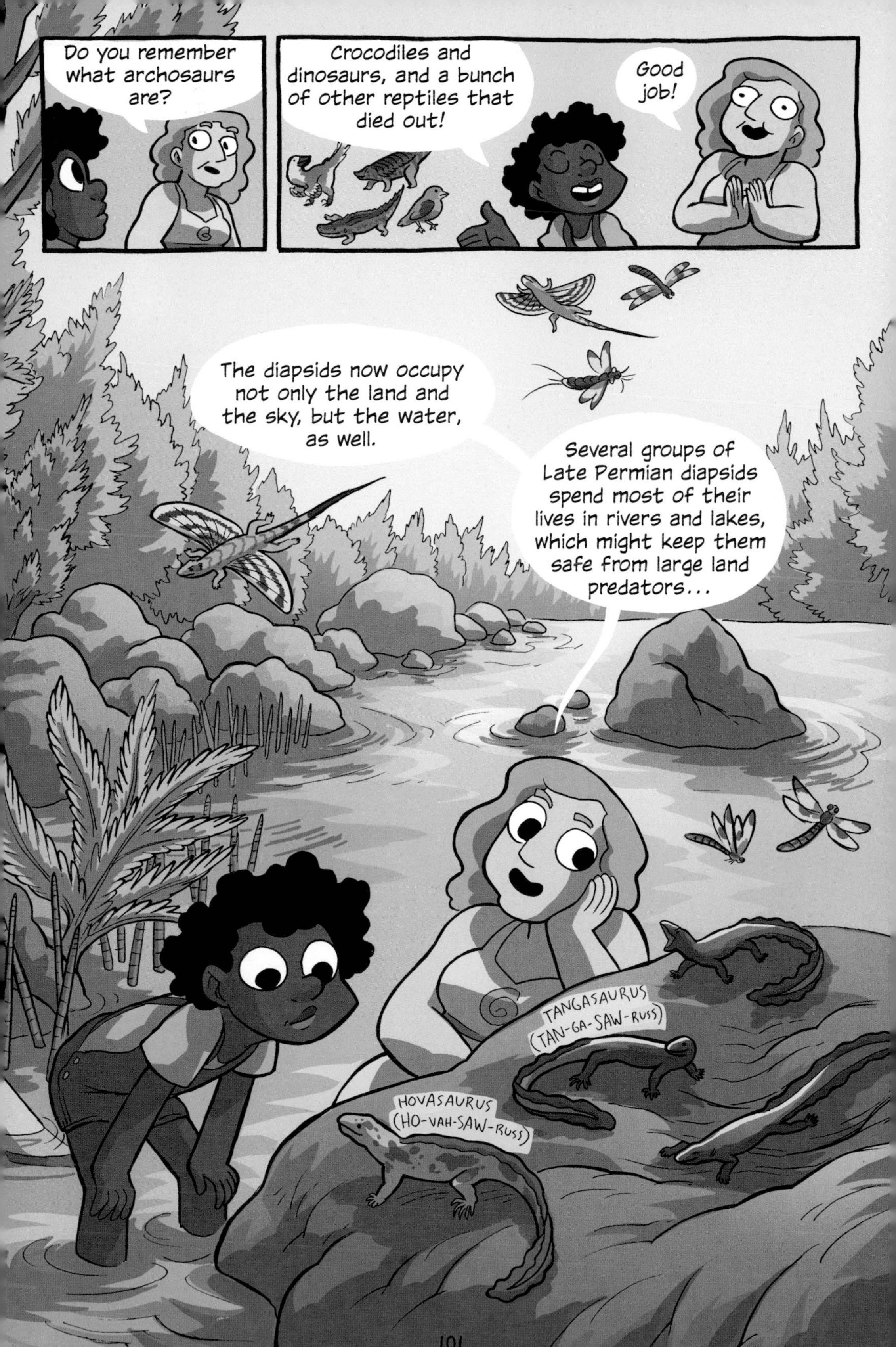
Do you remember what archosaurs are?
Crocodiles and dinosaurs, and a bunch of other reptiles that died out!
Good job!
The diapsids now occupy not only the land and the sky, but the water, as well.
Several groups of Late Permian diapsids spend most of their lives in rivers and lakes, which might keep them safe from large land predators...
TANGASAURUS (TAN-GA-SAW-RUSS)
HOVASAURUS (HO-VAH-SAW-RUSS)

...but puts them right in the jaws of one of the largest amphibians ever found, Prionosuchus (pree-ON-oh-SOO-kuss).*
This amphibian could grow up to 30 feet long, though that length was probably pretty uncommon.
Most were probably only about six feet long, which would make them slightly smaller than another large freshwater predator, **Nigerpeton** (NYE-jur-PEH-ton).
NIGERPETON
*Note: Prionosuchus actually lived about 20 million years before the end of the Permian, but it was just too cool to leave out!

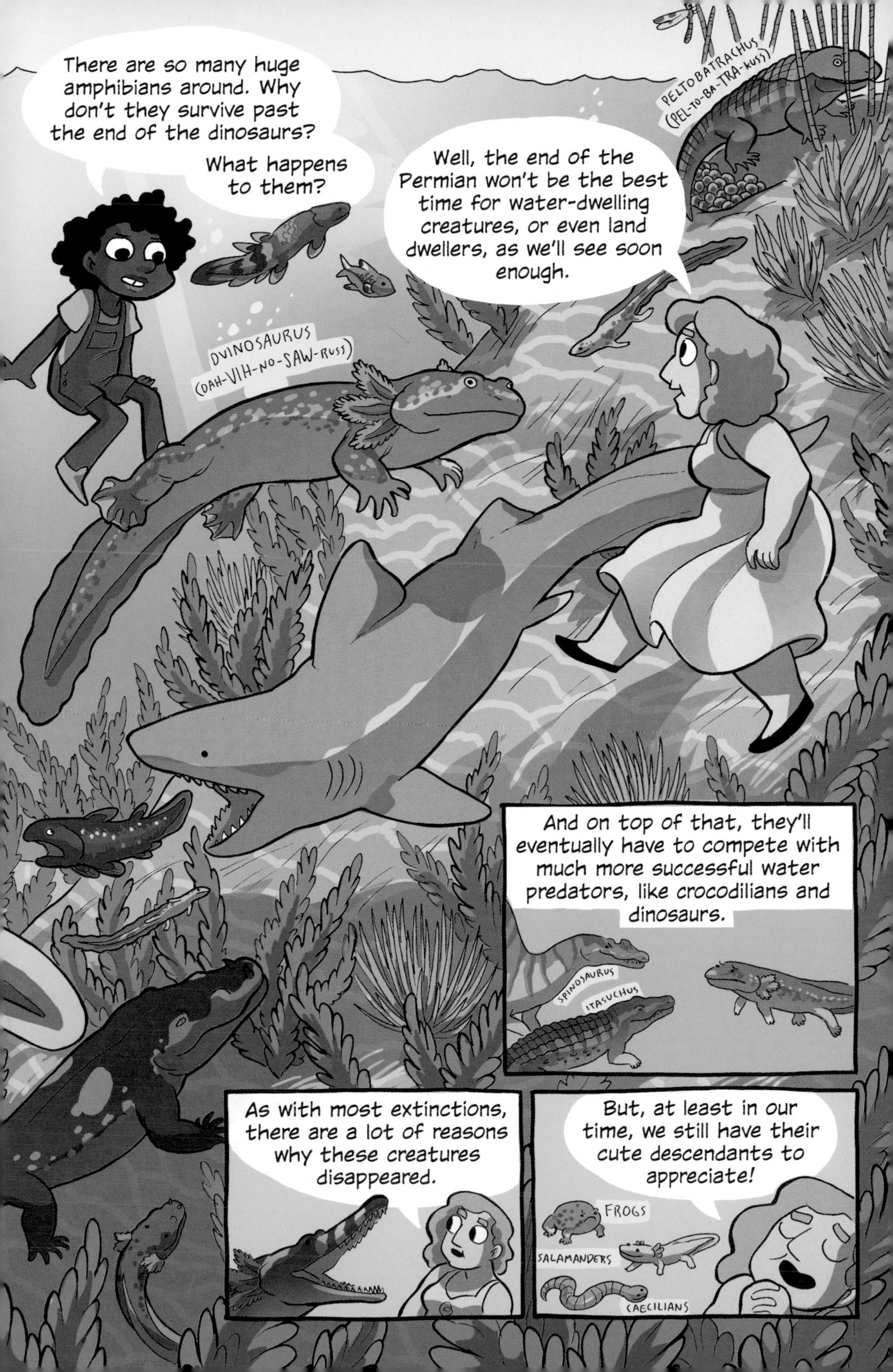
There are so many huge amphibians around. Why don't they survive past the end of the dinosaurs?
What happens to them?
PELTOBATRACHUS (PEL-TO-BA-TRA-KUSS)
Well, the end of the Permian won't be the best time for water-dwelling creatures, or even land dwellers, as we'll see soon enough.
DVINOSAURUS (DAH-VIH-NO-SAW-RUSS)
And on top of that, they'll eventually have to compete with much more successful water predators, like crocodilians and dinosaurs.
SPINOSAURUS
ITASUCHUS
As with most extinctions, there are a lot of reasons why these creatures disappeared.
But, at least in our time, we still have their cute descendants to appreciate!
FROGS
SALAMANDERS
CAECILIANS

However, there are some groups that have no modern descendants to appreciate.
The Paleozoic is the only time we'll get to appreciate the reptiliomorphs, such as this **Bystrowiana** (bis-TRO-ee-AH-na).
As you can see, some reptiliomorphs have gotten sweet upgrades, like rows of armor along their backs that protect against the large predators of the Permian.
URALERPETON (YOO-RAH-LUR-PEH-TON)
What kind of predator would a creature this big have to worry about...
KARPINSKIOSAURUS (KAR-PIN-SKEE-OH-SAW-RUSS)
CHRONIOSUCHUS (KRO-NEE-OH-SOO-KUSS)
PELTOBATRACHUS (AMPHIBIAN)

And the amniotes have upgraded as well, like the spiky **Scutosaurus** (SKOOT-oh-SAW-russ) and its cousins.
They'd certainly be intimidating to any predator that wanted to try its hand...
...or should I say claw...
...at taking them down.
Okay, you keep talking about these land predators, but I haven't seen any!
That's because I've been saving my favorites for last.

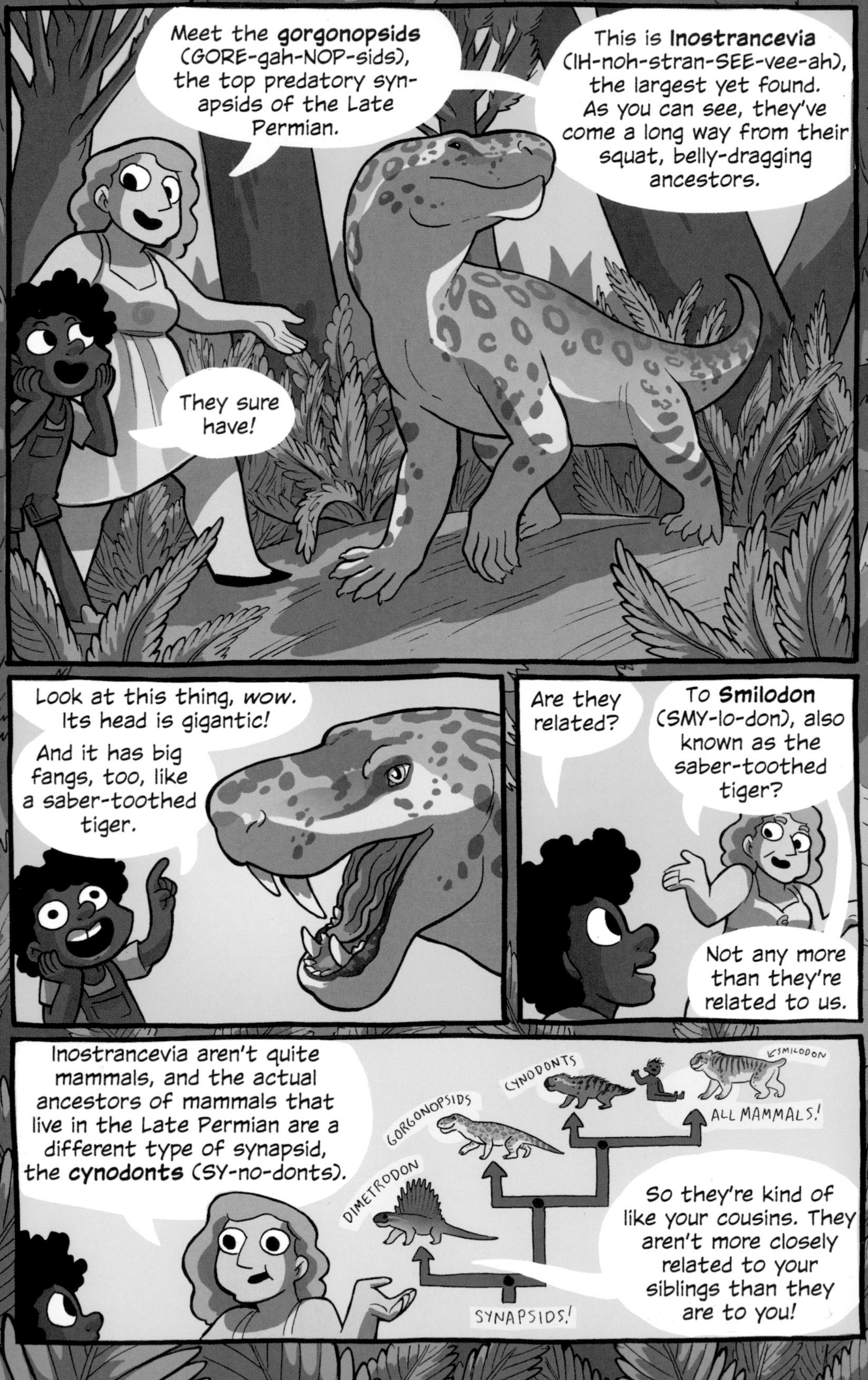
Meet the **gorgonopsids** (GORE-gah-NOP-sids), the top predatory synapsids of the Late Permian.
This is **Inostrancevia** (IH-noh-stran-SEE-vee-ah), the largest yet found. As you can see, they've come a long way from their squat, belly-dragging ancestors.
They sure have!
Look at this thing, *wow.* Its head is gigantic!
And it has big fangs, too, like a saber-toothed tiger.
Are they related?
To **Smilodon** (SMY-lo-don), also known as the saber-toothed tiger?
Not any more than they're related to us.
Inostrancevia aren't quite mammals, and the actual ancestors of mammals that live in the Late Permian are a different type of synapsid, the **cynodonts** (SY-no-donts).
CYNODONTS
SMILODON
GORGONOPSIDS
ALL MAMMALS!
DIMETRODON
SYNAPSIDS!
So they're kind of like your cousins. They aren't more closely related to your siblings than they are to you!

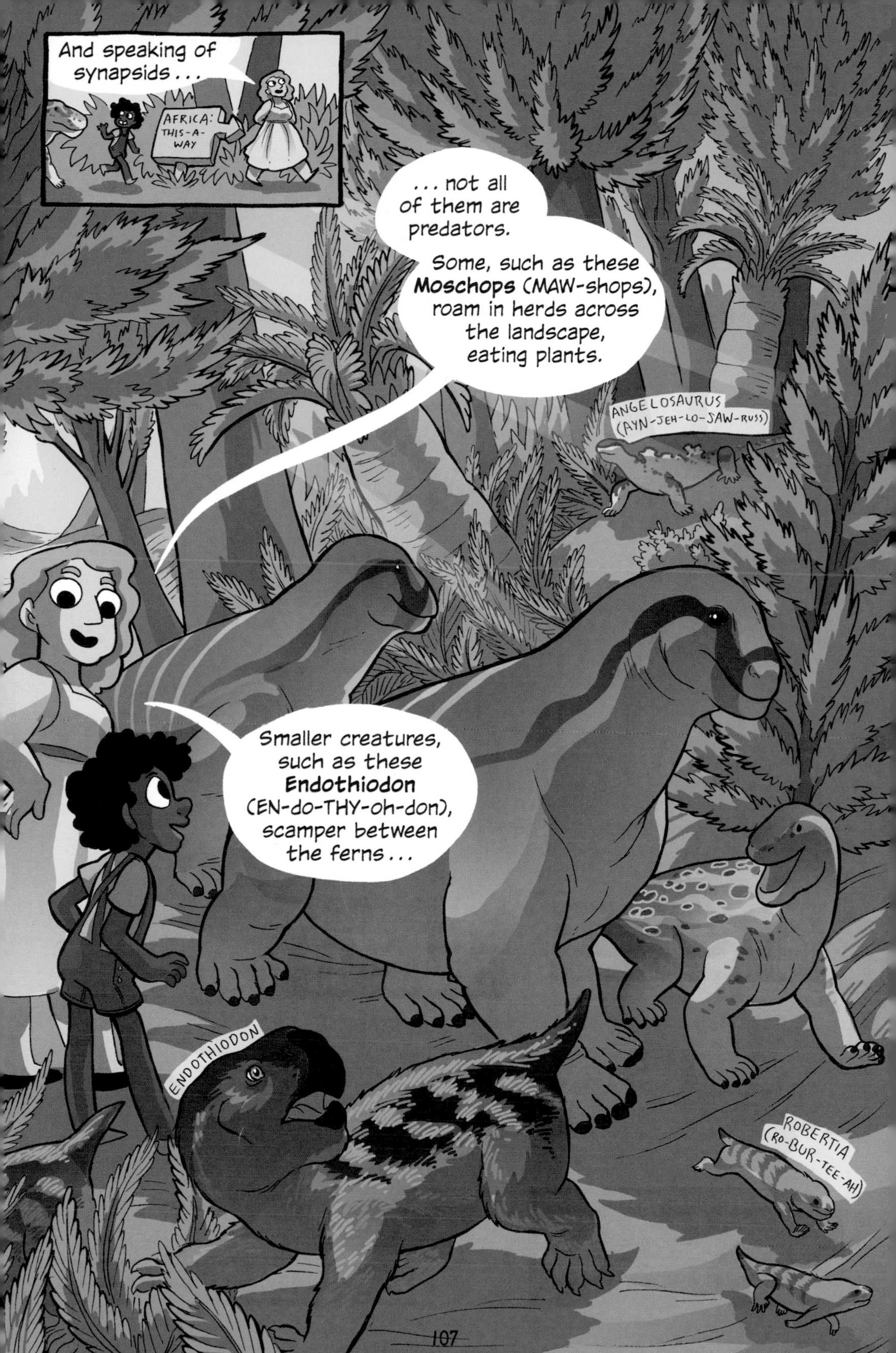

And speaking of synapsids . . .
AFRICA: THIS-A-WAY
. . . not all of them are predators.
Some, such as these **Moschops** (MAW-shops), roam in herds across the landscape, eating plants.
ANGELOSAURUS (AYN-JEH-LO-SAW-RUSS)
Smaller creatures, such as these **Endothiodon** (EN-do-THY-oh-don), scamper between the ferns . . .
ENDOTHIODON
ROBERTIA (RO-BUR-TEE-AH)

...and the even smaller **Diictodon** (dye-ICK-toh-don) burrowed beneath their feet.

Aw, these things are so cute! And they're furry!!

Yes, they're a bit closer to mammals than the gorgonopsids are, so they have several very mammal-like features.

That includes something that's very important to mammals: good hearing!

SNAP

Other Permian creatures can hear fairly well, but these mammal-ish synapsids have taken it further than most other animals have.

They use three little bones that used to be a part of their jaws to sense vibrations.

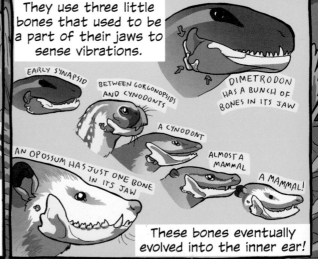

EARLY SYNAPSID

BETWEEN GORGONOPSIDS AND CYNODONTS

DIMETRODON HAS A BUNCH OF BONES IN ITS JAW

A CYNODONT

AN OPOSSUM HAS JUST ONE BONE IN ITS JAW

ALMOST A MAMMAL

A MAMMAL!

These bones eventually evolved into the inner ear!

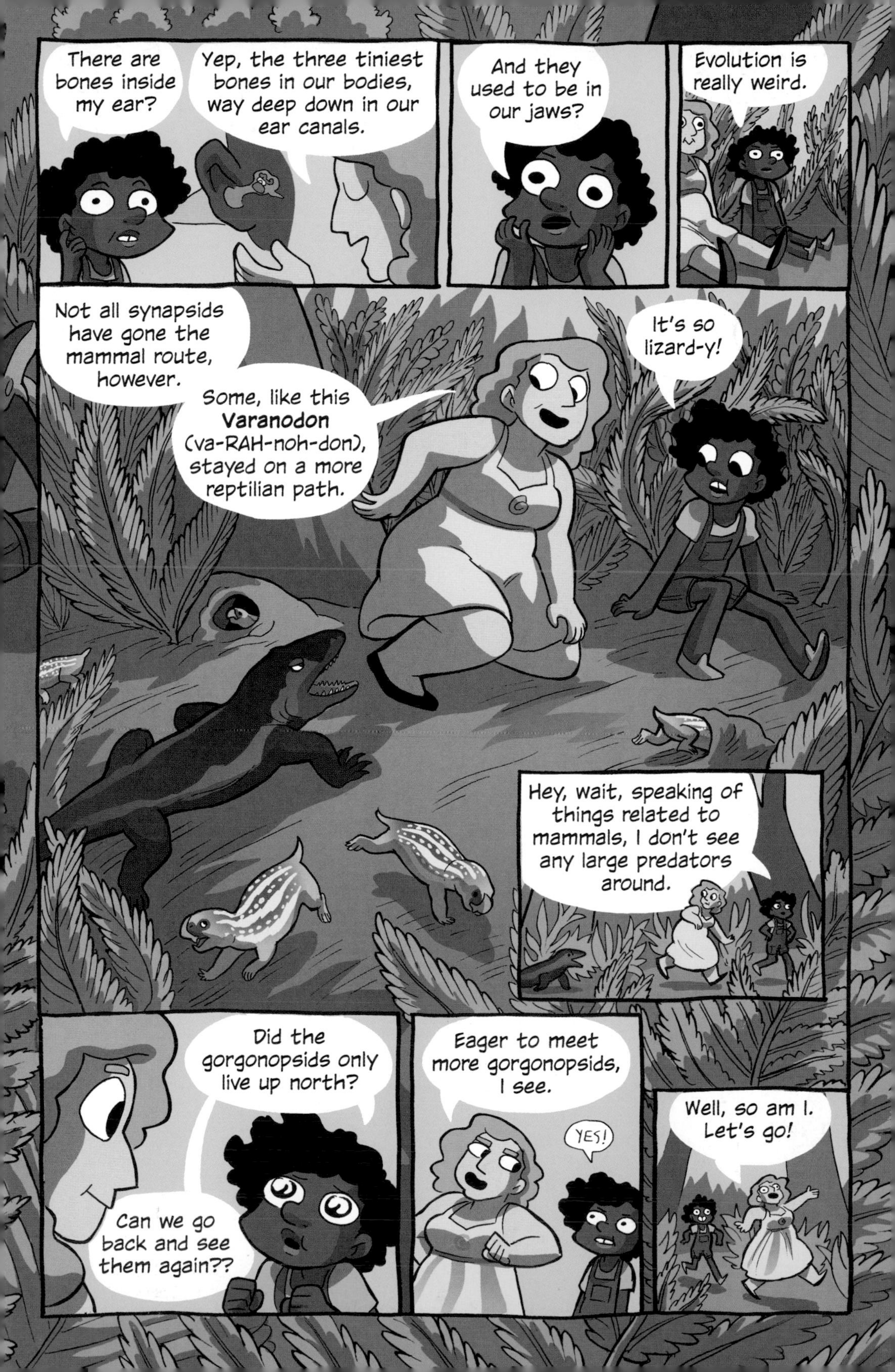
There are bones inside my ear?
Yep, the three tiniest bones in our bodies, way deep down in our ear canals.
And they used to be in our jaws?
Evolution is really weird.
Not all synapsids have gone the mammal route, however.
Some, like this **Varanodon** (va-RAH-noh-don), stayed on a more reptilian path.
It's so lizard-y!
Hey, wait, speaking of things related to mammals, I don't see any large predators around.
Did the gorgonopsids only live up north?
Can we go back and see them again??
Eager to meet more gorgonopsids, I see.
YES!
Well, so am I. Let's go!

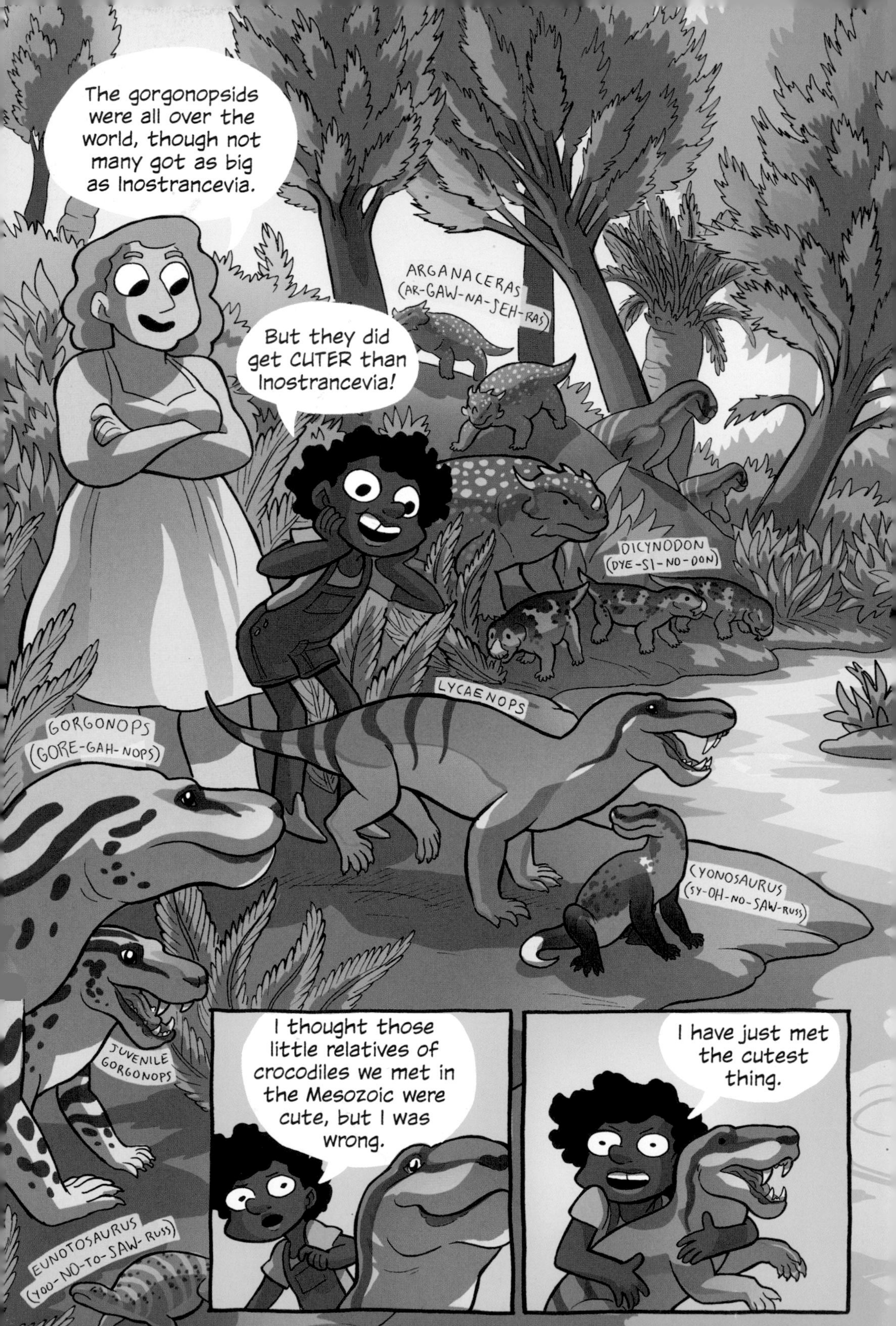
The gorgonopsids were all over the world, though not many got as big as Inostrancevia.
But they did get CUTER than Inostrancevia!
ARGANACERAS (AR-GAW-NA-SEH-RAS)
DICYNODON (DYE-SI-NO-DON)
LYCAENOPS
GORGONOPS (GORE-GAH-NOPS)
YONOSAURUS (SY-OH-NO-SAW-RUSS)
JUVENILE GORGONOPS
EUNOTOSAURUS (YOU-NO-TO-SAW-RUSS)
I thought those little relatives of crocodiles we met in the Mesozoic were cute, but I was wrong.
I have just met the cutest thing.

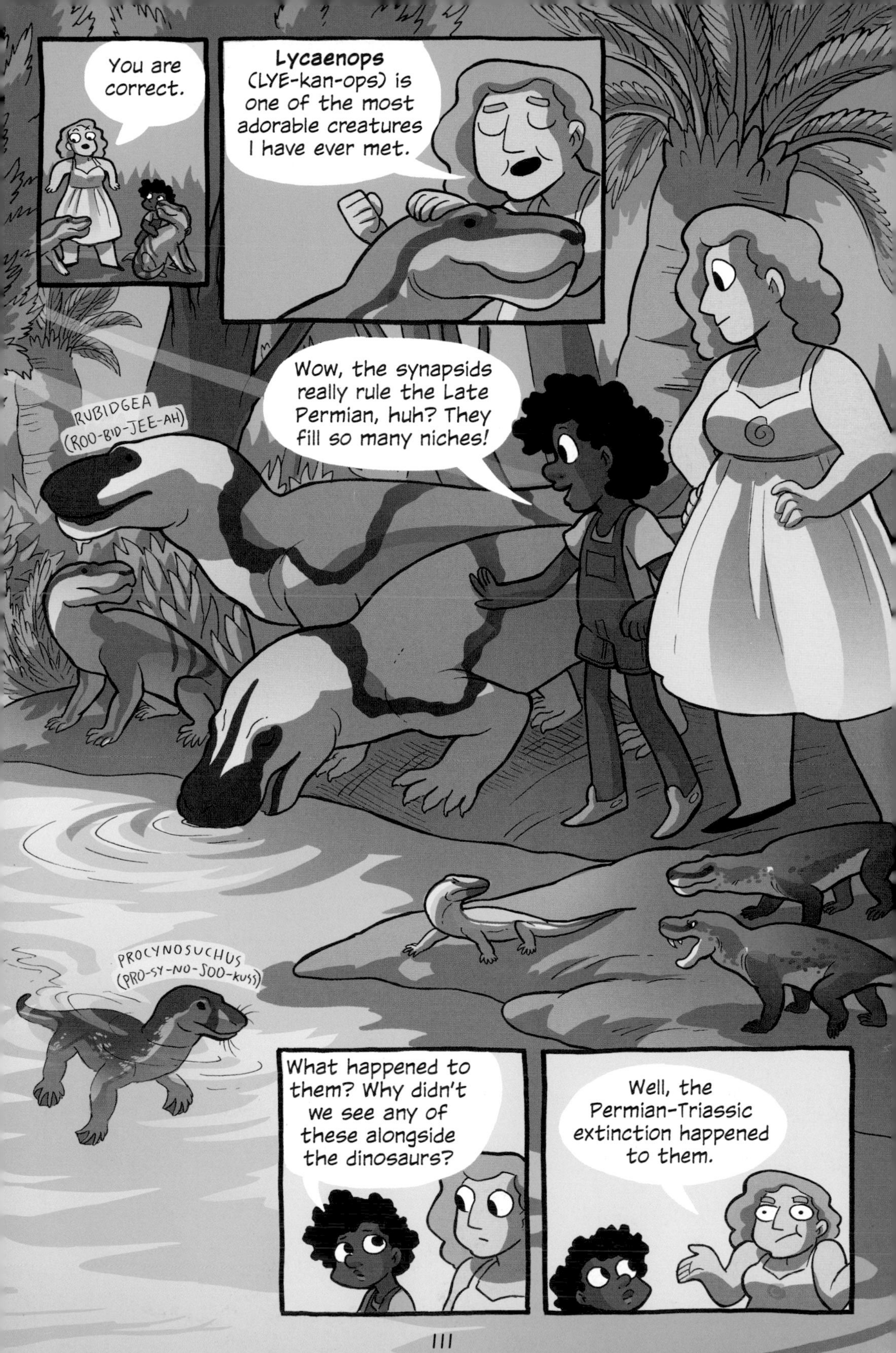
You are correct.
Lycaenops (LYE-kan-ops) is one of the most adorable creatures I have ever met.
Wow, the synapsids really rule the Late Permian, huh? They fill so many niches!
RUBIDGEA (ROO-BID-JEE-AH)
PROCYNOSUCHUS (PRO-SY-NO-SOO-KUSS)
What happened to them? Why didn't we see any of these alongside the dinosaurs?
Well, the Permian-Triassic extinction happened to them.

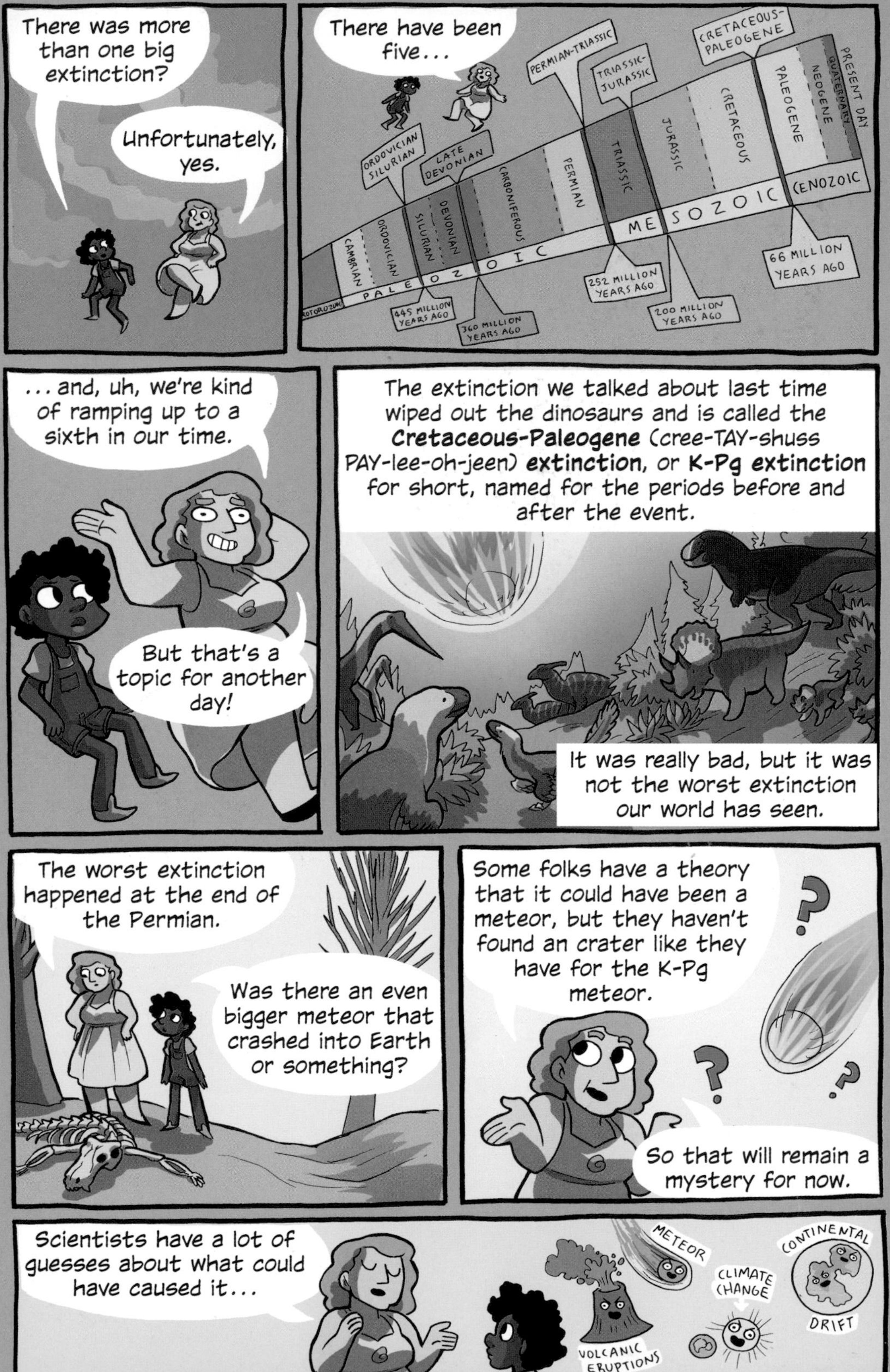
There was more than one big extinction?
Unfortunately, yes.
There have been five...
PERMIAN-TRIASSIC
CRETACEOUS-PALEOGENE
TRIASSIC-JURASSIC
ORDOVICIAN SILURIAN
LATE DEVONIAN
PRESENT DAY
QUATERNARY
NEOGENE
PALEOGENE
CRETACEOUS
JURASSIC
TRIASSIC
PERMIAN
CARBONIFEROUS
DEVONIAN
SILURIAN
ORDOVICIAN
CAMBRIAN
PROTEROZOIC
PALEOZOIC
MESOZOIC
CENOZOIC
445 MILLION YEARS AGO
360 MILLION YEARS AGO
252 MILLION YEARS AGO
200 MILLION YEARS AGO
66 MILLION YEARS AGO
...and, uh, we're kind of ramping up to a sixth in our time.
But that's a topic for another day!
The extinction we talked about last time wiped out the dinosaurs and is called the **Cretaceous-Paleogene** (cree-TAY-shuss PAY-lee-oh-jeen) **extinction**, or **K-Pg extinction** for short, named for the periods before and after the event.
It was really bad, but it was not the worst extinction our world has seen.
The worst extinction happened at the end of the Permian.
Was there an even bigger meteor that crashed into Earth or something?
Some folks have a theory that it could have been a meteor, but they haven't found an crater like they have for the K-Pg meteor.
So that will remain a mystery for now.
Scientists have a lot of guesses about what could have caused it...
METEOR
CONTINENTAL DRIFT
CLIMATE CHANGE
VOLCANIC ERUPTIONS

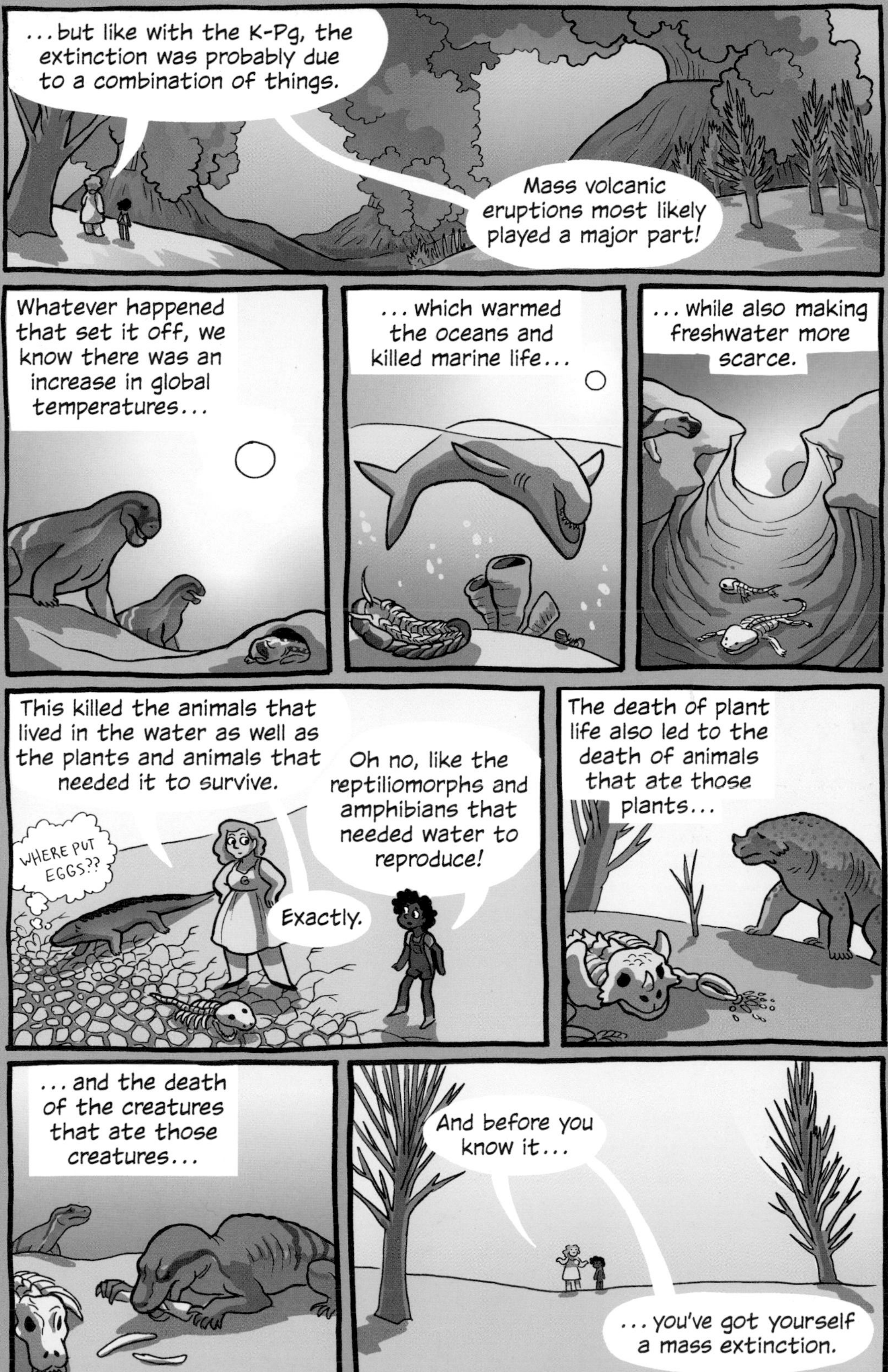
...but like with the K-Pg, the extinction was probably due to a combination of things.
Mass volcanic eruptions most likely played a major part!
Whatever happened that set it off, we know there was an increase in global temperatures...
...which warmed the oceans and killed marine life...
...while also making freshwater more scarce.
This killed the animals that lived in the water as well as the plants and animals that needed it to survive.
WHERE PUT EGGS??
Oh no, like the reptiliomorphs and amphibians that needed water to reproduce!
Exactly.
The death of plant life also led to the death of animals that ate those plants...
...and the death of the creatures that ate those creatures...
And before you know it...
...you've got yourself a mass extinction.

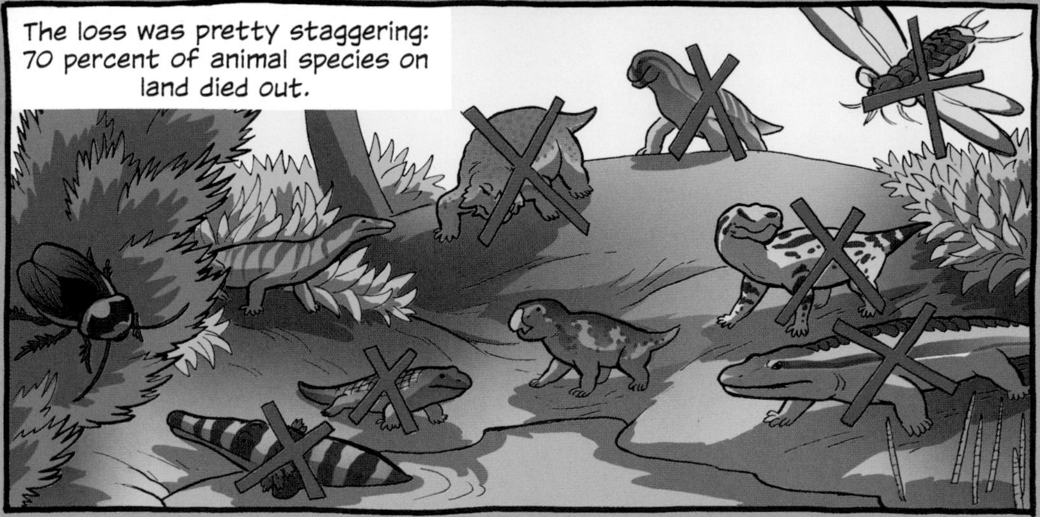

The loss was pretty staggering: 70 percent of animal species on land died out.

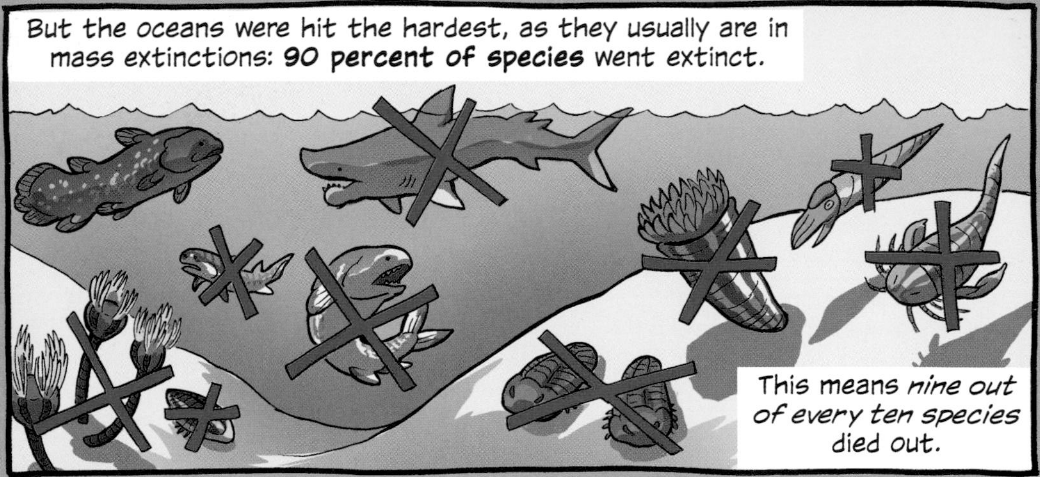

But the oceans were hit the hardest, as they usually are in mass extinctions: **90 percent of species** went extinct.
This means *nine out of every ten species* died out.

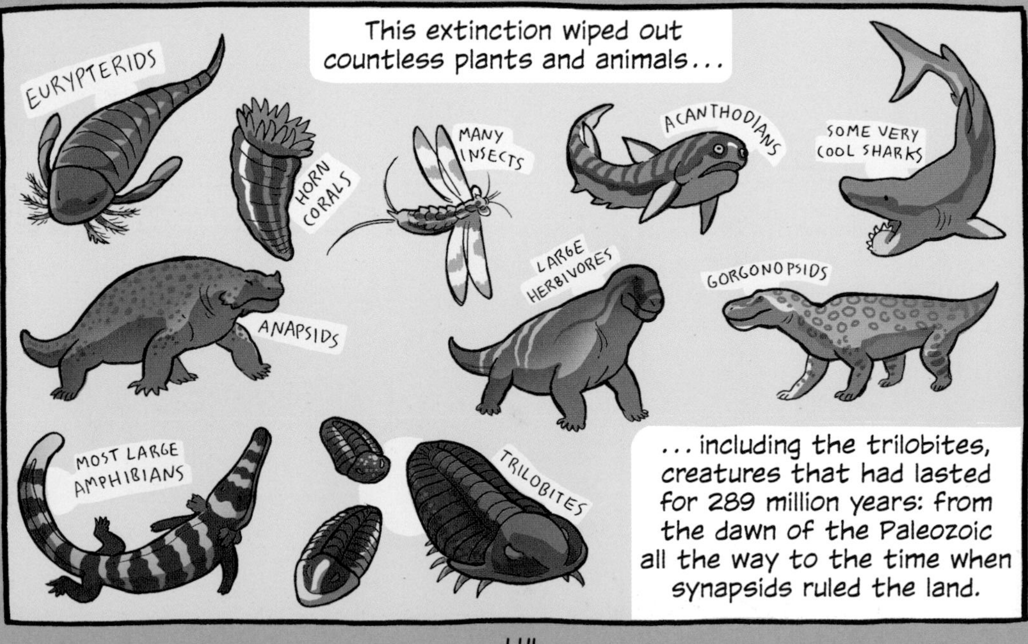

This extinction wiped out countless plants and animals...
EURYPTERIDS
HORN CORALS
MANY INSECTS
ACANTHODIANS
SOME VERY COOL SHARKS
ANAPSIDS
LARGE HERBIVORES
GORGONOPSIDS
MOST LARGE AMPHIBIANS
TRILOBITES
...including the trilobites, creatures that had lasted for 289 million years: from the dawn of the Paleozoic all the way to the time when synapsids ruled the land.

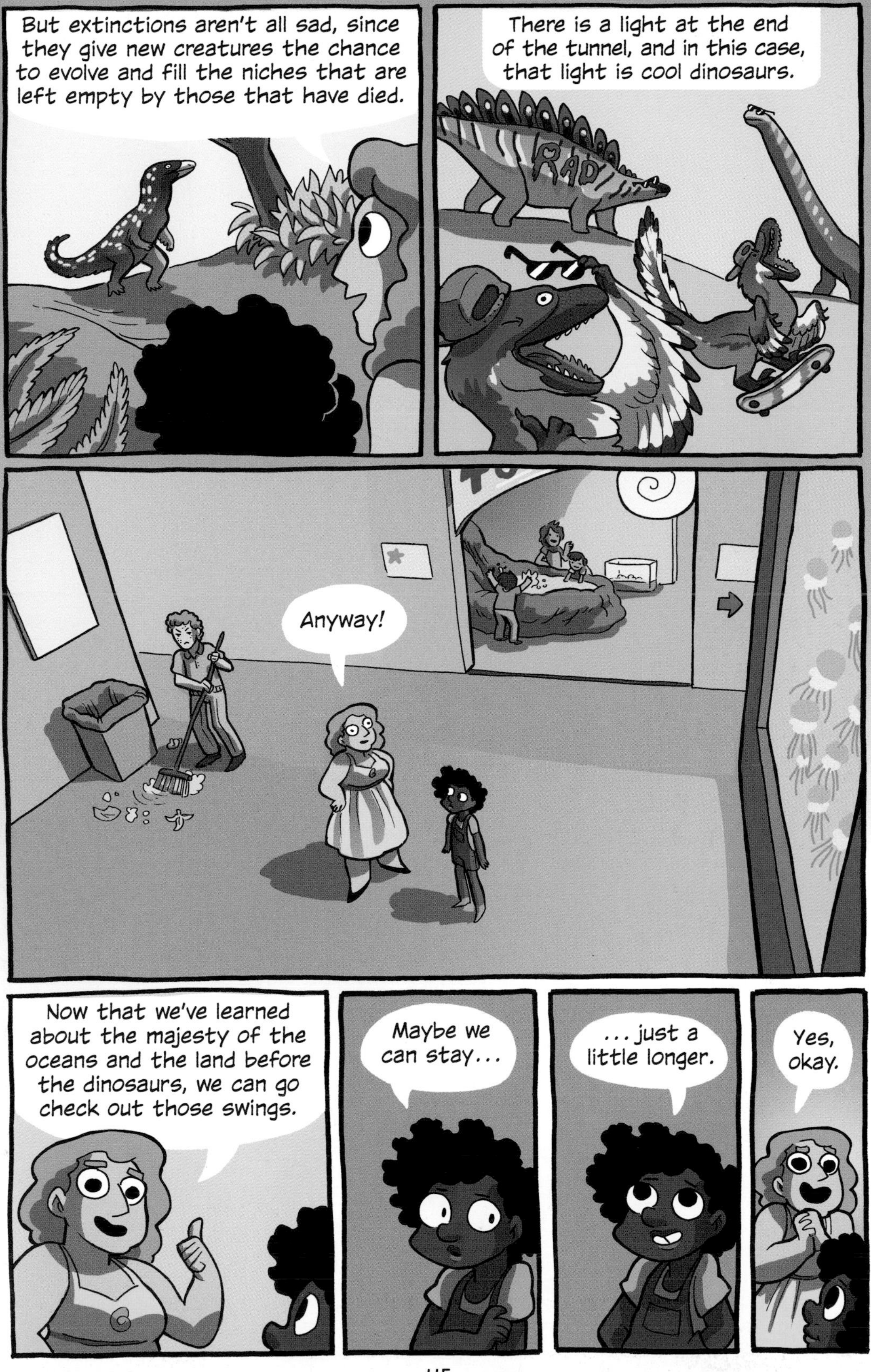

But extinctions aren't all sad, since they give new creatures the chance to evolve and fill the niches that are left empty by those that have died.
There is a light at the end of the tunnel, and in this case, that light is cool dinosaurs.
RAD
Anyway!
Now that we've learned about the majesty of the oceans and the land before the dinosaurs, we can go check out those swings.
Maybe we can stay...
...just a little longer.
Yes, okay.

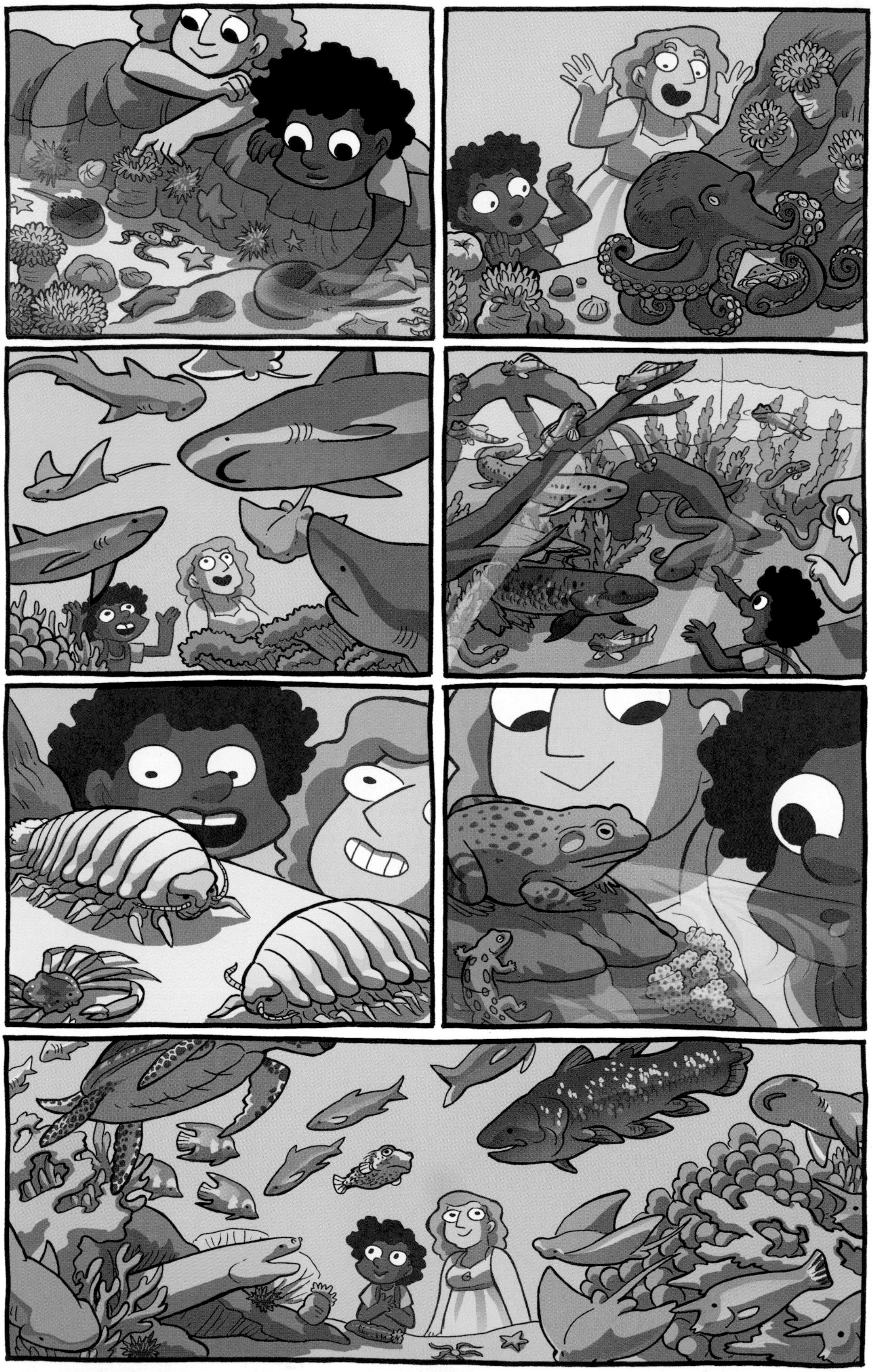

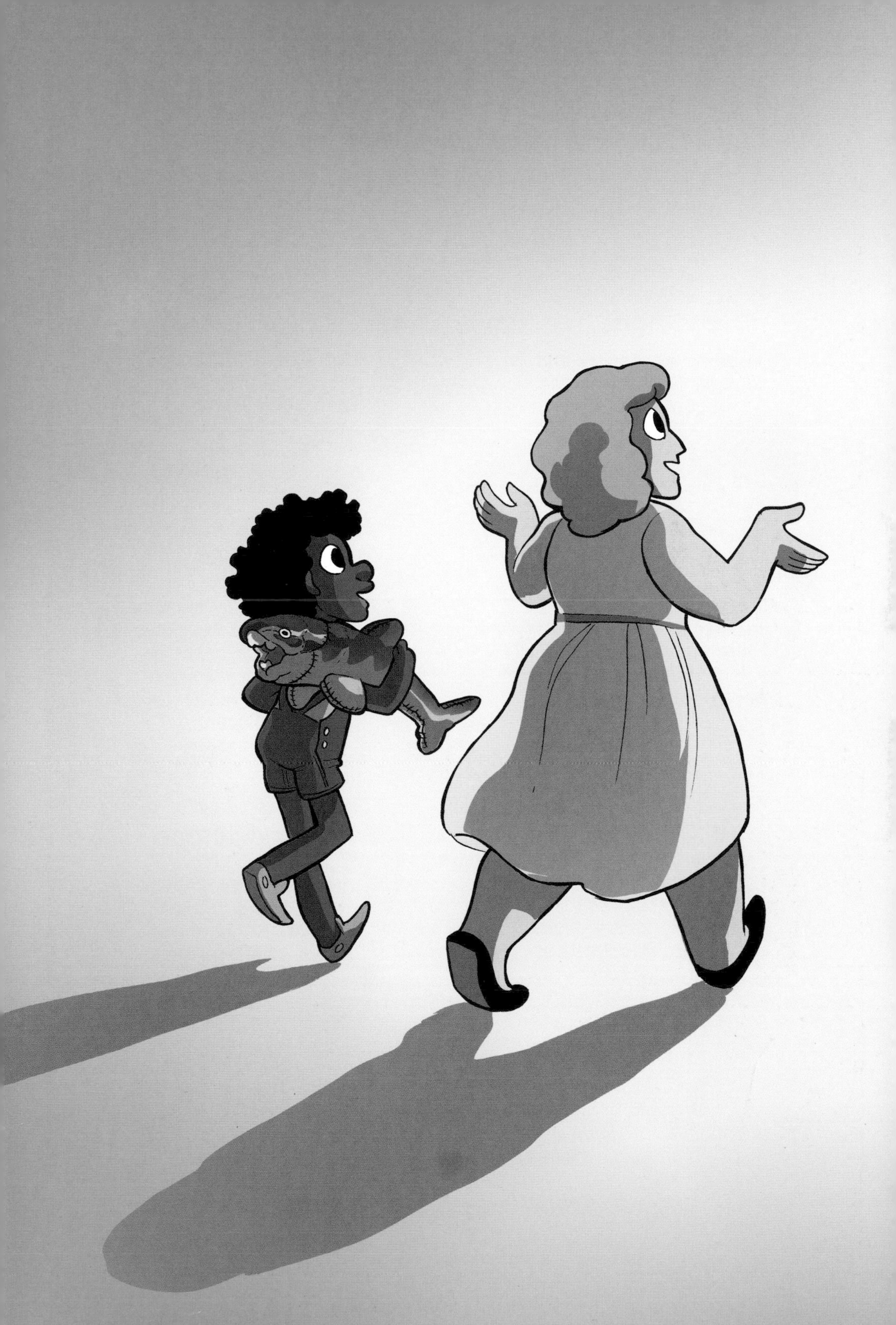

See if you can sort the animals in the aquarium into their different groups!

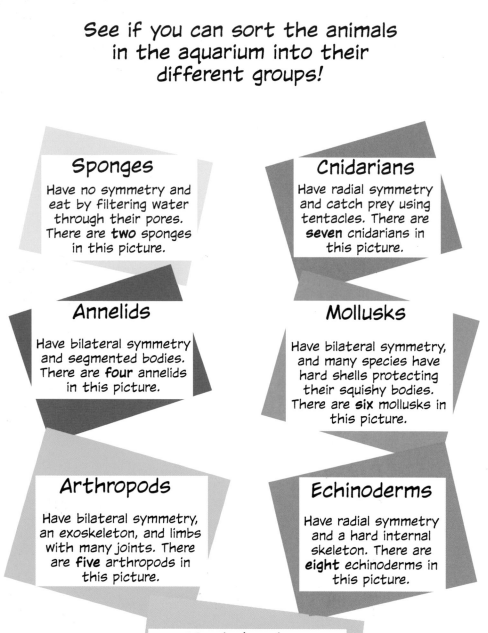

Sponges
Have no symmetry and eat by filtering water through their pores. There are **two** sponges in this picture.

Cnidarians
Have radial symmetry and catch prey using tentacles. There are **seven** cnidarians in this picture.

Annelids
Have bilateral symmetry and segmented bodies. There are **four** annelids in this picture.

Mollusks
Have bilateral symmetry, and many species have hard shells protecting their squishy bodies. There are **six** mollusks in this picture.

Arthropods
Have bilateral symmetry, an exoskeleton, and limbs with many joints. There are **five** arthropods in this picture.

Echinoderms
Have radial symmetry and a hard internal skeleton. There are **eight** echinoderms in this picture.

Vertebrates
Have bilateral symmetry, an internal skeleton, and a spine. There are **five** vertebrates in this picture.

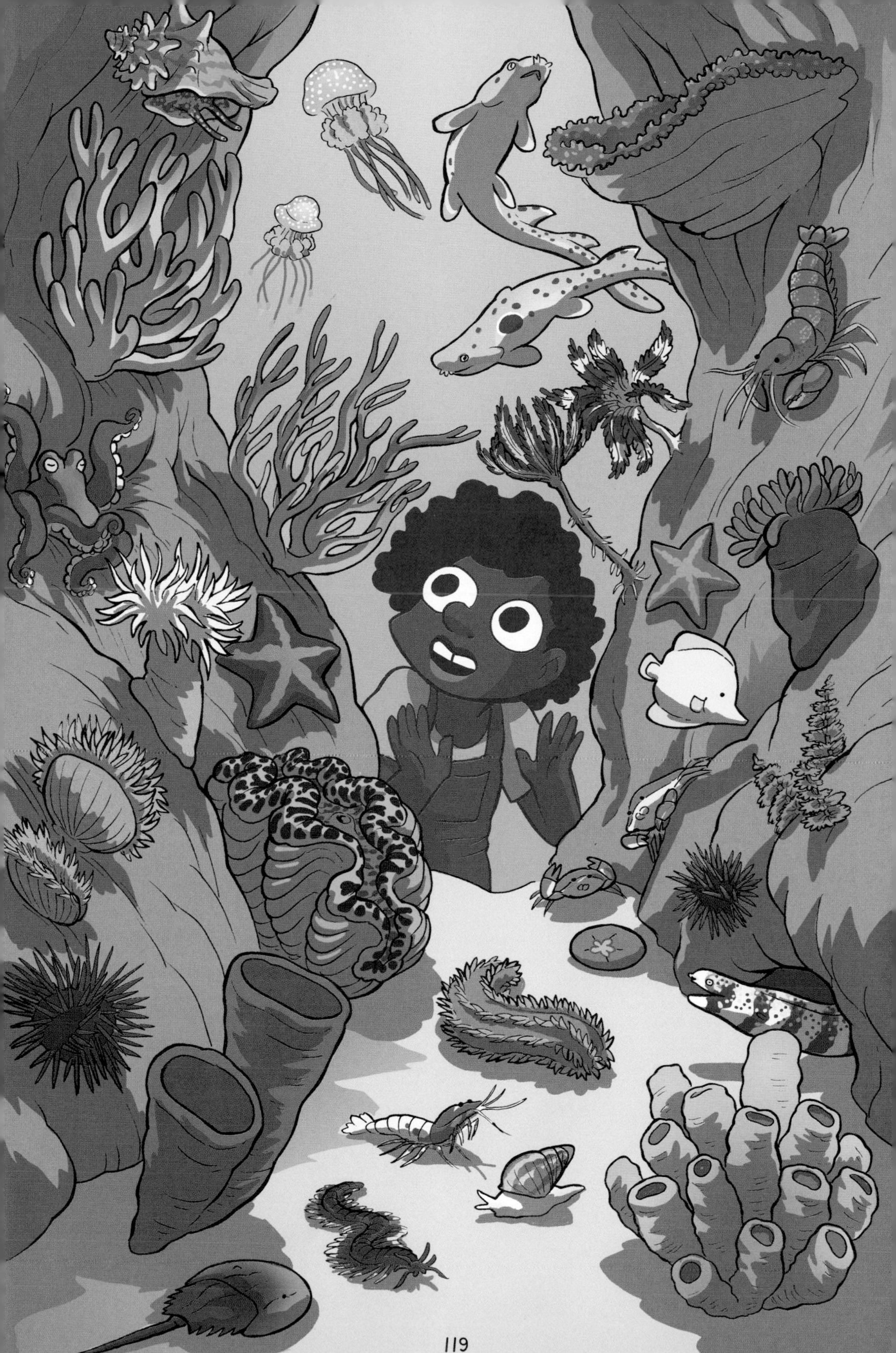

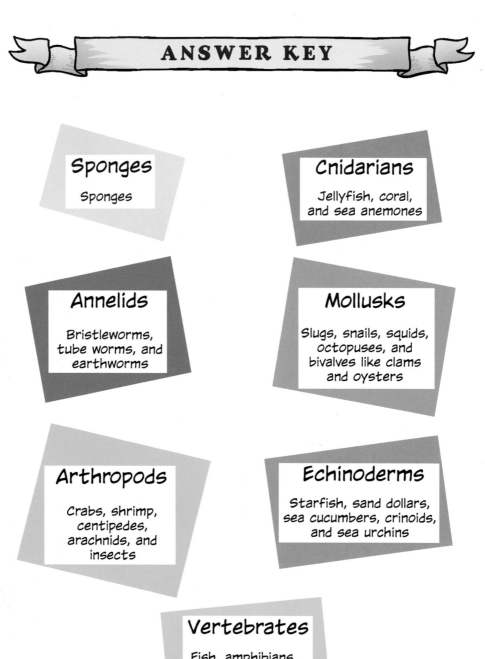

Sponges

Sponges

Cnidarians

Jellyfish, coral, and sea anemones

Annelids

Bristleworms, tube worms, and earthworms

Mollusks

Slugs, snails, squids, octopuses, and bivalves like clams and oysters

Arthropods

Crabs, shrimp, centipedes, arachnids, and insects

Echinoderms

Starfish, sand dollars, sea cucumbers, crinoids, and sea urchins

Vertebrates

Fish, amphibians, reptiles, birds, and mammals

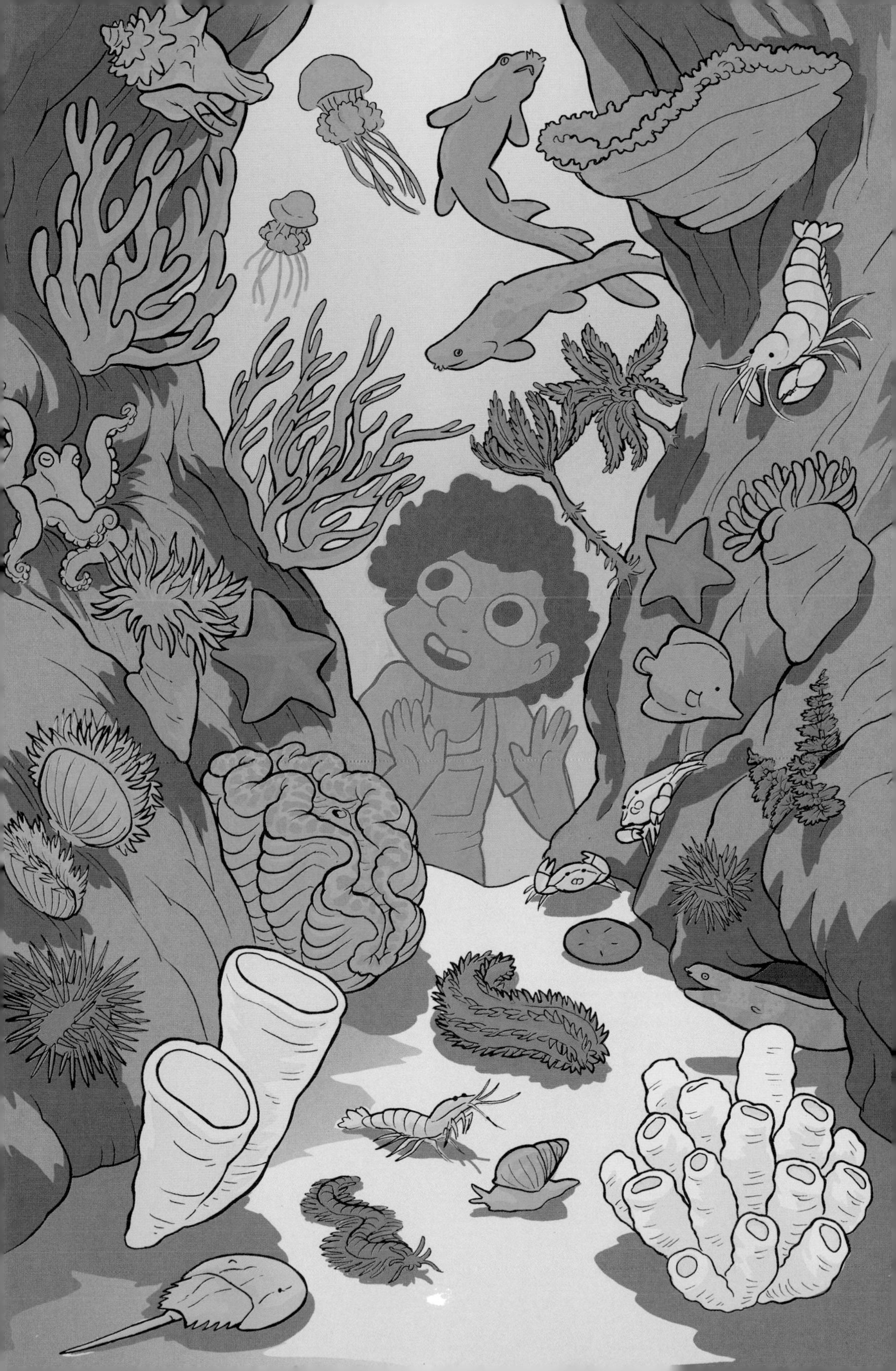

GLOSSARY

Algae: Plants that live in water. This does not include plants that evolved to live on land and then decided to move back to the water.

Amniote: A creature that lays amniotic eggs, which are eggs that have a tough, leathery shell. The shell protects the eggs from dehydrating, meaning they can be laid outside of water, unlike the eggs of amphibians, which always have to be laid in water.

Anapsid: Tetrapods that have no holes in their skulls behind the eye. Most of these died out at the end of the Paleozoic, and they have no modern descendants. Turtles are technically anapsids, but probably evolved from a diapsid ancestor, making them diapsids!

Annelid: Squishy segmented tube animals. Leeches, earthworms, polychaetes, and tube worms are all annelids.

Arthropod: An animal with an exoskeleton and a segmented body, named for its many-jointed legs. Insects, arachnids, millipedes, eurypterids, and crustaceans are examples of arthropods.

Asymmetry: Not having any symmetry. No side of something that is asymmetrical is the same as any other side. Sponges are an example of animals that are asymmetrical.

Bilateral symmetry: When there are two symmetrical sides to a creature or object. Humans and butterflies are both bilaterally symmetric.

Cambrian: The first period in the Paleozoic era, when most groups of animal life first evolved.

Carboniferous: The fifth period in the Paleozoic era, named for the abundance of carbon that was preserved in this time. This is because plants were thriving in this time, but there were not many insects or fungi around to decompose the plants that died. So a lot of plants were left lying around, creating an abundance of carbon, making this time period very carbon-iferous!

Chordate: An animal with a notochord, which is a thin protective layer around the nerve cord that runs along its back. Sharks, fish, and humans are all examples of chordates.

Cnidarian: Radially symmetric animals that use tentacles to grab floating nutrients or other animals. Jellyfish, coral, and sea anemones are examples of cnidarians.

Ctenophore: An animal that looks like a jellyfish, but is not a jellyfish. They produce beautiful flashing lights and lack the stinging cells that many cnidarians (such as jellyfish) have. They move around using rows of small tentacles, and most don't have large tentacles like jellyfish do.

Devonian: The fourth period in the Paleozoic, known as the "Age of Fishes," because many amazing fish (such as Dunkleosteus) lived in this time.

Diapsid: A tetrapod that has two holes in its skull behind its eye. This means there are more places for jaw muscles to attach, giving it a strong bite. Examples include lizards, non-bird dinosaurs, birds, and crocodiles.

Dorsal fin: A fin on the back of many fish. Sharks and orcas both have prominent dorsal fins.

Echinoderm: A radially symmetric animal that has a hard internal skeleton covered in a squishy layer, a bit like how humans have an internal skeleton and squishy outer layer. Examples include starfish, sea urchins, sea cucumbers, sea lilies, and sand dollars.

Fossil: Any trace of an organism preserved in rock.

Invertebrate: Any animal that isn't a vertebrate, which is a creature that has a backbone. Echinoderms, annelids, arthropods, cnidarians, ctenophores, sponges, and mollusks are invertebrates.

Mesozoic: The era that came after the Paleozoic, and it means "middle-life" because it is between the era that had the oldest known life and the era that has the newest. All non-bird dinosaurs lived and died in the Mesozoic.

Metamorphosis: When an animal's body changes dramatically through the course of its life. Usually metamorphosis happens in stages that each look very different. Butterflies, for instance, start as caterpillars, then wrap themselves up in cocoons, and emerge as butterflies.

Mineral: Chemicals that form tough crystals. If many different minerals come together, they form a rock.

Mollusk: An animal that has a squishy body, a radula, and often a hard shell. Octopuses, snails, and clams are all examples of mollusks.

Multicellular: An organism whose body is made up of more than one cell.

Ordovician: The second period in the Paleozoic era, during which mollusks ruled the seas and plants first started growing on land.

Organism: Anything that is alive.

Paleozoic: The era that came before the Mesozoic. It means "ancient life" because most of the oldest known animals evolved during this era.

Pectoral fins: A pair of fins on the sides of a fish and other animals that live in the water. They also evolved into arms in tetrapods.

Permian: The sixth and last period in the Paleozoic era. The land during this time was ruled by synapsids, which are close relatives of mammals.

Permian–Triassic extinction: The largest mass extinction that's ever happened. It came at the end of the Permian, right before the start of the first period in the Mesozoic era, the Triassic. Most large synapsids and aquatic creatures died, which made way for new creatures to conquer the land: dinosaurs!

Photosynthesis: The process plants use to turn sunlight, water, and carbon dioxide into food.

Porifera: A group of asymmetrical filter-feeding animals known as sponges.

Predator: An animal that hunts other animals for food.

Proboscis: A tubelike mouth that some animals use to suck up food.

Radial symmetry: When something has several identical chunks arranged around its center, like a pie in which each slice looks the same as the others. Starfish and jellyfish are both examples of creatures with radial symmetry.

Radula: A tooth-covered "tongue" found in the mouths of mollusks. It helps them scrape tasty food from surfaces.

Seed: A baby plant covered in a protective outer coat.

Silurian: The third period in the Paleozoic era, during which the first vascular plants evolved and animals started to live on land.

Spore: A microscopic cell that some plants and fungi create to reproduce. They release the spore on the wind, and when it lands, it grows into a clone of its parent. Mosses are an example of a plant that uses spores to reproduce.

Synapsid: A tetrapod that has one hole in the skull behind the eye, which means its jaw muscles have more places to attach and it has a strong bite. Mammals are an example of a synapsid, along with dimetrodon and gorgonopsids.

Unicellular: Creatures that are made up of just one cell.

Vascular plant: Land plants that have special tubes that move water and nutrients through the plant like veins. This means the plant can grow bigger. Examples of vascular plants are trees, club moss, and any plant that creates a flower.

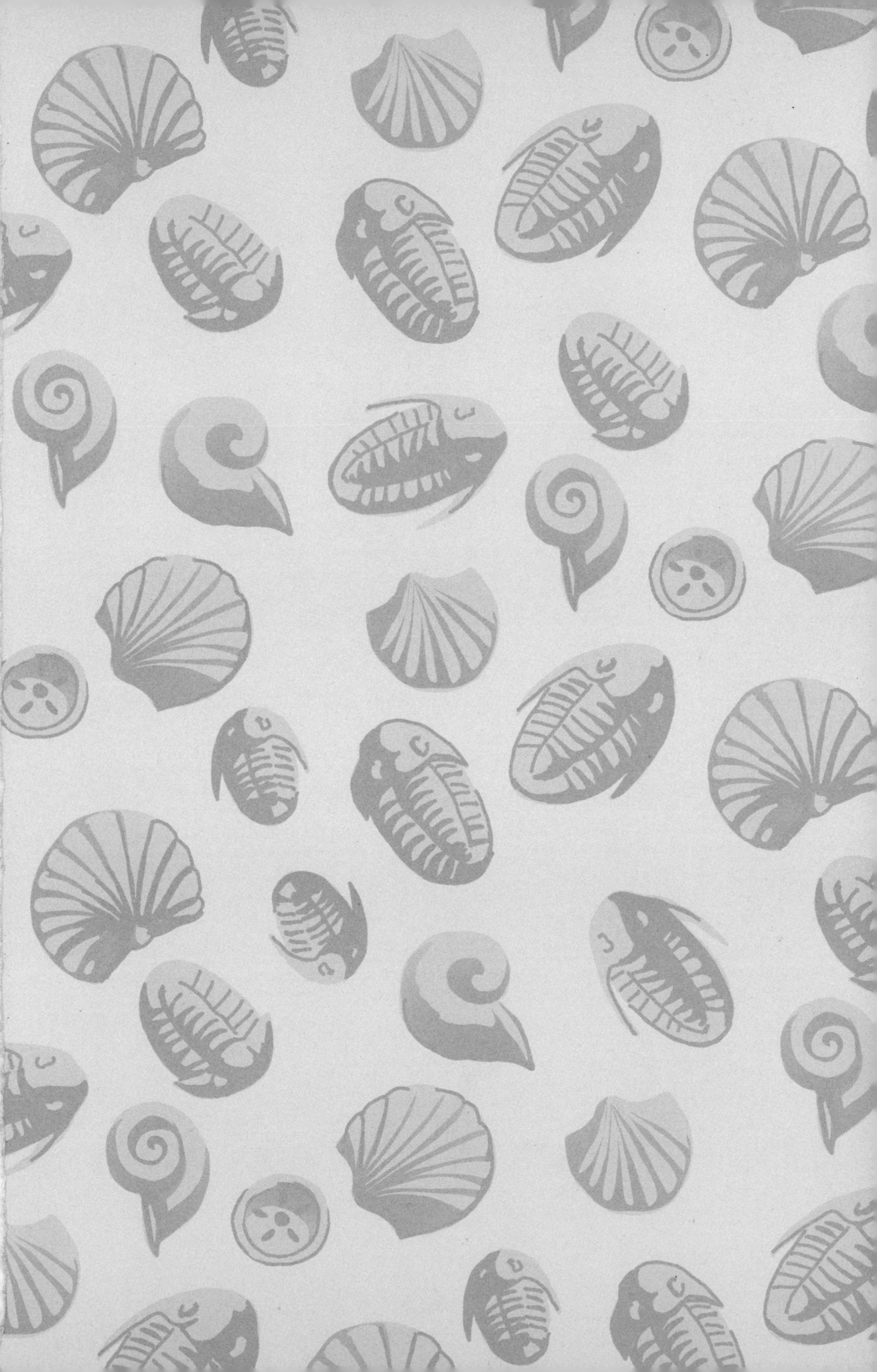

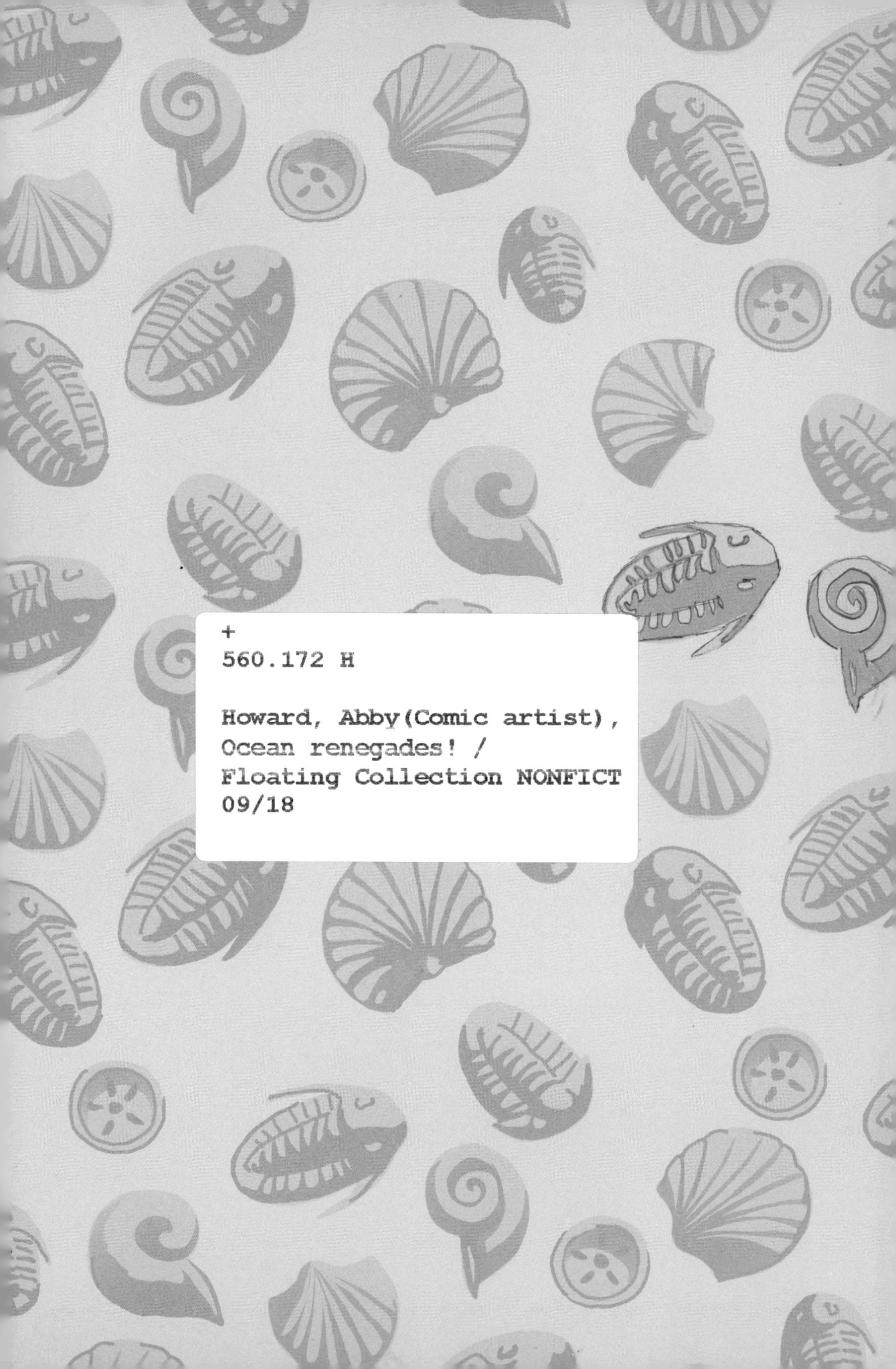